D1244516

WITHDRAWAL

Poverty and Brain Development During Childhood

Poverty and Brain Development During Childhood

AN APPROACH FROM COGNITIVE PSYCHOLOGY AND NEUROSCIENCE

Sebastián J. Lipina

Jorge A. Colombo

AMERICAN PSYCHOLOGICAL ASSOCIATION

WASHINGTON, DC

#X124950

Published by
American Psychological Association
750 First Street, NE
Washington, DC 20002
www.apa.org

To order
APA Order Department
P.O. Box 92984
Washington, DC 20090-2984
Tel: (800) 374-2721; Direct: (202) 336-5510
Fax: (202) 336-5502; TDD/TTY: (202) 336-6123
Online: www.apa.org/books/
E-mail: order@apa.org

In the U.K., Europe, Africa, and the Middle East, copies may be ordered from
American Psychological Association
3 Henrietta Street
Covent Garden, London
WC2E 8LU England

Typeset in Goudy by Stephen McDougal, Mechanicsville, MD

Printer: Data Reproductions, Auburn Hills, MI
Cover Designer: Berg Design, Albany, NY
Technical/Production Editor: Harriet Kaplan

The opinions and statements published are the responsibility of the authors, and such opinions and statements do not necessarily represent the policies of the American Psychological Association.

Library of Congress Cataloging-in-Publication Data

Lipina, Sebastián J.
  Poverty and brain development during childhood : an approach from cognitive psychology and neuroscience / Sebastián J. Lipina and Jorge A. Colombo.
    p. cm.
  Includes bibliographical references and index.
  ISBN-13: 978-1-4338-0445-8
  ISBN-10: 1-4338-0445-X
  1. Child development deviations. 2. Poverty—Psychological aspects. 3. Brain—Growth. 4. Developmental neurophysiology. 5. Cognitive neuroscience. I. Colombo, Jorge A. II. Title.

  RJ135.L57 2009
  362.198'92—dc22   2008044360

British Library Cataloguing-in-Publication Data
A CIP record is available from the British Library.

Printed in the United States of America
First Edition

July 14, 2009

HUMAN BRAIN
DEVELOPMENT SERIES

CONTENTS

LIST OF TABLES AND FIGURES

TABLE

FIGURES

FOREWORD

This book is a wake-up call addressed to scientists and policymakers. The poor children of the world, particularly in the developing world, are at risk. The risk is not only for the clear economic and health problems of being poor but also that their brains will fail to develop to their full potential. As this volume points out, the risk from multiple influences of systemic poverty is that these children will suffer not only from loss of opportunity but from poor development of their nervous systems. Although it is not easy to disentangle the influences of malnutrition, abuse, health, low verbal input, and sensory deprivation as potential causes of deficits in brain development, together they clearly take a toll in reduced potential from which many children are unable to recover despite evidence for brain plasticity in later years.

Most scientists in the developed world are unfamiliar with the situation confronting the poor in underdeveloped countries. This book could help remedy that lack of understanding and lead to more concerted efforts to provide improved conditions for the world's poor. In recent years, the U.S. public has begun to realize the consequences of a poor start in education. However poorly implemented, the goal of No Child Left Behind is to provide good education for every child.

Chapter 5 of this volume reviews efforts to develop interventions that could reach large numbers of poor children. Although no one program seems to fit all, the authors extract some of the principles needed for successful interventions. In chapter 6, they enumerate what public policy changes would be required to implement the interventions reviewed in the previous chapter.

As the authors recognize, the connections are distressingly weak between the research described in chapter 2, which deals with brain changes in development, much from nonhuman animal research; that described in chapter 4, which discusses efforts by cognitive neuroscience researchers to delineate the mental operations most influenced by poverty; and the science and policy surrounding interventions discussed in chapters 5 and 6. They point out that much research is needed to elaborate these connections and show in specific terms how the various forms of deprivation influence neural mechanisms so that the most likely remedy could be determined. I was surprised that the most powerful and sweeping deficit seems to be the deficit in children hearing their own language spoken. This is also the easiest to remedy with noninvasive interventions: Parents can initiate speech to their children in the earliest months of life, incorporating positive statements in addition to what corrective language is needed to direct their child's behavior.

Strong scientific evidence exists that speech directed by humans toward infants even before the age that the child begins to speak (e.g., 7 to 10 months) can shape phonemic structure,[1,2] together with the evidence that these changes can be monitored with simple behavioral and electronic assays, provides a basis for training parents to present this input. This kind of intervention is one basis for the Harlem Children's Zone parent college.[3] Evidence also shows that the extent of parent language directed toward children is correlated with vocabulary, literacy, and success in school.

It was equally surprising to me that measures of executive control (self-regulation) were not as strongly related to later success as I would have thought. Nonetheless, this also is an area where noninvasive intervention through parents or preschool can be implemented, as is pointed out in chapter 5. These two surprises suggest how important a role summaries of wide-ranging research, such as those provided by this volume, can have in guiding how best to direct our research and policy efforts in future years.

In chapter 5, the authors deal with the results of intervention efforts, particularly the Head Start program in the United States. They suggest that classroom exercises built on models of cognitive function (e.g., Vygotsky or Montessori) may be the basis for establishing improved preschool performance that can have influence later in life. They also discuss experimental efforts based on specific neural models that influence attention, literacy, and numeracy. It remains to be seen if the large-scale classroom demonstrations based on overall views of child learning and the targeted improvements found in laboratory studies can be synthesized into a strong theory-based intervention strategy appropriate for each child.

In the final chapter, the authors provide some suggestions for policymakers. The mood for such actions is promising. For example, Barack Obama gave a speech in Washington, DC, on urban poverty, citing the Harlem

---

[1]Kuhl, P. K., Stevens, E., Hayashi, A., Deguchi, T., Kiritani, S., & Iverson, P. (2006). Infants show a facilitation effect for native language phonetic perception between 6 and 12 months. *Developmental Science, 9*(2), F13–F21.
[2]Werker, J. F., Gilbert, J. H. V., Humphrey, K., & Tees, R. C. (1981). Developmental aspects of cross-language speech-perception: *Child Development, 52*(1), 349–355.
[3]Tough, P. (2008). *Whatever it takes*. New York: Houghton Mifflin.

Children's Zone as an effective model for improving urban neighborhoods and education. As president, he announced, he would replicate the model to 20 other cities. Staff would be trained, communities would engage in planning, and the federal government would pick up half the tab, with the balance sought from private agencies and supporters. He admitted it would cost "a few billion dollars a year," but to do nothing at all, he added, would be unacceptable.[4] This volume shows that the problems present in the United States and throughout the developed world are dwarfed by the even larger problems and opportunities presented by the poor in developing countries. The way in which even modest input from science energized the Harlem Children's Zone may, along with this volume, provide impetus for new research designed to produce change on a worldwide scale.

Michael I. Posner
Series Editor

---

[4]*Remarks of Senator Barack Obama: Changing the odds for urban America.* (2007, July 18). Retrieved December 29, 2008, from http://www.barackobama.com/2007/07/18/ remarks_of_senator_barack_obam_19.php

Poverty and
Brain Development
During Childhood

OVERVIEW

If the mysery of the poor be caused not by the laws of nature, but by our institutions, great is our sin.

—Charles Darwin

Child poverty and development are complex, multidimensional phenomena. Study of these phenomena involves an analysis of varied biological and psychosocial components and processes within a continuous, dynamic interaction (Beddington et al., 2008; Bronfenbrenner & Ceci, 1994; Westermann et al., 2007). Both poverty and development have been studied by different scientific disciplines. That keeps the debate open on whether there are universal biological and psychosocial underlying processes or whether these processes are context dependent. Poverty increases a child's exposure to both biological and psychosocial risks that are most likely to affect developmental and social opportunities. Inasmuch as the strategies that typically have been implemented do not appear to have modified the fate of poor children significantly, the international community should be challenged to commit to improving present and future human development (United Nations Children's Fund [UNICEF], 2005). More than 1 billion of the world's children are affected by severe deprivation (Gordon, Nandy, Pantazis, Pemberton, & Townsend, 2003). In this context, *deprivation* refers to inadequate height and weight for age; lack of or limited access to drinkable water and sanitary facilities; no immunization against diseases; no medical treatment in cases of diarrhea; overcrowding; lack of education between the ages of 7 and 18 years; and no access to radio, television, telephone, or newspapers at home. Even though this level of severe deprivation does not appear to affect developed countries, child poverty rates in the world's wealthiest nations vary from less than 3% to more than 25%. For instance, 47 million children from the nations belonging to the Organisation for Economic Cooperation and Development live below their national poverty lines (UNICEF, 2000), and in the United States, 28.6 million children (39%), and 12.7 million children (17%) live in low-income families and poor families, respectively (Douglas-Hall & Chau, 2007). The lack of political and economic ability to deal with these problems is incomprehensible, given the ready availability of a large body of basic and practical information aimed at modifying the most preventable risk factors. Perhaps one problem is that the world's political and socioeconomic structure tends to generate these risk factors.

Economic and sociological disciplines also refer to deprivation in studies dealing with the impact of poverty on child cognitive development: These cite lack of income and material resources as causing basic needs to go unattended and limiting the full development of human populations. When considering the concept of deprivation, it is essential that one adjust the concept of poverty and its operational definition according to each research context. In promoting of interdisciplinary exchanges, one must consider child development and poverty as multidimensional phenomena. For instance, in the fields of economics and sociology, only recently has child poverty been differentiated from poverty in general, with significant implications for children's rights and basic needs (UNICEF, 2005). This conceptual definition stresses the multidimensional and interrelated nature of child poverty besides suggesting that economic safety is only one of its components.

Debates regarding the causes of child poverty and the ways in which poverty in general is to be measured mean that there is no uniform approach to conceptualizing and measuring child poverty (Minujin, Delamonica, Davidziuk, & González, 2006). The *income approach* (i.e., measuring poverty solely by specific level of income) is the most widely used to identify and measure poverty in several disciplines. This approach does not account for the fact that a child's basic needs are different and more extensive than those of an adult. The income approach gives little consideration to household structure, gender, age, or well-being. Several authors (see, e.g., Minujin et al. 2006; Roosa, Deng, Nair, & Lockhart Burrell, 2005) have argued that access to basic services and a protective environment depends more on developmental context than on household income. For example, children are disproportionately affected by health conditions involving access to sanitation. Lack of such access increases the likelihood of preventable injuries and infectious diseases. The same trend has been found in other factors, such as overcrowding conditions and lack of adequate home and academic stimulation, that are likely to alter child's long-term cognitive and emotional development (Evans, 2004; Walker et al., 2007). Thus, a particular household income is unlikely to guarantee the satisfaction of basic needs.

No widely accepted conceptualization of child-related poverty takes into account the relationship between children's material needs and their needs for affectionate support in relation to their developmental stage. The impact of child poverty on cognitive development varies according to the poverty measurements used (Hill & Michael, 2001). For example, in addition to poverty, low cognitive stimulation levels at home, strict parenting styles, and living in overcrowded conditions are high risk factors for poor cognitive performance during the earliest development years. This suggests the need to consider current conceptual and methodological advances in the study of child development, including studies using cognitive neuroscience research methods.

Some of these concerns have influenced some international organizations and researchers to begin to see child poverty as a phenomenon that must be defined and measured along several dimensions of deprivation (Minujin et al., 2006). For instance, severe deprivation levels in some developing countries require consideration of human rights—placing an emphasis on the principles of nondiscrimination, equality, and participation in the decision-making process. This means providing adequate nourishment, shelter, and basic education; avoiding preventable morbidity and premature mortality; and ensuring social inclusion by encouraging families to take part in community life (Minujin et al., 2006). To date, the impact of poverty on cognitive performance has been mainly conducted with income used as the only factor in determining child poverty. Severe deprivation, however, is missing from current research. In particular, studies analyzing the impacts of poverty at the neurocognitive level have applied only variations of income-based or basic needs-based definitions. Thus, although the need to improve child poverty–related conceptualizations and measurement among researchers is on the increase, it is still lacking in many research studies.

The diversity of poverty effects are also mediated by accumulation of risk factors at home, at school, and in community institutions and organizations (Walker et al., 2007). The term *risk factors* here refers to both biological and psychosocial hazards likely to compromise child development at any of the analysis levels—for example, intrauterine growth restrictions, undernutrition, specific nutritional deficits, infectious diseases, environmental toxic exposures, parental home stimulation, sensitivity, and responsivity. A majority of these risks could be prevented through appropriate policies, so restricted views on child poverty and development increase the likelihood of not improving children's opportunities. Thus, a multidimensional view on poverty and development is important for designing interventions and evaluating their impacts.

More than 40 years of research on intervention and educational programs for children living in poverty have yielded several specific conceptual and methodological recommendations (S. Ramey & Ramey, 2003). Projects based on these recommendations, using appropriate designs with adequate controls as well as conceptual and methodological frameworks based on complex and ecological approaches, have produced the best effects. However, not all children benefit in the same way from their participation in this type of program. Crucial individual differences are due fundamentally to multiple interactive factors, including the early status of children in terms of their biological inheritance and risk accumulation as well as variations in the development context quality (National Institute of Child Health and Human Development & Early Child Care Research Network [NICHD], 2005; C. T. Ramey & Ramey, 1998). Recent findings on how children's genotypic nature modulates their cognitive performance—after specific training of their attention networks—constitute a promising research trend in the intervention area (Rueda, Rothbart, McCandliss, Saccomanno, & Posner, 2005).

Both basic and applied research works remain crucial, not only for a more in-depth knowledge about how poverty influences development but also in designing actions aimed at improvement. Although scientific contributions are not expected to replace social and political actions against poverty, they are expected to inform those actions. This book incorporates several conceptual and methodological approaches, developed in the context of neuroscientific disciplines such as developmental cognitive neuroscience and cognitive psychology, on the basis of proven experimental and applied methodologies aimed at analyzing poverty impacts as well as cognitive optimization through interventions.

In the past 4 decades, several experimental projects and programs have contributed significantly to the understanding of how material and social deprivation influences brain organization. These influences are at different analysis levels, from the molecular up to the learning process levels. The study of early cognitive development involves the consideration of several components and processes taking place at different times and at various analysis levels (Sirois et al., 2008). Hence, environmental deprivation factors could either modify or alter a child's cognitive development inasmuch as changes in some components are likely to affect ongoing development. This impact could vary according to the amount and timing of deprivation as well as the individual susceptibility, quality, and cultural nature of developmental contexts (NICHD, 2003, 2005).

The concept of deprivation varies depending on the scientific discipline involved. In the context of neuroscientific experimental animal models, *environmental deprivation* refers specifically to the controlled manipulation of different material and social conditions in laboratory animals, aimed at modulating several inputs (Grossman et al., 2003; A. H. Mohammed et al., 2002). The use of animal models and controlled conditions is needed to be able to analyze the most elementary levels of brain components and processes, such as molecules, dendrites, and synapses. The findings may have limited application to human contexts. Nonetheless, they do allow an understanding of basic neural processes. Researchers need to analyze the effects of specific deprivations (e.g., access to the mother at specific times) on different molecular or cellular components of the brain cortex (Markham & Greenough, 2004).

With regard to impact caused, as already mentioned, there is an agreement about the fact that poverty involves multiple alterations and impacts on physical growth and on cognitive and socioemotional development. Specifically with regard to brain development and function, recent studies have shown that poverty affects people from birth to adulthood. For example, the 2003 and 2005 studies performed by the NICHD showed that the quality of home environment predicted children's performance in sustaining attention, memory, and inhibitory control tasks.

There is a need to evaluate how the environment may influence basic cognitive processes involved in school and social functioning (Noble, McCandliss, & Farah, 2007; Thorell, Lindquist, Bergman Nutley, Bohlin, & Klingberg, 2009). Recent studies have shown the impact of a socially disadvantaged home on cognitive performance in tasks requiring basic operations related to different brain networks. For instance, Mezzacappa (2004) has verified a pattern of associations between children's basic cognitive functions of attention and their socioeconomic status—for example, socially disadvantaged children performed less proficiently under all conditions in an attention task. Lipina and colleagues (Lipina et al., 2004; Lipina, Martell, Vuelta, & Colombo, 2005) found that infants and preschoolers from socially disadvantaged homes performed less proficiently in tasks requiring working memory, inhibitory control, attention, flexibility, and planning. Blair and Razza (2007) examined the role of self-regulation in emerging learning among preschoolers from low-income homes. They found that although children's self-regulatory competencies—executive function, effortful control, and false belief—were moderately correlated, each tended to account for a unique variance in mathematics and literacy measurements. In a recent series of studies, Noble, Farah, McCandliss, and colleagues have assessed several neurocognitive systems of children from preschool through preadolescent ages to determine socioeconomic contributions to performance and neural activation (Farah et al., 2006; Noble et al., 2007; Noble, Farah, & McCandliss, 2006; Noble, Norman, & Farah, 2005; Noble, Wolmetz, Ochs, Farah, & McCandliss, 2006). These studies show that socioeconomic background differences were associated with disparities in language performance and executive function systems. In addition, some studies show the influences of parenting (Landry, Millar-Loncar, Smith, & Swank, 2002) and parents' educational levels (Ardilla, Rosselli, Matute, & Guajardo, 2005) on the development of the executive functions of children from different cultures as well as the socioeconomic modulation of maternal speech on early vocabulary development (Hoff, 2003).

Finally, in the first developmental imaging studies applied to the analysis of poverty effects on brain function, Noble et al. (2007); Neville and colleagues (Pakulak, Sanders, Paulsen, & Neville, 2005; Sabourin, Pakulak,

Paulsen, Fanning, & Neville, 2007; Raizada, Richards, Meltzoff, and Kuhl (2008); and Kishiyama, Boyce, Jimenez, Perry, and Kinght (2009) have studied how socioeconomic status modulates children's brain activity during attentional processing when the child is reading, speaking, and listening. Using functional magnetic resonance imaging, a technology allowing coevaluation of brain activation and cognitive performance, Noble et al. have shown an interaction between socioeconomic status and phonological awareness and activation of the left fusiform brain area, an area related to reading skill. Neville and colleagues have shown that socioeconomic status of 3- to 5-year-old children modulates scalp-recorded event related potentials in connection with semantic and phrase structure violation and auditory attention (see also Raizada et al., 2008). The implemented approaches have opened a promising area of analysis: Activation represents a crucial dimension in terms of the characterization and development of basic cognitive processes and of the possibilities of modifying them by exercise, training, and education.

Interest has been growing in the potential contributions of cognitive neuroscience to education (Ansari & Coch, 2006; Goswami, 2006; Posner & Rothbart, 2005, 2007b). These discussions also apply to interventions aimed at improving disadvantaged children's cognitive and psychosocial performance. The revived interest in brain studies in relation to education is based on results from laboratory studies involving behavioral training and remediation of basic cognitive processes in healthy as well as sick children.

For example, Rueda et al. (2005) have designed and applied an executive attention-training program for 4- and 6-year-old healthy children. The authors showed that trained groups obtained a more mature performance in the Attentional Networking Test; a generalization effect on an intelligence test; and, using event related potentials, changes in the pattern of brain activations within an area related to attention. Also, with regard to an examination of differences in temperament and genotype, these authors have found that a specific allele of the DAT1 dopamine gene transporter was associated with stronger effortful control, suggesting that attention training was more effective in children with lower levels of executive control. The study showed both genotype and training influence performance on tests of attention and intelligence. Klingberg and colleagues (Klingberg et al., 2006; Klingberg, Forssberg, & Westerberg, 2002) have designed a working memory training paradigm and then evaluated its effectiveness in school-age children and adolescents with attention-deficit/hyperactivity disorder. Results showed that intensive, adaptive computerized working memory training gradually increased the amount of information that children could maintain on line (see also Thosell et al., 2009). McCandliss, Beck, Sandak, and Perfetti (2003) examined the reading abilities of school-age children with deficient decoding skills before and after an intervention in the context of a controlled randomized design. Findings indicated that participation in the program resulted in gains in decoding, phonemic awareness, and passage comprehension skills. Shaywitz et al. (2004) and Temple et al. (2003) designed and applied phonologically mediated reading interventions combining behavioral and imaging approaches that showed that children participating in the intervention protocols made more significant gains in reading and fluency skills than children in control groups. Moreover, increased activation in related brain areas proved to be associated with behavioral gains. Wilson, Dehaene, et al. (2006) and Wilson, Revkin, Cohen, Cohen, and Dehaene (2006) have designed an adaptive, computerized game for dyscalculia remediation, inspired by cognitive neuroscience research specifically conducted on the current understanding of brain representation of numbers. These studies involved typically developing children or those with specific difficulties, and results suggest that application of this software was successful in increasing a sense for numbers over a short study period.

The application of cognitive neuroscience frameworks to interventions aimed at improving socially disadvantaged children's cognitive development are even more recent. Currently, approaches by McCandliss et al. (2003); Wilson, Dehaene, et al. (2006); and Wilson, Revkin, et al. (2006) are being applied in schools in both New York (B. D. McCandliss, personal communication, March 2007) and Europe (see http://www.unicog.org).

On the basis of previous studies, Colombo, Lipina, and colleagues (e.g., Colombo & Lipina, 2005) have designed and applied a controlled, randomized, multimodular intervention program that includes cognitive exercise, nutritional supplementation, teacher training, and health and social counseling for parents to be applied to a sample of healthy 3- to 5-year-old children from disadvantaged homes. Results have shown that participation in 32 sessions per year, combined with an iron and folic acid supplement, improved both control and monitoring processing in the intervention groups. Finally, the Tools of the Mind curriculum has been shown to improve executive functions in a socially disadvantaged preschool sample from low-income urban schools (Diamond, Barnett, Thomas, & Munro, 2007).

Cognitive neuroscience studies described in this volume have been useful in identifying effects of poverty on specific basic cognitive processes. These processes are strongly associated with the early development of literacy and numeracy competencies from kindergarten onward. The same processes have been subject to the design and implementation of intervention programs whose results encourage researchers to transfer those programs to children in poverty. Obviously, there is a need to (a) demonstrate the limits of generalization and (b) determine how long it takes for interventions to succeed in altering affective networks. However, the current findings in cognitive neuroscience may help scientists and policymakers improve their approaches aimed at optimizing the quality of life of socially disadvantaged children.

The present volume reviews the impact of different types of early deprivations on structural and functional brain organization. We also describe how poverty affects cognitive and socioemotional development and then analyze the potential contributions of neuroscientific disciplines to the design of early interventions aimed at optimizing the cognitive performance of socioeconomically disadvantaged children. We hope this book will be useful for students and colleagues interested in this field.

The book is organized into six chapters. Chapter 1 reviews conceptual and operational definitions of poverty. Chapter 2 reviews the effects of material and social deprivation on molecular, cellular, and network levels of brain functioning. This analysis focuses on results obtained from studies of rodents and primates and includes discussions on brain plasticity, critical periods, and brain modification achieved by learning experiences as well as specific skill training. These issues are considered relevant to the understanding of the different analysis levels of cognitive and socioemotional development. Chapter 3 describes the effects of poverty on physical and mental health and their underlying mechanisms as risk factors. Chapter 4 discusses current results on the impact of poverty on human brain functioning. Current behavioral and neuroimaging experiments are analyzed, with a special emphasis placed on methodological and technical issues. Chapter 5 describes and analyzes examples of intervention programs aimed at modifying brain activation patterns and/or the cognitive performance of healthy children with and without socioeconomically disadvantaged backgrounds as well as children affected by either attention-deficit/hyperactivity disorder or dyslexic and dyscalculic disorders. The cognitive performance of children living in poverty is examined from neuroscientific and cognitive frameworks on the basis of experiments that have been carried out in different countries. Advantages of and differences from other intervention programs are discussed. Finally, chapter 6 presents several issues linked to the contributions of cognitive neuroscience and cognitive psychology to public policies for socially disadvantaged children, including a brief discussion of technological and ethical concerns. In addition, specific recommendations to officers and educators working with disadvantaged children are included.

We thank all those whose work is cited in this volume, and we gratefully acknowledge the support from Michael I. Posner to encourage its writing. We also thank Mary K. Rothbert and the reviewers for their contributions to this volume and Françoise Martins de Sousa and Valerie Melia for their work on English correction and translation. Lansing Hays, Maureen Adams, and especially Ron Teeter and Harriet Kaplan in the Books Department of the American Psychological Association have been helpful as we have put together this volume. We also acknowledge support from the National Research Council of Argentina, the FONCYT (Argentina), Fundación Conectar (Argentina), and the Centro de Educación Médica e Investigaciones Clínicas "Norberto Quirno."

1

CONCEPTUALIZATION AND MEASUREMENT OF POVERTY

This chapter deals with the definition of poverty and its assessment. Because of the intrinsic heterogeneity of human groups, even within the same culture, a definition based on a single set of variables only—for example, variables dealing with economy, basic needs satisfaction, human rights, and so on—may limit researchers' consideration of other significant aspects pertaining to poverty. This limitation could affect not only the way we understand poverty but also the design of social programs and policies.

In the study of poverty's impact on child development, four aspects are in need of close consideration. First, definition methods predominate that are based on either family income or any possible combination of income with social stratification, including education level and whether parents have jobs (Brooks-Gunn & Duncan, 1997; Gordon, Nandy, Pantazis, Pemberton, & Townsend, 2003; Minujin, Delamonica, Davidziuk, & González, 2006; United Nations Children's Fund [UNICEF], 2005). In these methods, a series of basic needs are defined a priori, and then research proceeds by checking on whether such needs are met within different population groups. This causes difficulties—for example, if privations are approached as an adult problem only. Second, measurement using specific analysis units such as the children or the family group fails to take into account aspects of the impact of privation on children's physical, intellectual, emotional, and social needs. Third, even when observation of a child's privations includes concern for the child's developmental processes (Brooks-Gunn & Duncan, 1997), those observations do not necessarily include an understanding of brain mechanisms. Fourth, studies aimed at analyzing child privations (Gordon et al., 2003) have not appropriately considered processes such as how privations influence the opportunities available to a child during stages of brain development.

The last two aspects are vital because brain development has not as yet been adequately incorporated into studies of poverty. On the one hand, investigations into child development and poverty insist on examining the intensity of privations and the importance of the time when privations occur (Duncan, Brooks-Gunn, & Klevanov, 1994). On the other hand, experimental research on brain development makes it clear that environmental privation and environmental enrichment modulate different aspects of both the structure and functioning of the central nervous system during the whole life cycle (see chap. 3, this volume). Studies within both cognitive neuroscience and developmental psychology allow identification of how cognitive processes relate to brain development, suggesting progressive interdependence and interrelationship (Diamond, 2007; Garon, Bryson, & Smith, 2008). For example, the rudimentary ability to select a given stimulus and focus one's attention on it is present in early childhood. Once this ability has been stabilized, children start controlling which stimuli they attend to. In other words, while the brain attentional networks are developing, this ability becomes more and more voluntary and less dependent on the immediate environment (Posner & Rothbart, 2007b). This development takes place during the first 12 to 18 months of postnatal life. During this period, privation or an inadequate environment could have a distinct impact on the child's attention. According to several studies, the exposure of pregnant mothers to drugs (whether legal or illegal) could result in alterations of children's cognitive performance and emotional behavior during subsequent developmental phases (Cichetti, Kaufman, & Sparrow, 2004; Espy, Kaufmann, & Glisky, 1999; Wasserman, Liu, Pine, & Graziano, 2001; see also chaps. 2 and 4, this volume).

Thus, any definition or measurement of child poverty should take into account the needs of cognitive and brain development. In this context, knowledge stemming from developmental cognitive neuroscience and developmental cognitive psychology has the potential to contribute to the design of actions directed toward the prevention of problems related to poverty, recovery from those problems, and optimization of development for children exposed to conditions of poverty.

CONCEPTS OF POVERTY

Although poverty affects more than 40% of the world population (United Nations Procurement Division, 2005) and 50% of children worldwide (UNICEF, 2005; see Figure 1.1), poverty is not a simple, easily understood concept. Researchers from different scientific disciplines, public agencies, and nongovernmental organizations (NGOs) have defined and measured poverty in several ways by applying different methods. Historically, the theoretical and practical goals of studies defining and measuring poverty have been aimed not only at the analysis of the multiple underlying processes involved and their effects on humans but also at identifying the features that could foster the design of genuine actions and policies aimed at modifying the impact of poverty on children.

Several stages can be identified in the history of studies analyzing the impact of poverty on child development during the late 20th century. Generally speaking, studies carried out before the 1980s sustained one-dimensional static concepts, such as socioeconomic status (SES) indexes that involved either family income alone or in combination with parental educational and occupational backgrounds. Studies carried out later in the 1990s began to conceive of poverty as a multidimensional phenomenon, analyzing it as a dynamic process in terms of its impact on several dimensions of cognitive development and physical growth (McLoyd, 1998). At about the same time, both the beginning and duration of privation of fundamental needs began to be considered critical factors for developmental outcome (Brooks-Gunn & Duncan, 1997). These conceptual changes led to new studies that started by analyzing impacts in terms of when in development they occurred (McLoyd, 1998) and the risks to which the child was exposed (Bhargava, 1998; Burchinal, Roberts, Hooper, & Zeisel, 2000; Evans, 2004; Walker et al., 2007). For example, several studies showed a positive association between the number of years living in poverty, established on the basis of income, and quality of life in the home environment (Garret, Ng'andu, & Ferron, 1994). Other studies showed that children living in homes in persistent poverty tended to have lower IQs as well as more behavioral disorders. It was also found that poverty of long duration had stronger effects than an occasional exposure to poverty (Duncan et al., 1994).

Current conceptual definitions of poverty used by both economists and sociologists—in official studies, NGO studies, and several child development studies—refer to a set of psychological, physical, and cultural needs, the satisfaction of which is a minimum condition for an adequate quality of human life (Boltvinik, 1999). In this definition, needs and satisfiers are the main dimensions; they form a system in which (a) some satisfiers are likely to meet several requirements, (b) the satisfaction of some necessities can be conditioned to the cancellation of others, and (c) any unsatisfied need is likely to cause multiple effects.

When establishing what poverty is, researchers and NGO officers assign a normative level of satisfaction to each type of need. In cases where the normative values of satisfaction are derived from the notion of human dignity and the universality of human rights, those necessities are considered to

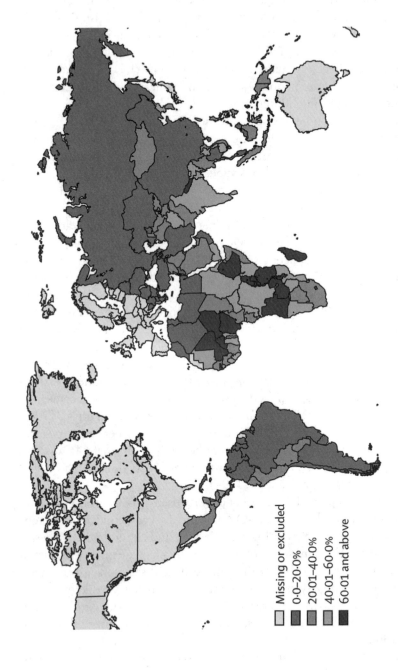

Figure 1.1. Percentage of disadvantaged children under 5 years, by country, in 2004. From "Developmental Potential in the First 5 Years for Children in Developing Countries," by S. Grantham-McGregor, Y. B. Cheung, S. Cueto, P. Glewwe, L. Richter, B. Stuup, and the International Child Development Steering Group, 2007, *Lancet, 369*, p. 66. Copyright 2007 by Elsevier. Reprinted with permission.

be absolute and their satisfiers to be both basic and universal—although in terms of history and culture, concepts such as "requirements" are not static. In each society, basic satisfiers vary according to the predominant cultural rules and material availability (Townsend, 1979). Thus, the lack of specific satisfiers would seriously decrease people's full participation in social life— that is, they would face social exclusion if they did not have these satisfiers. Furthermore, the study of child development has been confined to North America, Europe, and Australia, which include approximately only 10% of the children worldwide. That is, such studies have failed to consider the majority of children in Asia, Africa, Latin America, and the Pacific Islands, who live under conditions differing drastically in terms of developmental opportunities (LeVine & New, 2008).

The concept of poverty is therefore the result of a comparison between a personal or a family circumstance and a set of universal (absolute) and specific (relative) needs and satisfiers. Basic needs can be classified according to their form of satisfaction—for example, economic, political, cultural, and social. As already mentioned, definitions based on economic frameworks could involve different dimensions. For instance, *nourishment* refers to the availability of drinking water, food, and means for both preparation and consumption. *Health* and *biological reproduction* include access to public health services, home sanitation, and household hygiene. *Housing* includes criteria such as an appropriate house size on the basis of the number of family members living in it, appropriate materials and maintenance, services, furniture, and basic equipment for everyday life. *Socialization* and *basic education* refer to school, health, and work education as well as clothes, footwear, personal care, and public transportation. Finally, having access to basic information services such as TV, telephone, and regular mail have been recently included.

Needs considered not to depend directly on home economic conditions, such as affection, participation in social activities, identity, and freedom, are not easy to include in empirical studies or in intervention strategies aimed at optimizing the life of disadvantaged populations. Nevertheless, the satisfaction of noneconomic needs is also modulated indirectly by household economic circumstances. Not satisfying any one of these noneconomic (more cultural) the needs could result in being considered poor. Consequently, poverty could assume a dimension with either biological or cultural dominance.

Although measures of child poverty are dominated by income criteria, child welfare indicators differ inasmuch as they need to reflect children's specific positions among adults in the context of their family. This point of view requires specific poverty measurements in terms of welfare, rights, and developmental factors (White, Leavy, & Masters, 2002). For example, on the basis of results from high-quality intervention programs for children living in poverty, several researchers have identified a set of primary mechanisms for child development. These principles include environmental exploration, the expression of basic cognitive and social skills, the stimulation of language and symbolic communication, adult reinforcement of children's achievements, and the avoidance of inappropriate punishments (C. T. Ramey & Ramey, 1998; S. Ramey & Ramey, 2003).

In addition, recent studies within the realms of both cognitive psychology and developmental cognitive neuroscience have suggested that poverty's impact on different cognitive development aspects varies according to the maturation patterns of different neural networks, such as those supporting language, control, and monitoring processes (see chap. 4, this volume). Those studies suggest the possibility that both language and cognitive control systems are more susceptible to environmental influences than other networks. This contention supports other studies that show that the influence of parenting on the development of executive functions in children differs among cultures (Landry, Millar-Loncar, Smith, & Swank, 2002) and depend in part on the influence of SES on early vocabulary development (Hoff, 2003). Hence, beyond parents' education level and income, some structural aspects of households and materials availability as well as variables linked to the style of child raising are important in considering the impact of poverty (Bradley & Corwyn, 2005; Farah et al., 2008; Guo & Harris, 2000).

Numerous studies have shown that income has an impact on child development independent of the level of parental education (Duncan et al., 1994). Less is known about the impact of income in combination with such other indicators as unemployment, unstable employment, or income loss that do not necessarily place a family in poverty (Huston, McLoyd, & García Coll, 1994). Studies that have analyzed the isolated impact of income suggest that it has specific effects on different developmental dimensions. For example, verbal and nonverbal cognitive skills seem to be more affected by the income level than behavioral disorders when other family conditions, such as maternal education, age at childbirth, or parental employment are controlled (Brooks-Gunn & Duncan, 1997; Duncan & Brooks-Gunn, 2000). Associations between income and SES are also likely to vary by race and ethnicity as well as location in either an urban or a rural setting (Huston et al., 1994). Thus, poverty criteria perhaps should be changed to take into account experiences of the family linked with income, such as parental education or family structure (Duncan & Brooks-Gunn, 2000).

Even when income or SES measurements are computed accurately, they will not reflect poverty as an intense and painful psychological experience, and, indeed, a loss of freedom (Narayan, Chambers, Shah, & Petesch, 2000). Other methodological obstacles, such as the influence of the relationship between researchers and poor people on communication and information gathering, are also important. Finally, recent studies on child privation indicators based on basic needs criteria that have been carried out in developing countries worldwide suggest the need to analyze both the sole and combined contribution of physical and mental health on child development under the impact of poverty (Gordon et al., 2003; Minujin et al., 2006).

Studies on rights, security, empowerment (i.e., social capital), and psychological experiences in poverty have garnered less attention than studies focused on income or economic stratification. However, the inclusion of these other measures introduces significant analysis issues, inasmuch as the members of a family can perceive the same comfort—or discomfort—levels differently. For instance, some studies with adolescent participants have shown that the psychological experience of economic stress could be a mediator of the impact of poverty on psychological well-being (McLoyd, Jayaratne, Ceballo, & Borquez, 1994). Furthermore, the experience of poverty can also be modulated by social comparisons between peers at school, the characteristics of neighborhoods, and media (Huston et al., 1994).

More recently, qualitative methodologies have been applied to analyze how adults and children subjectively experience either poverty or specific privations. For example, a recent study by the World Bank in 52 countries, titled *Voices of the Poor* (Narayan et al., 2000), provides insight on this issue. This study shows effects of poverty on the psychological well-being of adults in several situations, such as precarious and transitory employment; isolated, unsafe, and stigmatized dwellings; hunger, fatigue, and chronic illness; gender inequities; social discrimination, exclusion, and isolation; abuse; institutional exclusion; weakness of social organizations; and lack of information and education. UNICEF (1999) has also identified indicators of well-being that are important to children, such as perception of peace in their society, perceived family harmony, quality of food, access to schooling, ability to play safely, and whether others look down on them.

It seems clear that all researchers studying child poverty, as well as those who design interventions, should take into account the different definitions of poverty in their methodological and analytical designs. Even current studies using such improvements as applying the income-to-need ratio indicator (e.g., Noble, Norman, & Farah, 2005) have not necessarily included the noneconomic dimensions likely to modulate poverty impact, nor have they considered the best times for an intervention depending on the stage of evolution within the life cycle.

MEASURING POVERTY

To understand the efforts to measure poverty, it is important to distinguish between direct measurements and indirect ones and between absolute and relative measurement. In the following paragraphs, we discuss each of these.

Direct Measurements

The direct method identifies the presence or absence of basic needs satisfaction and resources. Specifically, the measurement process involves an identification of privations of food, dwelling, health, education, transportation, drinking water, and systems for elimination of waste. Identification of basic needs is guided by the hypotheses that (a) all needs are considered basic in the sense that they identify a circumstance of critical privation, and (b) all needs are equally significant.

Different privation indicators are used to generate several indexes of unsatisfied basic needs (UBN)—one of the most-used direct methods, with variable degrees of homogeneity for different samples. Indexes are likely to vary in terms of the number of indicators that authors decide to include in their analyses. The UBN method allows the comparison of several degrees of dissatisfaction between groups and the design of national poverty maps.

Other direct poverty measurements frequently used in child development studies are parental employment and education as well as different determinants of SES, which represent a constellation of more central events than side events, as income-based criteria do, for example (see the next section, "Indirect Methods"). Thus, the UBN and SES indicators try to represent life conditions more directly in terms of both household, community, sanitary, and social conditions. Contrary to the income method, *stratification* approaches propose a hierarchical ranking based on home access and some combination of comfort values (i.e., *satisfiers*; McLoyd, 1998).

Despite these direct methods allowing identification of privations at several household levels (i.e., housing, education, occupation, overcrowding, etc.), methods that are usually used to identify long-term poverty, several authors have suggested that any identification of poor households should acknowledge that poverty is also a privation syndrome and that a compound of a few indicators does not allow a comprehensive identification. For instance, a recent study analyzed the effects of poverty on Argentine infants' cognitive performance (Lipina, Martelli, Vuelta, & Colombo, 2005; see also chap. 4, this volume). A UBN index including six basic needs indicators identified significant performance differences between socioeconomically disadvantaged and more advantaged children. In this study, a home was considered to be poor when at least two of the following conditions had been found: more than three people per room (i.e., overcrowding); disadvantaged housing (i.e., inappropriate building materials and maintenance); lack of services, furniture, and basic everyday life equipment; lack of toilet; presence of at least one child over the age of 6 who did not go to school; and four or more people economically dependent on a household head who had attended school for less than 7 years. Nevertheless, this type of analysis fails to include a consideration of specific child-oriented privation factors.

Furthermore, direct methods do not necessarily confirm correlations between the indicators, and poor families could meet the poverty criterion with only two indicators. This means that direct methods could change over time in the number of privations (Beccaria & Minujin, 1991; Boltvinik, 1995). Identifying privation is a task to be performed on the family group as a whole—

that is, this is not a task to be performed at the level of some family members or family subgroups, such as children. This means that aside from its usefulness in identifying links between general privation and child cognitive performance, partial identification fails to discriminate peculiar cognitive components in the resulting subgroups.

Indirect Measurements

The indirect method consists of calculating an income threshold that allows satisfaction of basic needs for food and other services such as education, health, transportation, and clothing. This method has attracted the attention of policymakers inasmuch as it has been developed on the basis of concrete physiological needs and thus is considered a valuable tool that is frequently used by governments (Roosa, Deng, Nair, & Lockhart Burrell, 2005). Because it is based on a threshold representing an absolute amount of money rather than a percentage of the median income, theoretically speaking everyone could be above that threshold.

Differences exist in the estimation and use of thresholds between industrialized and developing countries. For example, in some Latin American countries (e.g., Argentina), governments also use a second threshold to identify people living in extreme poverty conditions. This threshold only includes the income necessary to satisfy daily protein and energy in the diet, excluding needs related to education, health, and transportation. Although the direct method identifies long-term poverty, the indirect method allows detection of families who, in spite of enjoying good-quality dwellings and access to services, are no longer able to adequately satisfy their needs because of income drops. In Latin America and Eastern Europe, where financial crises take place cyclically, the latter represent a subgroup of "new poor" people resulting from increases in unemployment rates, reduction of income, and increase of unstable working positions.

All indirect definitions of poverty, including those based on income, bring about artificial dichotomies. That is, thresholds fail to reflect distances between poor and nonpoor people (Huston et al., 1994). This is a natural result of creating a dichotomy from a continuous variable. Thus, families whose income is US$1 below the threshold corresponding to their family size are not qualitatively different from similar-sized families whose incomes are US$1 above the same threshold. Nevertheless, one of those family groups is considered to be living in poverty whereas the other group is not (Roosa et al., 2005).

In addition, there is a significant concern about the availability and reliability of income information to be found in almost all studies on poverty. Respondents are often reluctant to report their income when answering an open-ended question. Furthermore, the income question becomes more sensitive when participants receive some type of public support because quite often, they will not talk about additional income they may be receiving out of fear that they will lose their subsidy privileges. Moreover, because many low-income workers are involved, at least partially, in a cash economy, no tax records exist to document their income (Roosa et al., 2005). At the same time, it is also possible that low-income workers are probably unaware of how much they earn per month or per year. For these reasons, categorical income ranges have been widely used as a means for reducing nonresponse questions on income.

Besides the absence of reliable information on family income, one of the most significant limitations of the indirect method is the need to obtain detailed knowledge about the way the members of a family use money to meet their basic needs, a fact requiring a systematic evaluation in order to estimate historic and geographic variations—that is, longitudinal methodologies. Furthermore, because the analysis unit is a family rather than an individual, equivalence scales are required to assess the nutrient needs for each family member. Even when periodic surveys include items related to family consumption, indicators likely to separate out privation aspects specifically linked to children's needs are not included. Methodological development requires investments not only in human resources—for example, survey takers' training—but also in materials and modifications to the relevant processing. In other words, besides interdisciplinary research and financing requirements, political and economic decisions need to be made. Adequate investigation of poverty is likely to be expensive, a fact that agencies studying poverty need to be aware of.

Absolute Measurements

Absolute measurements identify the basic needs below which people are disadvantaged (Iceland, 2003). They also include family income and poverty threshold components (e.g., typical thresholds, income-to-needs-ratios, family budgets; Roosa et al., 2005). Despite variations among countries, the family income threshold includes the gross annual income from sources such as earnings, pensions, and interest, and the poverty threshold is calculated using government-issued data to determine the minimum cost of food required for a family survival. Absolute poverty is also characterized by a severe privation of basic human needs, depending not only on income but also on access to social services.

In the application of absolute measures, a common approach to studying adaptation of families to poverty requires the use of raw income as a continuous variable. Measured in this way, income may not be useful unless both linear and nonlinear effects are considered (see Figure 1.2, p. 23). Some studies have shown both linear and nonlinear effects of family income in relation to children's school performance. For example, level of income appears to have the most significant impact during early childhood (Duncan,

Yeung, Brooks-Gunn, & Smith, 1998). Researchers have estimated that in low-income families, a US$10,000 average income increase over the first 5 years of a child's life, but not later, is associated with a 2.8 increase in the odds that the child will complete high school. Thus, the same increase in income may have a greater proportionate influence on the life of the child when that child is 3 than when he or she is 6.

The use of family income as a means for understanding the effects of poverty on child development requires careful and systematic analysis in order to address several issues. For example, Duncan et al. (1994) suggested that because of social stratification, some approaches, such as SES, evidence a relatively small variance when examining a specific group, so these methods are much more useful for stratifying people in the general population than within particular groups. Family income in absolute terms is less stable because it may change with job loss or promotion, and its influence may depend on the stage of development of the child, as mentioned previously. Some researchers have introduced an *income-to-need ratio*, obtained by dividing the total family income by the federal poverty threshold, as an indicator of the income required to meet basic needs. Because this ratio can be used as a continuous score, it allows recognition of the variation in income in relation to assessed needs (Roosa et al., 2005). This approach was recently applied by Noble and colleagues (e.g., see Noble, Norman, & Farah, 2005; see also chaps. 4 and 5, this volume) to identify variations in cognitive development due to socioeconomic factors.

Other absolute measures are basic family budgets that reflect the real income a family needs in order to have access to a nonpoverty standard of living. Housing, childcare, health care, transportation, taxes, food, and other needs, as well as the number and ages of adults and children living in each household, are included. Estimates are based on current costs for a specific geographic area, and no artificial multipliers are used. However, despite the potential usefulness of these indicators for studying child poverty, this measurement has not been used in family and child research. Compared with current poverty thresholds, the use of family budgets could provide a more valid indicator of the point at which family income becomes a stressful factor in multiple regions or cities (Roosa et al., 2005).

Absolute measures of income thresholds are usually considered objective because regardless of any standard of living, there exists a given sum of money below which people face economic hardship and privation (Iceland, 2003). Furthermore, poverty thresholds provide a simple way for drawing a line between poor and nonpoor people, so they can be applied evenly to persons in different areas of a country. Absolute measurements also allow for comparisons to be made on an annual basis as well as across historical periods. Additionally, as far as policymakers are concerned, absolute measures represent simple tools for determining program eligibility (Roosa et al., 2005). Nonetheless, poverty thresholds do not adequately account for differences in poverty levels within and across groups and among geographic areas (Brady, 2003), a fact that includes the consideration of specific indicators on the privations children actually suffer. Cost of living can vary significantly across geographical areas, mainly in developing countries; this is why some researchers believe that national standards for studies examining the influence of poverty on developmental dimensions may be of little use. Additionally, official thresholds do not necessarily include government benefits such as food stamps, health benefits, or working or housing subsidies. So family budgets based on those subsidies are significantly different from historic budgets with regard to the portion of income spent on food, shelter, goods, and services.

As already mentioned, family needs are dynamic in nature and change as children grow, but developmentally linked needs differences are not reflected in poverty thresholds (Linver, Brooks-Gunn, & Kohen, 2002). Timing, duration, and frequency of exposure to poverty, measured in terms of absolute criteria, may be important for understanding the effects of poverty on child development. For instance, it has been well documented that persistent poverty drastically increases the likelihood of child maladjustment (Duncan et al., 1994). Some studies have shown that recent financial difficulties or transitions cause more distress and damage in adaptive skills than chronic poverty status does (Keegan Eamon, 2000; Korenman, Miller, & Sjaastad, 1995). However, other studies have shown that transitory poverty due to a job loss is less significant than chronic poverty in terms of cognitive and socioemotional impacts (McLoyd et al., 1994). Some authors have argued that although poverty thresholds or any other income-based indicators seem to be disadvantageous, they tend to be used whenever the time dimension of poverty is considered (Duncan et al., 1994; Keegan Eamon, 2000). For example, Keegan Eamon (2000) has measured separately (a) persistent poverty (the average time a child has spent under the poverty threshold), (b) poverty transitions (the number of transitions from below to above the poverty threshold or the other way round), and (c) recent poverty (whether a child has lived under the poverty threshold over the past year). Linver et al. (2002) summed up how many years children live below the poverty threshold as an indicator of persistent poverty. In turn, Korenman et al. (1995) resorted to a 13-year long-term and a 1-year short-term income-to-needs ratio to represent both persistent and recent poverty in a longitudinal study using data from the U.S. National Longitudinal Survey of Youth.

Relative Measurements

Absolute measurements, focusing as they do on basic needs, do not account for perceptions of what poverty means or the subjective and subtle ways in which those who experience it define poverty. Relative measures overcome this problem indirectly by using comparative privation models, which theorize that poverty exists only as a relative fact in relation to a given

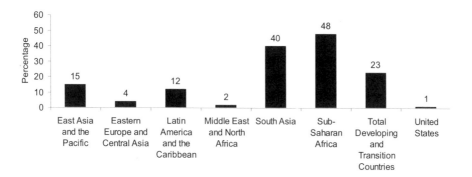

Figure 1.2. Percentage of people living on less than US$1 per day, by world area, in 1998. From *Poverty in America* (p. 60) by J. Iceland, 2003, Berkeley: University of California Press. Copyright 2003 by the Regents of the University of California. Adapted with permission.

society's level of economic and social development (Iceland, 2003). Relative measurements define poverty as a percentage of the mean, or median, household income for a specific country. They fit into the view that poverty is a function of how one person compares himself or herself with other people in his or her population. Thus, those measures are likely to account for changes in public perceptions of poverty and get inserted into national and historical contexts (Figure 1.2).

The major disadvantage of relative measurements is their lack of objectivity. In this case, poverty lines are more subjective—and often political—processes, depending on such issues as public opinion on what it takes to keep up with others. Furthermore, relative poverty is usually not computed for specific family sizes, meaning that a family falling under the selected percentage of the median income is considered poor, whether it is a 3-member family or a 12-member one. Finally, although relative poverty measures could readily be applied to almost any region in the world, because of their subjective nature, how useful it would be to use them in cross-cultural studies is unclear (Roosa et al., 2005).

Relative measurements also include several variants such as measurement of income-based stratification, economic distress, hunger, or food insecurity. *Economic pressure or hardship* is defined as the psychological distress resulting from financial difficulties (Barrera, Caples, & Tein, 2001). It has been shown to be related to family functioning and parenting, and, through these factors, to child adjustment. Economic pressure is assessed by the number of perceived economic hardships a person or a family has experienced. In the United States, Roosa et al. (2005) have identified the following three commonly used parent-report measures: (a) the *general economic pressure* measurement, which focuses on the strains caused by the overall family financial situation (e.g., whether it is difficult for a family to pay its bills each month); (b) the *unmet material needs* measurement, which asks each parent whether a family has enough money to meet their needs, including home, clothing, household items, car, food, medical care, and recreational activities items; and (c) the *specific economic pressures* measurement, used to determine whether parents have taken actions to adjust to their financial difficulties. These three variants have been used as (a) individual or multiple outcome predictors; (b) collectively, as indicators of a latent construct; and (c) when multiple responders are involved, to form a family score (Conger & Brent-Donnellan, 2007). Measures of economic pressure or hardship provide psychological meaning to poverty while linking research on poverty with the extensive literature on stress and coping (Roosa et al., 2005). Although these measurements allow researchers to understand variations in people's adaptation, they are not considered to be objective—that is, they are subject to common self-report biases. In addition, although they have been used with economically distressed and predominantly low-income subject samples, they have rarely been carried out among exclusively socially disadvantaged subject samples.

Self-reports of hunger, especially in developing countries, might contribute to a better understanding of variations in child stress and in coping abilities within families. Given the food-related privation and insecurity that critically affect the well-being of families and children (Walker et al., 2007), these types of measurements are valuable inasmuch as they offer a first-person perspective on children's perceptions of their experiences with food privation, which may be more informative than parent's perceptions when focusing on child-devoted outcomes (White et al., 2002).

Measurements of *food security*—that is, whether there is access to enough good quality food for a healthy life—that determine whether households are food insecure or hungry allow assessment of factors that could have direct consequences on children's physical, cognitive, and socioemotional development while setting up a link to biological and psychological processes. These measurements may need to be analyzed using cross-cultural criteria because of the fact that methods of obtaining food vary from one culture to another (Roosa et al., 2005).

Social exclusion measurements refer to measuring the degree to which either a family or a child does not participate fully in their society (Richardson & Le Grand, 2002). As in other relative measurements, social exclusion is used as a marker of whether individuals can satisfy their needs as well as other people do in their society. However, social exclusion differs conceptually from other relative measurements. The former directly assesses behavioral and circumstantial social participation indicators—for example, that adults do not vote and have no access to health services or that children do not participate in extracurricular activities because they lack transportation means or appropriate materials. Relative poverty measurements assume that differences in participation exist because of economic privation. Social exclusion measurements have begun to be applied only recently; hence, more research is needed before a scientific agreement is reached. Some European studies have linked social exclusion to negative outcomes, including depression, poor physical health, and teenage pregnancy, but elsewhere, family and child researchers have only begun to use social exclusion measurements in the past few years (Roosa et al., 2005).

Collective Measurements

In general, methods used to study diversity among poor people focus on either the individual or the family. Other approaches take into account ecological analysis and consider poverty as a collective experience. For example, owing to high housing costs, low-income families living in urban areas often have few housing options, which leads to high concentrations of poor families dealing with the same difficulties in some neighborhoods (Roosa et al., 2005). At the same time, living in poor urban settings has been associated with low-quality community resources and with an increased likelihood for people to be exposed to violence (Brooks-Gunn, Klebanov, Liaw, & Duncan, 1995).

Considering the multidimensional nature of poverty, some studies have included collective poverty in combination with other indicators taken from census data—for example, unemployment rates, proportion of households receiving public assistance, proportion of single-mother households, racial or ethnic heterogeneity, and residential mobility—to create a composite measurement of neighborhood disadvantages (Roosa et al., 2005). Collective poverty disadvantages are used as indicators of challenges families must deal with because of their place of residence; they are also used in examining how a given community environment or family resources mediate relationships between these disadvantages and child outcomes (Elliot et al., 1996; Roosa et al., 2005). However, a critical issue in the use of collective poverty measurements is the lack of consensus on defining *neighborhood*, even within the same cultural context—that is, is it defined by city blocks, census block groups, census tracts, groups of census tracts, and so on?

Other studies have analyzed collective poverty by *school poverty rates*, defined as the percentage of pupils eligible to receive free- or reduced-price lunches. Schools with a large number of low-income pupils tend to have fewer resources, coupled with providing lower quality academic preparation than schools with fewer poor children (Shipler, 2004). Furthermore, a recent study has shown that pupils attending high-poverty schools evidence lower academic achievements, regardless of their family income (Abbott, Joireman, & Stroh, 2002). As Roosa et al. (2005) stressed, few research studies on family and child development use a school-based approach. Moreover, it is unclear whether poverty at school level predicts some child outcomes better than family or neighborhood poverty.

Child Poverty Measurements

As seen previously, conceptual and operational definitions of poverty fail to include indicators likely to take into account specific information on privations children are subject to or an association with their developmental phases and dimensions. That is, it has been assumed that children suffer from deficiencies and privations depending on the groups to which they belong. Nonetheless, only recent studies have advised that children must be taken into account as independent analysis units because they are exposed differently than adults (Gordon et al., 2003; Minujin et al., 2006; Roosa et al., 2005; White et al., 2002).

The studies cited in the previous paragraph have noted several conceptual problems that exist regarding collective measurement. The first one is that most measures are not child specific. Thus, analyses based on income and expenditure consumption usually assume an equal sharing of resources within a given household. However, child poverty is not only dependent on family income but also on the availability of infrastructure and services. Another significant issue is whether all people within a poor household should be considered poor. It is most likely that variations in child-specific consumption are highly dependent on variations in household size, type, and geographical contexts.

Some researchers have tried to overcome these obstacles in income- and stratification-based measurements. For instance, in a recent study on poverty among children in countries from Eastern Europe, the indicator used to measure poverty was the current household consumption tested against an absolute poverty threshold of US$215 income per month per family converted at the purchasing power parity exchange rates. This measure appeared to correlate well with nonincome indicators of child well-being (Menchini & Redmond, 2006). The authors observed that the higher the absolute poverty rates among children, the lower the national income and the higher the proportion of children in the population.

Several social indicators, such as health and education status (e.g., life expectancy and literacy) are among the most frequently used nonincome measurements; others are infant and child mortality and school enrollment. Over the past 15 years, different NGOs and government agencies have proposed several alternative measures. For instance, in 1995, the United Nations Educational, Scientific and Cultural Organization proposed a set of complementary measures (Hernandez, 1996) of the well-being of children, grouped into dimensions such as parental and community resources (e.g., literacy by gender, age, fertility, community—meaning gross national product per capita), access to health care services, safe drinking water, and education. In 1999, the London Department of Social Security (Bradshaw, 2006) proposed a set of well-being indicators such as low birth-weight rates, reduction in the rate of hospital admission owing to injuries, or an increase in the rate of children obtaining lower scores in language and arithmetic tests. Finally, with regard to subjective indicators, which can be specifically linked to either income poverty or, more generally, with well-being, the Canadian National Longitudinal Survey of Children (Corak, 1998) has presented subjective indicators distributed into seven modules: friends and family, school, feelings and behaviors, puberty, smoking, drinking and drugs, and activities (White et al., 2002).

Contrary to what happens in industrialized countries, the literature from developing countries stresses the multidimensional nature of poverty for children (White et al., 2002). In this context, the United Nations Procurement Division (2005) and UNICEF (2005) have placed more emphasis on the nonincome features of development, such as social outcomes and participation. However, a significant gap exists when it comes to surveying child mental health in developing countries, where no systematic collection of data is to be found despite the range of possible instruments available. Educational data on enrollments, repeating grades, and dropouts are common in developed countries. By contrast, educational outcome data are not widely available on a worldwide comparable basis, so biases may occur because of different curricula or cultural norms.

Cognitive skills data also have been collected from specific studies at the individual level in the context of household surveys. An interesting feature of these studies is that this approach views cognition as a dimension of poverty from the perspective of human rights. For instance, the Ghana Living Standards Survey included simple written tests that measured reading, arithmetic, and abstract thinking (Grosh & Glewwe, 1995). The Monitoring and Learning Achievement project, in which poverty measurement is based on the attainment of life skills (Chinapah, 2003), collected data on everyday health, hygiene, nutrition, and social and natural environment. However, other learning achievement measures might include children's emotional characteristics, such as feelings, attitudes, interests, and values (White et al., 2002). The Birth to Ten to Twenty study covered growth, nutrition, health, illness, psychosocial development, care and education, social context, environment and health, sexual maturity, and reproductive history (Richter, Cameron, Norris, Del Fabro, & MacKeown, 2004).

In 1996, Childwatch International designed a project aimed at defining indicators to monitor the implementation of the Convention of Rights using samples from Latin America and Africa. Those indicators were linked to specific articles of the Convention, such as net enrollment, rates of dropout or repetition of school years, and more general articles adjusted to each country. For instance, Zimbabwe indicators were grouped according to parent–child relationships, social and economic privation, protection and survival, juvenile justice, and rehabilitation.

Other studies have attempted to build a composite index of child development compatible with the Human Development Index used by the

United Nations Development Program, which included material well-being (e.g., household income, assets, and public subsidies), physiological well-being (e.g., nutrition, health care, and maternal health), economic status, sanitation, and social dimensions (e.g., political and cultural factors; Corrie, 1994).

Finally, during a recent study on child poverty in developing countries, Gordon et al. (2003) designed an operational measure of absolute poverty based on the concept of *privation*, which refers to a state of observable disadvantage in personal, physical, and mental conditions, as well as local and environmental facilities, social activities, and habits. The authors stated that although poverty and privation are linked concepts, the latter refers to conditions irrespective of income. They postulated that to measure absolute poverty among children, it is necessary to define the threshold measurements of severe privation related to basic human needs, such as food, safe drinking water, sanitation facilities, health, shelter, education, information, and access to services.

Even though it is of great importance to widen the comprehension of how poverty affects child development beyond economic indicators or basic needs indicators, studies reviewed in this section failed to take into account the interrelationship and interdependence between phases, contexts, and dimensions—that is, growth, intellect, constitution, emotional reaction, socialization, and so on.

CONCLUSION

A variety of methodologies aimed at defining and measuring poverty in general, and child poverty in particular, have been presented in this chapter. A majority of these methods do not adequately include children as entities independent from adults. Methods that do take several child privations into account fail to include material and affective needs in terms of the different dimensions and stages of child development. With regard to child poverty, many researchers agree that owing to the complex nature of poverty, multidimensional measurement methods have to be adopted. This represents a task that would require the combined use of different indicators, general as well as specific (Harpham, 2000).

A demand for multidimensional definitions and measurements imposes an obligation to carefully select the measuring procedures, such as questions, hypotheses, and study objectives, both basic and interventionist, aiming at the analysis of child developmental processes. Promotion of collaborative work among research groups and NGOs devoted to the area in question would be most necessary. An example of this is the international workshop that was organized recently by the Comparative Research Program on Poverty and the Childwatch International Research Network. This workshop focused on the nexus between children and poverty and how both factors affect not only different child dimensions but development of future generations (see http://www.crop.org). Specifically, the workshop addressed the interdisciplinary effort needed to set up a real dialogue between researchers and practitioners to identify children's environmental requirements. In this regard, different neuroscientific disciplines could be in a position to contribute to such an endeavor with a considerable amount of modern knowledge of brain functions (Lipina & McCandliss, 2007). We turn to this topic in the next chapter.

2

EXPERIMENTAL MODELS: EFFECTS OF PHYSICAL AND SOCIAL PRIVATION ON BRAIN DEVELOPMENT

Developmental brain organization processes involve different levels of complexity. Several levels must be considered for a better understanding of the environmental impact of privations on child brain development. Two phenomena are of utmost importance. One is *brain plasticity*, which refers to a collection of mechanisms involved in the organization and the reorganization of brain components and connections that take place throughout the life cycle (Lledo, Alonso, & Grubb, 2006). The second is the existence of critical or sensitive developmental periods. These define temporal windows during which environmental variables can affect the neurobiological and behavioral organization of the individual in a more or less persistent way.

Since the mid-20th century, two main findings have clearly arisen from research on plasticity and environmental impact: (a) Material and social privation during the first developmental stages place brain structure and function in jeopardy, and (b) different types of environmental enrichment—for example, either material and social stimulation or specific cognitive exercises—can help with prevention or rehabilitation of disorders caused by poverty among child populations. Technological advances have made the study of some of these aspects possible in our own species, but experimental animal models remain a critical means for the thorough exploration of the intricate neural substrate and its molecular, cellular, and systemic mechanisms.

BRAIN ORGANIZATION AND MATURATION

Genetics and experience are the two forces that drive brain development. Over the past few decades, neuroscience has begun to elucidate the impact of experience on the architecture, biochemistry, and gene expression of the neural circuits involved in cognitive and socioemotional functioning. As result of such studies, it has become increasingly apparent that a significant feature of the interrelation between experience and brain organization is the existence of sensitive periods that significantly transform the information-processing capabilities demanded by experience. Within this context, another fundamental aspect is that the quality of the child-rearing milieu—the child's physical and social experience—modifies brain development.

Brain functioning involves plastic mechanisms that change throughout the life span, both before and after birth. Understanding these mechanisms requires an appreciation of the neurobiological basis of brain development, which proceeds in interaction with the child's experience. Although the basic brain layout is relatively fixed by the time a child is 2 to 3 years old, both structure and function continue to evolve and be refined by experience (Nelson, 2002).

Early brain organization follows a sequence of productive and regressive phenomena, regulated by genetic programs and experience. This sequence includes generation of cells and cellular processes and their connectedness followed by partial elimination of both in a process that is supposed to result in a decrease of redundancy and increased information processing. This sequence proceeds by means of program- and experience-induced neuronal death and pruning and retraction of cell processes (Bystron, Blakemore, & Rakic, 2008; Grossman et al., 2003; Rakic, 2006; see Figure 2.1).

The origin of the constitutive elements of the neural tissue neurons and glial cells is found within a common embryonic area: the neuroectoderm. Specifically, the development of the mammalian central nervous system follows several organizational stages, beginning with the neurulation process (3rd to 4th prenatal week). This is when neuroepithelial precursor cells are found, each with a capacity to become neurons or glia. Cell division will provide the population of neuronal and nonneuronal cells. Embryonic cells proliferate progressively and actively, entering a central neural tube. Two progenitor cell types develop: *neuroblasts*, from which neurons are to be formed, and *glioblasts* that give rise to glial cells. Neurons and glia are endowed with their own structural and functional characteristics and form the interactive elementary building blocks for brain organization and functional coupling.

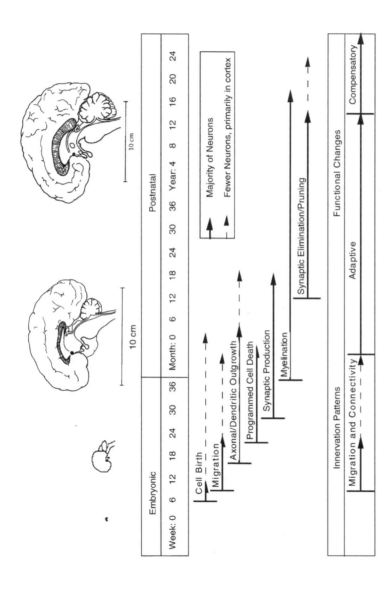

Figure 2.1. The stages of brain development (top) and windows of vulnerability (bottom). Developmental processes occur in phases, setting the stage for potential periods of vulnerability. Early insults in life (bottom) will be assimilated into innervation patterns, whereas a later prepubertal insult will cause functional changes that are more adaptive. From "Trajectories of Brain Development: Point of Vulnerability or Window of Opportunity?" by S. L. Andersen, 2003, *Neuroscience and Biobehavioral Reviews, 27*, p. 5. Copyright 2003 by Elsevier. Reprinted with permission.

It should be noted that although most brain neurons interrupt their mitotic division once they have achieved their final differentiation stage, except in hippocampus and olfactory bulb (Altman & Das, 1965; Goldman & Nottebohm, 1983; E. Gould, Reeves, Graziano, & Gross, 1999), glial cells do not. Concepts regarding glial cells have undergone drastic changes since the original descriptions that attributed to them only a supportive role. Indeed, glial cells are organized in complex, conditional networks with ionic, electrical, and amino acid involvement in glial–glial and neuronal–glial interactions. Additionally, glial cells participate in several trophic processes during brain development and brain reorganization after an injury (Verkhratsky & Toescu, 2006).

As the rostral portion of the neural tube enlarges because of cell proliferation, the brain begins to differentiate into various subcortical structures, followed by the growth of the cerebral cortex, in turn regulated by a variety of transcription factors—that is, proteins that directly or indirectly affect the initiation of the process whereby the DNA sequence in a gene is copied into both the messenger RNA and genes (Molnar et al., 2006). Adverse experiences likely to affect these processes directly or indirectly could significantly alter basic brain organizational patterns and functions. As an example, prenatal exposure to either methyl mercury or ethanol is likely to interrupt the neurogenesis process, thus leading to different types of mental retardation manifested throughout the first stages of mental development (Choi, 1989).

As previously mentioned, experimental studies carried out on different species have shown the postnatal generation of a small number of neurons in the *dentate gyrus*—one of the interlocking gyri that constitute both the hippocampus and the olfactory bulb (Lledo et al., 2006). Moreover, the proliferation and survival of these new cells appear to be highly modulated by environmental conditions. For instance, Rampon et al. (2000) have been verifying patterns of the environment-dependent expression of a large number of genes related to neuronal synaptic plasticity and neural transmission processes. However, as far as humans are concerned, both the age at which new cortical neurons are generated as well as their functional benefits remain a matter for debate (Bhardwaj et al., 2006).

Cerebral cortex development depends on the radial and tangential migration of successive waves of new cells taking place between the 6th week and the 3rd month after birth. Except for early neuronal cells scattered throughout what is going to become the first cortical layer, the cerebral cortex appears to follow a predominately inside-out organization pattern. Cells generated earlier migrate from the proliferation loci toward the surface of the cortex. As the immature cells migrate, different intrinsic and extrinsic signals modulate their genetic expression. As described by A. H. Mohammed et al. (2002), extrinsic signals such as extracellular proteins, cellular adhesion molecules, and trophic and growth factors are likely to either activate or suppress the expression of specific genes, thus affecting the final organization of the cortical neuropil. As previously mentioned, environmental factors could affect these processes deeply and, consequently, the normal development of the cerebral cortex (Grossman et al., 2003; Van den Pol, 2006).

A stage of neuronal differentiation involving the development of axons and dendrites takes place once a cell has completed its migratory process (Rakic, 2006). Dendritic growth and synapse formation and elimination follow cell migration and differentiation. Besides all the above-mentioned factors involved in cell migration, cell differentiation, neural circuit formation, cell maturation, and maintenance of synaptic contacts are dependent on neural activity patterns. Thus, even though visual deprivation experiments have shown that sensorial experience contributes to appropriate cortical modeling and connectivity, such phenomena also depend on several intrinsic cues (Majewska & Sur, 2006). More specifically, during prenatal and early postnatal development, cerebral cortex exhibits a synchronized oscillatory electrical activity, which could be essential for generating neural circuits (Khazipov & Luhmann, 2006).

On the basis of histological studies, different authors have proposed five stages in the synaptic formation process of the primate cerebral cortex (Grossman et al., 2003). The first two stages, determined by intrinsic mechanisms common to the whole neocortex, take place during embryonic life, involving a low synaptic density. A third stage of synaptic accumulation has been observed by the time of birth. At a fourth stage, synaptic density remains at a high level until the onset of puberty, which is followed by a period of synaptolysis, followed by a fifth stage that begins after sexual maturity, characterized by a slow process of synaptic density reduction. Whether the functional role of synaptic density changes through development is still a neuroscientific issue for debate (see, e.g., Bruer, 2006), even though researchers agree that this question is related to the continuous organization of the connectivity supporting information processing in the brain. During postnatal stages, cell processes and neural circuits are continuously adjusted on the basis of experience.

The sequence of intrinsic and extrinsic signals that trigger *apoptotic processes* (developmental, neural, or both) differs from those forms of neurodegeneration induced by *excitotoxicity* (death from toxins). Nearly half of the neurons in the mammalian central nervous system are eliminated by apoptosis, which involves functionally connected mature neurons as well as young cells before they are integrated into neural networks. According to Grossman et al. (2003), late periods of apoptosis appear to be associated with the removal of cells that fail to actively contribute to the function of neural networks, coupled with a process of selection of appropriate patterns of synaptic activity.

In the human brain, the peak of synaptic overproduction and pruning varies according to cortical areas. In the visual cortex, synapse formation peaks between 4 and 6 postnatal months, followed by a gradual reduction

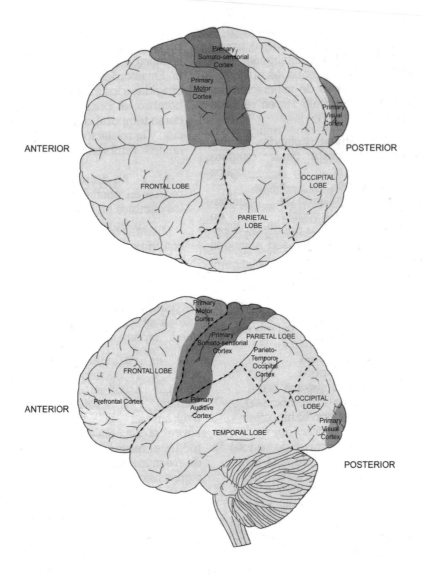

Figure 2.2. Superior (top) and lateral (bottom) views of main human brain lobes and association cortices.

toward adult numbers between 4 and 6 years of age. By contrast, the rate of synapse formation in the prefrontal cortex middle frontal gyrus is attained at about 12 postnatal months. Adult numbers are not obtained until mid to late adolescence (Nelson, 2002; Figure 2.2).

Once axons have been formed, the myelination process begins. As in the synapse formation process, development varies between brain areas. From both the sensory and motor areas, axon myelination process begins during the last prenatal quarter, whereas association areas—for example, frontal cortex—myelinate between the 1st and 2nd decades of life (Nelson, 2002).

CRITICAL AND SENSITIVE PERIODS

The structural and functional organization of the cerebral cortex is also modulated by the presence of either critical or sensitive periods. A *critical period* is a specific time during which either a brain structure or a function develops readily. Thereafter, acquisition is much more difficult and eventually less successful. During this period, specific, appropriate stimuli are needed for the brain to progress through developmental stages properly. *Sensitive period* refers to a time when the human brain is especially sensitive to particular classes of external stimuli. The sensitive period is also a temporarily opened time window during which the brain is particularly receptive to experience that contributes to brain organization. Gradually, this window closes, and the neural organization becomes irreversible (Siegler, DeLoache, & Eisenberg, 2003; Thomas & Johnson, 2008).

More than 60 years have been devoted to the study of such phenomena. The origin of this area of research can be located in the ethological studies describing how early experiences are likely to have a permanent impact on behavior, following the seminal studies performed by Konrad Lorenz and colleagues in the 1930s (see, e.g., Lorenz, 1965). A classic example is the study of social imprinting in birds: Fledglings, once exposed to members of their species when they are just out of the shell, will develop adaptive attachment behaviors and appropriate gender preferences (Knudsen, 2004). Studies with birds, cats, dogs, monkeys, and humans suggest that critical periods constitute a significant phenomenon in the brain development of various species. Recent studies have disclosed that these periods are not necessarily fixed in terms of timing and object specificity. For example, the critical period for the imprinting of any domestic bird could be extended if the appropriate stimulus is missing; alternatively, imprinting can be reversed under certain learning conditions. This suggests that closure of this critical period is likely to constitute the natural consequence of a given learning process rather than being strictly finite. This line of evidence has led different researchers to prefer the use of the term *sensitive period* to *critical period* (Michel & Tayler, 2005).

Several studies performed in humans show the expression of multiple sensitive periods in sensory systems as well as in connection with several aspects of speech development and musical perception (in the auditory field) and in face recognition (in the visual field; Patel, 2003; Peretz & Zatorre, 2005). An important feature in the development of these sensory systems is that sensitive periods are not synchronized among sensory modalities. In spite of such differences in developmental timing, basic plastic mechanisms appear to be similar. The end of a sensitive period is often associated with the age at which a set of neural circuits subserving a given neural processing becomes specialized. For instance, in humans between 6 and 12 months of age, electrophysiological patterns associated with face recognition processes become specific for a given stimulus. In addition, and at approximately the same age, the number of cortical areas activated by the viewing of faces seems to decrease. This suggests that the end of the sensitive period of a neural substrate for a given modality processing coincides with the attainment of specialization (M. H. Johnson, 2005).

In the case of neural circuits involved in complex behaviors, the closure of sensitive periods seems to depend on whether they relate to circuits performing either fundamental or high-level computations. For instance, the sensitive period for circuits combining visual inputs from both eyes comes to an end long before circuits responsible for recognizing biologically significant objects (Pascalis et al., 2005). According to Knudsen, Heckman, Cameron, and Shonkoff (2006), experience-dependent plasticity (see next section) of high-level circuits depends on the type of information provided by those circuits and is unable to attain completion until such circuits become stable.

IMAGING-BASED STUDIES AND BRAIN DEVELOPMENT

Data from animal experiments and human postmortem studies have allowed analysis of the basic processes underlying brain development. However, histological studies provide only limited evidence regarding late brain maturation because it may be related to variability among individuals over time and the evolution of several neural functional systems. In this sense, technique-based imaging studies have contributed to serial observations of several brain developmental processes. For example, the National Institute of Mental Health's pediatric brain imaging project (Lenroot & Giedd, 2006) has proposed main long-term goals for the mapping of developmental trajectories of brain development, the study of genetic and environmental influences on these pathways, and the use of this knowledge to guide interventions aimed at optimizing brain development.

The first magnetic resonance imaging (MRI) cross-sectional studies on normal developmental changes showed that volumes of *gray matter* (i.e., neuron bodies and dendrites), generally decline once a child is more than 6 or 7 years old and keep decreasing during adolescence, whereas *white matter* (i.e., myelinated fibers) increases linearly over time (Toga, Thompson, & Sowell, 2006). However, the first longitudinal studies showed a linear increase in white matter up to age 20 coupled with a nonlinear change pattern in cortical gray matter. For example, Giedd et al. (1999) demonstrated a preadolescent increase for the frontal and parietal lobes and an adolescent rise for the temporal lobe. In another longitudinal MRI study conducted on healthy children, Gogtay et al. (2004) observed that total brain size reached 95% of maximum size by age 6, although cortical and subcortical components changed significantly throughout childhood and adolescence. Gray matter volume

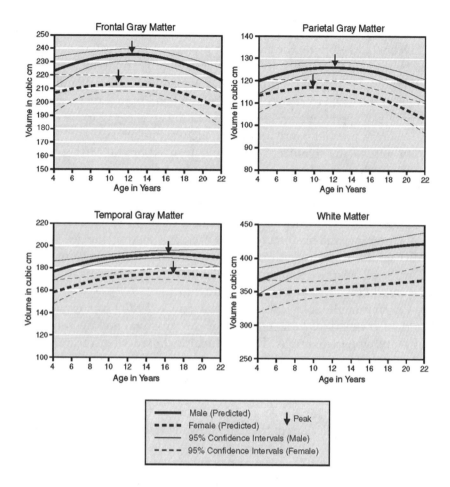

Figure 2.3. Frontal gray matter, parietal gray matter, and temporal gray matter volumes: 243 scans from 145 subjects (scans acquired at approximately 2-year intervals). The arrows indicate peak volume. From "Brain Development in Children and Adolescents: Insights From Anatomical Magnetic Resonance Imaging," by R. K. Lenroot and J. N. Giedd, 2006, *Neuroscience and Biobehavioral Reviews, 30*, p. 724. Copyright 2006 by Elsevier. Reprinted with permission.

tends to follow an inverted-U developmental course, with volumes reaching peaks at different times in different brain areas (Figure 2.3). These developmental trajectories appear to follow a regionally specific pattern: For example, areas subserving primary functions attain maturity earlier than higher order association areas.

In contrast to the inverted-U shape of gray matter developmental trajectories, white matter as a whole generally increases throughout childhood and adolescence—growth is similar in frontal, temporal, and parietal lobes. Furthermore, proximal pathways tend to be myelinated before distal pathways, and a similar evolution is observed in association areas: Sensory areas are myelinated before motor areas, and projection areas before association areas (Volpe, 2000). Finally, in normally developing children, Sowell et al. (2004) showed a cortical thinning of approximately 0.15 to 0.30 millimeters per year in the language areas of both temporal and frontal lobes, whereas a growth rate of approximately 0.40 to 1.50 millimeters per year was observed in other areas, predominantly in frontal and occipital areas.

In spite of the significant findings evidenced by the MRI technique, these studies have not been able to explain the cellular changes involved in the brain maturation processes (Toga et al., 2006). The MRI procedure measures changes in volume and density of brain structures, but so far it lacks enough resolution to identify cellular changes such as dendritic remodeling, synaptic pruning, and myelination. However, gray matter changes described in MRI studies correlate with the postmortem sequence of regionally variable increased synaptic pruning and myelination observed during adolescence and early adulthood, as described by Huttenlocher (1979).

Obvious methodological limitations exist regarding the capability to draw tight correlations between cell—at the structural and neurochemical levels—and system functions. These difficulties arise for both technical and theoretical reasons because they may be related to either distributed neural networks or to interactions of neurons, glial cells, neurotransmitter systems, and synaptic function within any given brain area (Colombo, Reisin, Miguel-Hidalgo, & Rajkowska, 2006). Yet, despite these limitations, some studies have suggested correlations between functional capacities and the size of certain brain structures. A partial view of these studies is summarized below.

In animal research literature, studies with various species of birds, voles, kangaroos, rats, and pigeons have shown that despite their evolutionary histories and genetic backgrounds, there is a common relationship between relative hippocampal size and spatial ability (Sherry, Jacobs, & Gaulin, 1992). For instance, Krebs et al. (1989) showed that the volume of the hippocampal complex relative to brain and body size was significantly larger in species of birds that store food. With regard to human studies, Haier, June, Yeo, Head, and Alkire (2004) found that more gray matter was associated with higher IQ in frontal (Brodmann's areas [BAs] 10, 46, and 9), temporal (BAs 21, 37, 22, and 42), parietal (BAs 3 and 46), and occipital (BA 19) lobes in adults. Applying a different approach, Maguire et al. (2000) found that taxi drivers with extensive traffic experience had larger posterior and shorter hippocampal anterior areas than controls. Furthermore, hippocampal volume correlated with the amount of time spent as a taxi driver, supporting the concept that hippocampus stores spatial representations of the environment. These representations can expand regionally to accommodate further representational events in people with a high dependence on traffic-related demands.

EFFECTS OF EXPERIENCE ON BRAIN STRUCTURE AND FUNCTION

Although the history of brain modifications due to experience can be traced to ancient Greece (Rosenzweig & Bennett, 1996), it was in the 19th century that the first hypotheses appeared regarding how the nervous tissue responds to increased demands. For example, ethologists and biologists presented several examples of how wild animals differ from domesticated ones in brain measurements as evidence that evolutionary pressures are capable of reorganizing brain structure. Charles Darwin described increased brain size in wild rabbits compared with domesticated rabbits. The interest in brain size has been sustained by researchers and philosophers ever since.

Psychologist Donald Hebb (1949) postulated a theory of neuronal plasticity according to which when a neuron stimulates another one repeatedly, a change takes place in either one or both cells, so that the communication between them becomes increasingly efficient. Hebb's pioneering observations influenced other researchers who, in the early 1960s, began to study laboratory animals, mostly rodents, reared in complex versus standard and isolated environments. Results showed changes in brain chemistry and anatomy in young and adult animals owing to experience. These findings were not consistent with the prevailing view that during adulthood the brain is fixed and static and, therefore, not susceptible to modifications produced by environmental influences. On the contrary, it was found that housing adult rats in a complex environment—in terms of sensory and social stimuli—induced measurable changes in gross brain structure as well as at the molecular level (e.g., the acetylcholinesterase enzyme). These findings were followed by demonstrations of environmentally induced neurohistological changes, such as length of dendritic branching and spine density (Rosenzweig & Bennett, 1996). More recent studies have confirmed (a) the same pattern of environmental impact in several species, such as nonhuman primates (Kozorovitskiy et al., 2005); (b) increases in adult rates of neurogenesis; (c) changes in molecular events related to neurotransmission in different species (A. J. Bennett et al., 2002; Neddens, Brandenburg, Teuchert-Noodt, & Dawirs, 2001); and (d) several neuroprotective effects (Bezard et al., 2003; Fox, Merali, & Harrison, 2006; Winocur, Moscovitch, Fogel, Rosenbaum, & Sekeres, 2005), including cognitive training in nonhuman primate species (Lipina & Colombo, 2007).

Hebb (1949) also pioneered the concept of "enrichment" from an experimental point of view, starting from the description of improvements in the behavior of domestic rats in comparison with other rats raised in the laboratory under standard conditions. Then, in the early 1960s, two experimental approaches were developed to investigate the effects of experience on brain organization. In the first case, D. Hubel and T. Wiesel designed a program to examine the effects of selective visual deprivation during early stages of visual cortex development (A. H. Mohammed et al., 2002). Almost simultaneously, Rosenzweig and colleagues introduced the paradigm of complex environments as a measurable concept (Rosenzweig & Bennett, 1996). In early studies with rodents, the effects of exposure to environmental complexity were observed on whole brain weight, total brain contents of DNA and RNA, and total brain proteins. Further studies showed that environmental complexity was able to induce significant changes in biochemical parameters, dendritic branching, neuronogenesis, and gliogenesis as well as improving learning abilities in mature individuals (Grossman et al., 2003; Markham & Greenough, 2004; Rosenzweig & Bennett, 1996; Van Praag, Kemperemann, & Gage, 2000).

In these experimental contexts, a *complex environment* is characterized by comparing with conditions in standard laboratory cages. In general, animals living in a complex environment are placed in groups inside large cages, usually containing different types of objects. This allows them to develop complex social interactions as well as engage in exploratory and motor activities. Placement of inanimate elements and location of food are changed periodically to minimize habituation. Thus, this environment consists of the combination of social stimuli and novel, complex, inanimate stimuli (Figure 2.4).

It has been suggested that plasticity processes depend on at least two basic phenomena. One relates to particular experiences for all the members of a species for whom sensory stimuli guide brain development by selection and elimination of neural contacts (*plasticity expectant of experience*; Markham & Greenough, 2004; A. H. Mohammed et al., 2002). The visual system organization in Mammalia illustrates this concept. In most cases, when the eyes open at due time after birth, the visual cortex is organized and prepared to process stimuli significant for each species (e.g., light patterns). Initially, axons innervate the visual cortex in a superimposed way—that is, axons converge while performing a crossover. During development, axons are partially pruned, and cell columns of ocular dominance emerge in an alternating fashion on the basis of eye dominance for afferent information. So primary visual cortex cells are organized in a columnlike way, starting from the first cortical layer down to the white matter. Each column responds to an exclusive orientation axis. The development of ocular dominance columns involves a competition among axons channeling information from each eye. Following occlusion of one eye at birth, the ocular dominance columns innervated by the open eye develop in a wider way than the opposite-side columns. Furthermore, the cortical representation corresponding to the occluded eye exhibits an immature synaptic morphology whereas the opposite discloses a mature synaptic morphology (Grossman et al., 2003).

Brain changes depending on individual experience have been referred to as *plasticity dependent on experience* (Grossman et al., 2003). The complex environment paradigm has also been used to characterize these processes.

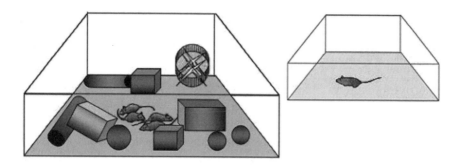

Figure 2.4. Rearing conditions in different experimental groups. Left: cage for enriched environment consisting of social interaction, stimulation of exploratory behavior with objects, and a running wheel. Right: cage for isolation. From *Vulnerabilidad social y desarrollo cognitivo: Aportes de la Neurociencia* [Social Vulnerability and Cognitive Development: Contributions of Neuroscience] (p. 60), by S. J. Lipina, 2006, Buenos Aires, Argentina: Jorge Baudino Ediciones. Copyright 2006 by Jorge Baudino Ediciones. Reprinted with permission.

Exposure of different species to enriched conditions, in comparison with either standard or deprived environments, has been associated with several structural changes in neurons and synapses (synaptic number and morphology, dendritic arborization, cell morphology), glial components (number of astrocytes and glial-synaptic contacts, myelination, cell morphology), brain vasculature, brain cortex weight and thickness, rate of hippocampal cell neurogenesis, availability and metabolism of both neurotrophic factors and neurotransmitters in different brain areas, and neurotrophic and neurotransmitter gene expression (Grossman et al., 2003; Markham & Greenough, 2004; A. H. Mohammed et al., 2002).

Functionally, the same type of exposure has been associated with alterations of postsynaptic potentials in the hippocampus dentate gyrus (Rosenzweig & Bennett, 1996). Another synaptic morphology with a proposed relevance to plasticity is the multisynaptic bouton, present in the presynaptic processes of cortical, hippocampal, and cerebellar areas. Thus, the formation of new contacts represents a common form of plastic synaptic change. These morphological effects are typically viewed as modifications of preexisting synapses, although they could also reflect either synapse remodeling intermediate stages or the formation or loss of different property-endowed synapses.

As mentioned previously, the experience-related activation of neural circuits is also likely to cause changes in the genetic expression of specific circuits. Protein products of such genes could cause long-term effects on the chemistry, excitability, and structure of the neurons involved. For example, induced gene products are in a position to regulate the formation or elimination of synaptic connections as well as the responsiveness of neurons to ei-

ther neural activity or to specific hormones, neuromodulators, or neurotransmitters (Kandel, 2001). Moreover, some genes are "on"—that is, their expression levels are susceptible to adjustment by experience—only for a limited (i.e., sensitive) period during the maturation process of a given circuit
(Corriveau, Huh, & Shatz, 1998).

The effects of experience on neural organization during development
are related to several mechanisms, the most significant of which are the molecular and cellular mechanisms that mediate neural plasticity during the
sensitive period, enabling circuits to undergo substantial changes in their
architecture, chemistry, and gene expression (Knudsen et al., 2006). During
the early stages of neural circuit formation, patterns and connective strength
take place in accordance with genetically encoded mechanisms. However,
connectivity patterns tend to be relatively imprecise and weak. This shaping, strengthening, and stabilization of neural connections includes cell- as
well as circuit-level mechanisms. Such changes tend to reinforce the initial configuration as well as limiting the formation of alternative connectivity patterns. Thus, early experience is particularly influential because of
a unique advantage, namely, lack of interference from a preexisting connectivity pattern.

Brain changes associated with exposure to environmental complexity
have been documented in a wide variety of species. Studies carried out with
fruit flies (*Drosophila melanogaster*) have shown that any exposure to environmental isolation or complexity affected neural events in central and medul-
lary bodies (Technau, 1984). These effects were observed in crickets as well
as in the African jewel fish. Moreover, social experience modulation of dendritic spines and branches in tectal interneurons (Coss & Globus, 1979) and
an increased cell proliferation in the olfactory system was verified in adult
crayfish placed in complex environments (Sandeman & Sandeman, 2003).
Similar effects on brain and behavior were described in gerbils, squirrels,
cats, monkeys, and bears after they were exposed to complex environments
(A. H. Mohammed et al., 2002).

Although the described effects were repeatedly verified in young animals, synaptogenesis also appears to occur throughout the lifespan. Exposure
to a complex environment has been shown to affect dendritic field dimensions in the visual cortex of young adult, middle-aged, and even elderly rodents. Furthermore, behavioral experience appears to induce anatomical
changes throughout the life span in the cerebellum and cerebral cortex of
rodents (Greenough, West, & DeVoogd, 1978).

Regarding the effects of exposure to complex and isolated conditions,
the main differences were found in the visual cortex of rodents, especially in
the deeper layers (E. L. Bennett, Diamond, Krech, & Rosenzweig, 1964),
with increased higher order dendritic branches in complex conditions compared with those found in isolated conditions (Grossman et al., 2003). Additionally, following exposure to complex environments, dendrites in pyrami-

dal neurons from Layers II and III showed increased branching and length terminal segments, and a larger postsynaptic thickening was observed in neurons from Layers III and IV (Grossman et al., 2003).

In addition to the effects described in the visual cortex, complex environments also induce neuroanatomical and biochemical changes in other brain areas of young and adult rodents, including frontal, parietal, and entorhinal cortices; hippocampus; and cerebellum (Grossman et al., 2003; A. H. Mohammed et al., 2002; Rosenzweig & Bennett, 1996). A considerable body of literature links the hippocampus to various plasticity factors and to learning and memory mechanisms such as gene expression and protein levels of neurotrophins, glucocorticoid receptors, the Alzheimer amyloid precursor protein, immediate early genes, serotonin receptors, α-amino-3-hydroxy-5-methyl-4-isoxazole propionic acid receptor binding, and neurogenesis (A. H. Mohammed et al., 2002).

Middle-aged rats that had spent at least 1 year in complex environmental conditions showed higher levels of nerve growth factor in the entorhinal cortex than isolated animals (A. H. Mohammed et al., 2002). Furthermore, several studies have suggested an involvement of these neurotrophins in the synaptic plasticity of the hippocampus and other brain areas, such as the somatosensory and visual cortex (McAllister, Lo, & Katz, 1995). Several neurotrophic factors, such as nerve growth factor, the brain-derived neurotrophic factor, and the neurotrophin-3, are abundantly expressed in pyramidal cells and dentate granule cells, a fact suggesting that neurotrophins are involved in mediating changes into the dendritic morphology following exposure to complex environments.

In this regard, the role of the hippocampus in learning and memory has been the focus of increased research interest involving the generation of new neurons. Using the proliferation marker bromodeoxyuridine, different studies have shown that enrichment increases neurogenesis in the dentate gyrus of adult mice and rats. This effect has been associated with learning (Shors et al., 2001), whereas stress experience has been related to the reduction of neurogenesis (E. Gould, McEwen, Tanapat, Galea, & Fuchs, 1997).

In addition to cortical and subcortical brain structures, the cerebellum has also been found to display plastic properties in response to environmental influences. Specifically, learning of a complex motor skill leads to an increase in the synaptic numbers of the cerebellar cortex and also to changes in the morphology of cerebellar Purkinje cells in rodents and monkeys (Kleim, Jones, & Schallert, 2003).

The multiple changes described above that take place in the brain following exposure to complex experiences may contribute to the enhanced cognitive function that has been observed in several behavioral tests. For instance, different studies have found that rats with hippocampal lesions exposed to an enriched environment improved their performances in several tasks related to locomotor activity in their home cage, reactivity to novelty, and checking up their reference memory in the Morris water maze (Galani, Jarrard, Will, & Kelche, 1997; A. K. Mohammed, Winblad, Ebendal, & Larkfors, 1990) and their learning ability in both the Hebb–Williams maze (Galani et al., 1997; A. K. Mohammed, Jonnson, & Archer, 1986) and the radial arm maze (Galani, Coutureau, &, Kelche, 1998). It is interesting that Galani et al. (1997) also found that these beneficial effects depended on the localization of the lesion and on the nature of the task.

Behavioral changes following exposure to enriched environmental conditions are not limited to the improvement of cognitive performance. One robust observation has been based on the effects of isolation. This is the case of rodents that after being reared in isolated environments interacted less with objects in a free exploration situation while displaying an increased locomotor activity coupled with a reduced habituation, which indicates increased arousal and emotionality (A. H. Mohammed et al., 2002). These behaviors correlated with neuronal and synaptic morphological changes in the medial amygdaloid nucleus (Ichikawa, Matsuoka, & Mori, 1993), auditory cortex, primary somatosensory cortex, and basal ganglia after an aversive learning (A. H. Mohammed et al., 2002). The above-mentioned observations suggest that depending on the complexity of environmental enrichment brain circuits would be affected with either more or less specificity involving different cortical areas and subcortical structures.

The temperaments of individual rats could also be altered by early social experiences. A good example is neonatal care by mothers who groom them extensively and facilitate their access to milk. In postweaning time, young rats who have had this experience explore their environment much more while becoming less anxious (Caldji, Tannenbaum, Sharma, Francis, & Plotsky, 1998). Additionally, cross-fostering studies suggest that these effects are regulated by environmental factors rather than genetic programming. For example, rats born to low-grooming mothers but raised by high-grooming ones become socially normal adults. Conversely, rats born to high-grooming mothers but reared by low-grooming ones become anxious and, eventually, low-grooming parents (Francis, Diorio, Liu, & Meaney, 1999). Finally, exposure to complex environments has also been associated with therapeutic and protective effects against impending threat and enduring effects of past and subsequent stressors (Fox et al., 2006).

Since the early work by H. Harlow with monkeys, several studies have shown the extent to which the disruption of an early affiliative bond has long-term effects on future social interactions in terms of affiliative and aggressive behaviors (Knudsen et al., 2006). It is interesting that the nature and severity of the effects caused by removing the mother in experimental settings change pursuant to the age of the litter at the time of separation. Once the litter is 6 months old, removing their mother does not appear to affect them. In contrast, should the mother be removed when the litter is only 1 month old, acute withdrawal syndrome and depression symptoms are observed, followed by an increased seeking of social comfort from other group members as well as a variety of atypical social behaviors, a great many of which persist into adulthood. Late attempts to remediate these consequences have had a limited impact. For instance, placing a surrogate mother within the social group during the 1st month of deprivation is effective at normalizing social contact time and self-comforting behaviors, whereas later replacements are less effective (Nelson et al., 2002). Once more, these results suggest the existence of a sensitive period regarding the emotional impact of nurturing relationships with a primary caregiver.

The concept of neural plasticity is also central to the design of neuroprotective and neurorestorative strategies applicable to the treatment or amelioration of several brain disorders. Recent studies with rodents and nonhuman primates have begun to apply experimental strategies aimed at protecting neurocognitive systems, either by premorbid specific training or exercising, or the application of the environmental complex paradigm. It seems highly pertinent to mention here several studies performed along this line of thought. Normal rats reared in a complex environment and thereafter receiving hippocampal lesions showed the retention of allocentric spatial memory for that environment (Winocur et al., 2005). Exposure of adult mice to an enriched environment or exercise during adulthood protected against neurotoxicity induced by a treatment with 1-methyl-4-phenil-1,2,3,6-tetrahydropiridine (MPTP; Bezard et al., 2003; Faherty, Raviie Shepherd, Herasimtschuk, & Smeyne, 2005; B. E. Fisher et al., 2004), a neurotoxin that has deleterious effects on working memory and inhibitory tasks performance. Clues to the effects of this neurotoxin at the nonhuman primate level were recently provided by a study we performed (Lipina & Colombo, 2007). We showed that cognitive exercising in tasks tapping inhibitory control and spatial working memory processes before a chemical lesion prevented impairment of cognitive performance in such tests, which normally occurs following the administration of MPTP neurotoxin at doses that induce a condition of parkinsonism (Figure 2.5). In summary, these findings support the idea that experimental analyses on either specific premorbid exercising or exposure to complex environment could provide a noninvasive means to interfere with cognitive impairment.

Increases in dendritic branching and number of synapses after exposition to complex environments persist for at least 30 days once an experiment is over (Briones, Klintsova, & Greenough, 2004; Rosenzweig & Bennett, 1996). Neuroanatomic changes after a motor training in terms of the number of synapses per neuron in cortical motor areas also persist between 1 and 2 months once training has been interrupted (Kleim, Vij, Ballard, & Greenough, 1997). These observations suggest that even in absence of continuous stimulation, the brain maintains residuals of previous experiences, which in turn may result in either positive or negative influences on future adaptive behaviors depending on the actual conditions of the environmental exposure.

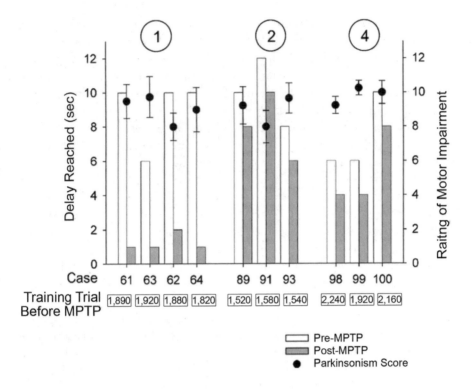

Figure 2.5. Maximum delay was reached in the spatial delayed response task before and after 1-methyl-4-phenil-1,2,3,6-tetrahydropiridine (MPTP) treatment in three different experimental conditions: one pre-MPTP run of exercises (1); two pre-MPTP runs of exercises (2); and four pre-MPTP runs of exercises (4). Note relative stability of motor scores among animals (solid dots), suggesting a motor-cognitive dissociation after premorbid training. sec = seconds. From "Premorbid Exercising in Specific Cognitive Tasks Prevents Impairment of Performance in Parkinsonian Monkeys," by S. J. Lipina and J. A. Colombo, 2007, *Brain Research, 1134,* p. 181. Copyright 2007 by Elsevier. Reproduced with permission.

Induction of structural changes of nonneuronal components such as glial cells and vasculature after a complex environment experience could also have an impact on brain functioning. For example, astrocytic hypertrophy following exposure to complex environment in rodents may indicate either an increased demand on synaptic microenvironment or alterations that impact on the neuronal information processing by modifying the functional organization in either a relatively transitory way or even more permanently (Briones et al., 2004). Yet the actual effect of the environmental impact on the dynamic interaction between neurons and glial cells has yet to be adequately studied. Owing to the growing understanding of the astroglial role in neuronal metabolism and trophism as well as in synaptic efficacy, it is intuitively predictable that much remains to be known about astroglial modifications as well as changes in brain microvasculature following exposure to environmental conditions (Grossman et al., 2003; Markham & Greenough, 2004; A. H. Mohammed et al., 2002).

Finally, neural plasticity in humans may also lead to use-dependent structural adaptations in the cerebral cortex gray matter in response to environmental demands (Toga & Thompson, 2005). At the MRI level, there is evidence that the brain may adapt dynamically to environmental cognitive demands. For instance, neuroimaging studies have shown structural changes after training in difficult motor tasks, such as juggling (Draganski et al., 2004), increased hippocampal volumes in taxi drivers with enhanced spatial traffic skills (Maguire et al., 2000), and increased gray matter in motor, auditory and visual–spatial brain areas in pianists (Gaser & Schlaug, 2003).

CONCLUSION

In summary, as Knudsen et al. (2006) have stated, several experimental studies have demonstrated that the early environments in which animals are reared exert significant influences on their temperament, social behavior, and cognitive skills. The importance of animal research lies in providing the means to elucidate fundamental, underlying, developmental, and neurobiological processes. In brief, brain organization is significantly influenced by experience and genetics, the hierarchical nature of brain development, and the existence of sensitive developmental periods followed by a decreasing neuroplasticity over time.

3

EFFECTS OF POVERTY ON DEVELOPMENT I: HEALTH, EDUCATIONAL, AND PSYCHOMETRIC PERSPECTIVES

In this chapter, aspects of the impact of poverty on child development during the first 2 decades of life are presented. The cognitive development dimension is considered only from the psychometric perspective in this chapter; the neuroscience approach is dealt with in the following one. This separate treatment is due mainly to differences between the two perspectives in their conceptualization of mental processing and evaluation of child performance.

An important change of approach has taken place in the scientific history of child poverty analysis with the inclusion of ecological studies on mediator mechanisms. First, identifying how poverty affects child development allows for a better understanding of the role of ecological influences. At the same time, this change reinforces a systemic approach that takes into account several factors linked to the child's biological history. This includes the prenatal stage as well as the later developmental contexts. Finally, this ecological approach has resulted in significant implications for the design criteria of interventions allowing scientific research to influence policy.

51

CONCEPTUAL AND METHODOLOGICAL ISSUES RELATED TO THE IMPACTS OF POVERTY AND THE ACCUMULATION OF RISK FACTORS

In a recent study, the National Institute of Child Health and Human Development and the Early Child Care Research Network (2005) analyzed the impact of poverty on the timing of child development from birth to age 9 by comparing children exposed to poverty at different times—for example, child was never poor, child was poor in early infancy, child was poor after infancy only, and child has lived in chronically poor homes. Children in the latter condition have had the lowest performance levels in language; school readiness; and standardized tests, scales, and inventories (e.g., the Reynell Developmental Language Scales, Woodcock–Johnson Psycho-Educational Battery, and Child Behavior Check List). Their scores differed significantly from those obtained from children raised in families who had experienced only short-term poverty. Mothers and teachers involved with children from chronically poor homes rated the children as having more externalizing and internalizing behavior problems than those in other groups. Chronically poor families were at a greater disadvantage than those exposed to transient poverty in terms of income and child-rearing quality. In addition, children who experienced poverty between 4 and 9 years of age had less favorable developmental outcomes than children whose families had been poor only during the child's first 3 years of life.

Given the multifactorial nature of poverty and cognitive development, an analysis of their associations in terms of impacts and mediators requires conceptual frameworks allowing multiple interactive factors and cofactors to be considered and controlled (Figure 3.1). Thus, several complementary methodological issues that potentially modulate associations should be taken into account, such as conceptual and operational poverty definitions (see chap. 1, this volume), paradigms used to assess cognitive processes (Hughes & Graham, 2002; Sternberg, Lautrey, & Lubart, 2003), the sociocultural backgrounds of the sampled participants (Rogoff, 2003; Sternberg, 2004), and consideration of developmental and ecological perspectives (Bronfenbrenner & Ceci, 1994; Evans, 2004; Keegan Eamon, 2001; Sameroff & MacKenzie, 2003; Sirois et al., 2008).

Over the past 80 years, studies of the impact of poverty on child development have generally focused on physical health and on cognitive performance as measured by standardized intelligence tests or mental maturation scales, school readiness, and socioemotional behavior (Bradley & Corwyn, 2002; Brooks-Gunn & Duncan, 1997; Evans, 2004; McLoyd, 1998). Advances in analytical methodologies have allowed researchers to include cumulative risk analyses. Despite the identification of individual factors, risks often occur together or cumulatively, with concomitant adverse effects (Burchinal, Roberts, Hooper, & Zeisel, 2000; Evans & English, 2002; Walker et al., 2007).

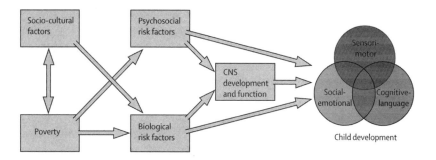

Figure 3.1. Pathways from poverty to poor child development. Sociocultural risk factors include gender inequity, low maternal education, and reduced access to services. Biological risks include prenatal and postnatal growth, nutrient deficiencies, infectious diseases, and environmental toxins. Psychosocial risks include parenting factors, maternal depression, and exposure to violence. Consequences of impairments in child development are likely to be intergenerational (not shown in figure). Poorly developing children are likely to remain in poverty as adults, thus continuing the pathways shown for their offspring. From "Child Development: Risk Factors for Adverse Outcomes in Developing Countries," by S. P. Walker, T. D. Wachs, J. M. Gardner, B. Lozoff, G. A. Wasserman, E. Pollit, J. A. Carter, and the International Child Development Steering Group, 2007, *Lancet, 369,* p. 146. Copyright 2007 by Elsevier. Reproduced by permission.

For example, Stanton-Chapman, Chapman, Kaiser, and Hancock (2004) examined the effects of risk factors present at birth on language development in a sample including more than 850 low-income preschool children. They found that at least one risk factor was present in 94% of the sample, and 39% had been exposed to three or more risk factors. Furthermore, results showed that on average, girls' language scores decreased by 2.3 points with each risk factor to which they had been exposed, and boys' scores decreased by 1.1 points (See Figure 3.2).

The same correlation pattern between the accumulation of risk factors and cognitive performance is evident in numerous examples. For example, Gorman and Pollit (1996) showed how an increase in risk factors in a Guatemalan school-age child population was associated with decreased growth curves for numeracy, general skills, nonverbal skills, and achievement scores derived from standardized tests. Mackner, Black, and Starr (2003) examined the cognitive development of normally growing but poor children and children whose infancy history evidenced failure to thrive. They found that performance persistently declined to 1.0 to 1.5 standard deviations below the normal value in both groups, but more significantly in children with failure to thrive.

Various ways to represent risk accumulation statistically have been proposed. For instance, Burchinal et al. (2000) examined three analytic meth-

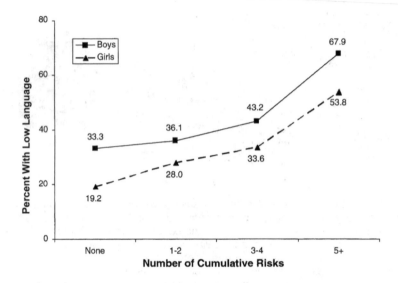

Figure 3.2. Percentage of children with poor language development by number of cumulative risks measured at birth. From "Cumulative Risk and Low-Income Children's Language Development," by T. L. Stanton-Chapman, D. Chapman, A. P. Kaiser, and T. B. Hancock, 2004, *Topics in Early Childhood Special Education, 24,* p. 234. Copyright 2004 by ProEd. Reproduced by permission.

odologies to describe child social risks. They found that the individual risk variables approach provided better predictions about developmental outcomes at particular ages; however, such an approach was less useful when it came to predicting patterns. In the same study, Burchinal et al. found that a risk factor approach derived from individual risk factors—for example, scores computed from the individual predictors, replacing individual variables as predictors in an analysis—provided a good prediction for developmental patterns by using moderate to large sample sizes. In addition, researchers have found that a third approach based on the design of a risk index—similar to the approach Gorman and Pollit (1996) applied—was useful to predict developmental patterns when both a large number of risk variables and a small sample size had to be dealt with. For instance, in a recent study, Appleyard, Egeland, Van Dulmen, and Sroufe (2005) used a longitudinal design to examine the cumulative effects on child behavior outcomes in adolescence of child mistreatment; interparental violence coupled with family disruption; low socioeconomic status (SES) in terms of family income, parental educational, and occupational backgrounds; and high parental stress occurring in early and middle childhood. Appleyard et al. found that the number of risks in early childhood predicted behavior problems in adolescence and provided evidence for a linear model of cumulative risk.

A number of methodological approaches have been used by researchers to study the impact of poverty on life span and timing. For instance, Duncan, Brooks-Gunn, and Klevanov (1994) used the poverty threshold methodology and the duration of poverty to create a dichotomous variable based not only on housing characteristics but also on the years a family lived in poverty. Keegan Eamon (2001) measured persistent poverty in terms of the percentage of a child's life spent under the poverty threshold as well as a number of transitions between poverty and nonpoverty statuses. Korenman, Miller, and Sjaastad (1995) used National Longitudinal Survey of Youth data measuring long-term (13 years) and short-term (1 year) income-to-needs ratio criteria to compare the effects of persistent poverty with those of recent poverty in a longitudinal study. More recently, Najman et al. (2008) used gross annual household income data at the child's birth and when he or she was 6 months, 5 years, and 14 years old to analyze the impact of episodic and chronic poverty on child cognitive development. Although there has been little consistency in the way researchers have included time when studying poverty timing, a majority of researchers have clearly defined their measurements and provided evidence of the applied rationale. In spite of the fact that all studies combining time with poverty have been based on poverty thresholds, nothing would prevent researchers from combining time factors with other measurements such as basic family budgets, as suggested by Roosa, Deng, Nair, and Lockhart Burrell (2005).

Other studies have stressed the importance of including a developmental, ecological perspective in cumulative risk analyses. For example, Keegan Eamon (2001) scrutinized theories explaining the adverse effects of economic privation on child socioemotional development using the Bronfenbrenner bioecological model (Bronfenbrenner & Ceci, 1994). The Bronfenbrenner model describes the child environment as being composed of a series of nested structures, including (a) *microsystems* (the immediate environment a child directly interacts with), (b) *mesosystems* (connections existing among microsystems), (c) *exosystems* (a social setting a child is not a part of that still affects him or her), and (d) *macrosystems* (the general cultural context into which all the other systems are embedded). This model also could be applied to cognitive development and even to the analysis of policies aimed at optimizing child development (Nayar & Lipina, 2007).

Studies on mediators and moderators of risk factors' effects on cognitive performance enriched and improved conceptual and methodological approaches when more sophisticated analytical tools became available (Bradley & Corwyn, 2002; Guo & Harris, 2000). Studies appeared identifying risk factors such as peri- and postnatal physical health, pre- and postnatal nutritional status, exposure to environmental toxic agents, access to prenatal health care systems, home environment (in terms of socioemotional, cognitive, and learning stimulation resources available as well as child rearing practices), parent mental health status, quality of educational services, and type of social resources available in both communities and neighborhoods (Adler & Newman, 2002; Brooks-Gunn & Duncan, 1997; Corcoran & Chaudry, 1997; Evans, 2004; Grigorenko, 2003; Guo & Harris, 2000; McLoyd, 1998).

In summary, studying the results of impacts, cumulative risks, and mediators supports the need for a more comprehensive prevention system, early intervention efforts, and investments related to children living in poverty. A literature review follows of some of the main findings on effects and mediators associated with the dimensions of child development.

INFLUENCES OF POVERTY ON PHYSICAL HEALTH

Worldwide, poverty has a strong association with decrease in physical health, and morbidity and mortality rates are strongly on the increase. In a recent study, Fotso and Kuate-Defo (2005) found several influence patterns, confirming not only that living in the poorest conditions increases the likelihood for suffering illnesses but also that community SES factors modify those impacts significantly. Community SES factors influence health through at least two main channels. One is by shaping the household-level SES (e.g., parent occupation); the other is by directly affecting social, economic, and physical environments, which in turn affect health outcomes. For instance, public services such as electricity, water, and transportation are likely to be less adequate in communities with lower SES, often causing deleterious consequences on children's health. Furthermore, the availability and quality of health, social, and economic services such as hospitals, schools, and markets usually differs by community SES characteristics. In some cases, when these services are available in poor areas, access is very likely to be limited because of inadequate or unsafe conditions and services.

However, the relationship between poverty and physical health may not be constant over time (Chen, Matthews, & Boyce, 2002), and health outcomes are also likely to be influenced by a number of factors. Although several studies have demonstrated multiple classes of evidence for SES gradients with respect to child health outcomes, whether and how they vary over time is a point that remains to be investigated. In a recent study, Chen, Martin, and Matthews (2006) found that the associations of SES (i.e., family income, parent education, and well-being) with overall health measures, such as parent ratings of child health, activity, and school limitations, are similar across childhood and adolescence, whereas associations of SES with specific, acute conditions vary across time, a fact that has been observed among representative U.S. samples. Specifically, for health measures such as parent's rating of general child health, activity limitations, and school limitations, Chen et al. (2006) found a linear gradient showing that lower SES was associated with poorer health and more limitations. It is interesting that they had the same findings regardless of whether poverty was measured through income or parent education. Finally, several factors not necessarily related to developmental processes contribute to overall health status. Among those factors are physical environments, access to and quality of health care, characteris-

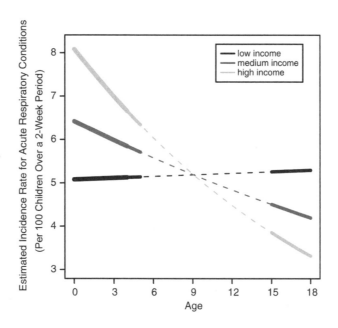

Figure 3.3. Graph depicting the Age × Income interaction for acute childhood respiratory illnesses. Authors tested the significance of the income slope at each year of age. The income gradient depicted in this figure is significant for the ages 0 to 4 ($p < .05$) and is marginally significant for ages 15 to 18 ($p < .10$). Thick solid bars indicate effects significant at the $p < .05$ level. Thin solid bars indicate effects at the $p < .10$ level. Dotted lines indicate nonsignificant differences for that age. From "Socioeconomic Status and Health: Do Gradients Differ Within Childhood and Adolescence?" by E. Chen, A. D. Martin, and K. A. Matthews, 2006, *Social Science & Medicine, 62,* p. 2166. Copyright 2006 by Elsevier. Reproduced by permission.

tics of the neighborhoods, social support, and family conflicts (Chen et al., 2002; Evans, 2004; Leventhal & Brooks-Gunn, 2000).

As previously mentioned, Chen et al. (2006) found evidence that relationships between SES and physical health vary with age in acute conditions. For instance, with regard to acute respiratory problems, they found a crossover effect that reverse SES gradients presented in early years whereas an expected SES-related gradient appeared during adolescence (Figure 3.3). In the case of acute respiratory conditions, a crossover effect was found such that a reverse SES gradient was verified in early years, whereas an expected SES gradient was found during adolescence. Thus, when their children are young, higher SES parents have a lower threshold for noticing respiratory symptoms and taking children for medical treatment. Alternatively, researchers have considered that this reverse gradient (childhood vs. adolescence) may be due to the so-called "hygiene hypothesis," which proposes that a decrease in childhood exposure to microbes and infections (often found among higher SES families) may increase predisposition to respiratory conditions such as allergies and asthma. In contrast, when children are adolescents, parents' reports on the children's respiratory illnesses may become less important because parents rely more on their children to identify symptoms. Thus, other factors may contribute to respiratory illnesses—for example, exposures to infectious agents because adolescents spend more time with peers, or the accumulation of early environmental exposures or unhealthy practices (e.g. smoking).

Lack of or insufficient prenatal care has been related to a reduced control over mothers' infections, which in turn may affect the developing brain. Viral infections in a pregnant mother could have long-lasting effects, such as an increased risk of mental disorders. For example, although the underlying mechanisms and processes have yet to be identified, several experimental models have suggested that respiratory infections in pregnant mothers could lead to behavioral and brain alterations in their children (Patterson, 2002). Fatemi et al. (1999) developed an experimental mouse model wherein the pregnant mother was given a human influenza virus respiratory infection at midgestation. They found a reduction in neocortical and hippocampal thickness as well as a reduction, in several areas, in the number of *reelin* (a protein involved in neuroblast migration) positive cells during fetal development. Many offspring also evidenced deficits in tasks requiring the filtering of sensory information in exploratory behavior. Offspring were also deficient with regard to social interaction (Shi, Fatemi, Sidwell, & Patterson, 2001). However, viral causes of brain dysfunction may involve multiple factors; hence, such causes are unlikely to be supported by simple cause-and-effect paradigms. Recent studies suggest that even though a virus presence in the brain is brief, this fact could cause long-lasting effects. This is, for example, the case with both *varicella zoster* (chicken pox) and polio viruses. Moreover, depending on the infected brain area, either a single virus could generate multiple neurological symptoms or multiple viruses sharing a common target could generate a single symptom. Thus, infected brain area and type and number of virus, as well as the immunological health status of mother and offspring, make it difficult to determine a clear viral responsibility for a brain disease, the symptoms of which could appear substantially later, after the original infection had been resolved. Once again, in this complex context, the use of animal models is crucial for understanding infections underlying brain dysfunction (Van Del Pol, 2006).

Finally, lower SES during childhood has been associated with poorer pulmonary function, poorer dental health, more injuries from domestic accidents, and delayed physical growth in childhood as well as increased risk for suffering from coronary heart disease, mortality due to stroke, and stomach cancer in adulthood (Adler & Newman, 2002; Chen et al., 2006; Guralnik, Butterworth, Wadsworth, & Kuh, 2006; Hamasha, Warren, Levy, Broffitt, & Kanellis, 2006; U.S. Department of Health and Human Services [USDHHS], 2000b).

EFFECTS OF POVERTY ON COGNITIVE COMPETENCIES: PSYCHOMETRIC AND EDUCATIONAL APPROACHES

The scientific history of the study of poverty-related effects on cognitive skills is more than 85 years old now (Bradley & Corwyn, 2002). Since the beginning, findings on the genetic and environmental influences on intelligence have been a subject of debate and have also raised concerns within the scientific community about the inappropriate use of these concepts increasing social and scientific concerns (J. S. Gould, 1981; Sternberg, 2005). However, researchers agree with the general idea of the difficulty of specifically defining the contribution of genetic and environmental factors in the development of cognitive processing (Bartels, Rietveld, Van Baal, & Boomsma, 2002; Scerif & Karmiloff-Smith, 2005). Turkheimer, Haley, Waldron, D'Onofrio, and Gottesman (2003) analyzed scores obtained on the Wechsler Intelligence Scale by a sample of 7-year-old twin pairs from varying socioeconomic backgrounds. They found that the proportions of IQ variance attributable to genes and environments varied nonlinearly with SES (as defined by family income and parental education). Specifically, after applying a model that included the components causing genotype additive effects as well as shared and nonshared environmental factors that interacted with socioeconomic instances, results suggest that in poor families, 60% of IQ variance was accounted for by the shared environment, whereas genetic contribution was close to zero. Furthermore, in nonpoor families, the result was just the opposite. As Noble, Norma, and Farah (2005) stated, these findings not only suggest that the genetic potential for learning is expressed more fully when children enjoy appropriate resources but also that environmental interventions could be particularly useful for children with low SES.

The most commonly described impacts of poverty on cognitive performance have been developmental quotients, children's verbal and achievement IQs, high incidence of learning disorders, school absence, and fewer years of school completed. These findings have been mainly described in children between 3 years and 8 years old. In children ages 6 months to 36 months, a decrease in both motor and achievement developmental quotients was also observed (Bradley & Corwyn, 2002; Brooks-Gunn & Duncan, 1997; McLoyd, 1998; Williamson, Salkie, & Letourneau, 2005). For instance, Stipek and Ryan (1997) assessed several cognitive competences among 233 preschoolers from low- and middle-income families through the Woodcock–Johnson Achievement Test; the Peabody Individual Achievement Test; the short form of the McCarthy Scales of Children's Abilities, including the Puzzle Solving, Word Knowledge, Numerical Memory, Verbal Fluency, Counting and Sorting, and Conceptual Grouping subtests; and motivation—this through subscales from the Feeling About School measurement. Results of cognitive performance showed not only lower scores among children from low-income families but also that they started school with significant learning disadvantages. Highly significant income differences were found in all eight cognitive assessments, including basic reading-related tests and number skills, problem solving, creativity, memory, and language skills. In contrast to the findings on cognitive performance, results suggested that low-income children were no less motivated to learn than their high-income counterparts.

Children from lower SES backgrounds build their vocabularies at slower rates than children from higher SES households. For instance, Hart and Risley (1995; quoted in Hoff, 2006) assessed vocabulary in 42 children from variable SES backgrounds and found SES-related differences in the vocabulary extent as of the beginning of speech development. Specifically, they showed that by the age of 3 years, the mean cumulative vocabulary for higher SES children was more than 1,000 words, whereas for lower SES children it was only around 500 words. It is significant that SES accounted for 36% of variance in vocabulary. Other studies have assessed spontaneous speech, mothers' report measurements, and standardized tests, showing SES-related differences. For example, in a recent study, Qi, Kaiser, Milan, and Hancock (2006) confirmed previous findings while assessing 480 African American and European American children 36 months to 52 months old from various SES backgrounds by applying the Peabody Picture Vocabulary Test, not only to provide norms but also to explore links between SES and language performance. They found that the degree of disadvantage among low-SES children was related to language abilities. Moreover, maternal education, marital status, and the number of children in the household were uniquely associated with child performance, suggesting mediating roles for such factors (see next section, "Mediator Mechanisms of Poverty Impacts"). Finally, other studies have described the same trends in SES-related influences on language and arithmetic outcomes—for example, grammatical development, communicative styles and skills, and arithmetic word problems (Hoff, 2006).

Physical risk conditions present in extremely poor environments could also influence the development of specific language skills. For example, Patrick et al. (2005) examined the correlations between early childhood diarrhea and specific language impairments in a sample of children from a Brazilian shantytown. The children had suffered from diarrhea in the first 2 years of life, and the researchers performed follow-up 5 to 10 years later during their 14-year prospective study. They found that diarrheal illnesses correlated with reduced semantic and phonetic fluency performance once maternal education, breastfeeding, and child schooling had been controlled for.

A recent analysis performed by Raver, Gershoff, and Aber (2007) on mediating models of income, parenting, and school readiness that included several ethnic groups from a U.S. national sample found that measures of children's reading, math, and general knowledge cohered in a similar fashion for African American, Hispanic, and White children. SES was not constant, but the authors applied analytical methods that considered SES baseline differences as a confounding factor. Similar trends have been observed for socioemotional aspects of school readiness—that is, child externalizing, internalizing, or self-regulatory behaviors—with social skills covarying similarly across the groups. In a second analysis (Gershoff, Aber, Raver, & Lennon, 2007), researchers scrutinized dual components of family income and material hardship together with parental stress mediators and positive parenting as predictors of child cognitive and social skills. Results from the path model applied showed unique parent-mediated paths from income to cognitive skills and from income and material hardship to socioemotional competence.

Regarding the progression of these effects in later developmental stages, with some exceptions (e.g., Najman et al., 2008) several studies have shown a decrease in the negative impact of poverty on adolescent IQ (Bradley & Corwyn, 2002; Brooks-Gunn & Duncan, 1997). However, the same trend is not necessarily verified when other cognitive processes measurements, such as processes involved in arithmetical problem solving and reading abilities, are analyzed. For instance, Keegan-Eamon (2002) used the mother–child data set from the National Longitudinal Survey of Youth to test a mediation model of the effects of poverty (defined in terms of family income) on mathematics and reading achievement of 1,324 adolescent girls and boys from several ethnic groups. Findings showed that poverty was indirectly related to a lower achievement stage through its associations with less cognitively stimulating and less emotionally supportive home environments, a fact that in turn was related to school behavioral problems. In addition, other direct and indirect relationships between poverty and achievement were described—for example, a cognitively less stimulating home environment was associated with lower reading but not lower arithmetical achievements. These results suggest that a further analysis of this developmental stage is required, with the incorporation of complementary or alternative indicators as well as other cognitive functioning measurements rather than only standardized intelligence tests (Bradley & Corwyn, 2002).

The English and Romanian Adoptee (ERA) Project is an ongoing, longitudinal, multimethod investigation of the development of children adopted into the United Kingdom from Romania in the early 1990s. During his 24 years in power, the Romanian dictator Nicolae Ceausescu banned abortion and the use of contraceptives as well as enacting a law stating that each family must have at least five children. Furthermore, families were given monetary incentives to have children. The simultaneous proliferation of infants and poverty caused many children to be admitted to state-run orphanages. Among the 150,000 children who lived in these institutions during the 1990s, many spent months or years in institutions where they were cared for on military-style schedules, with little or no playing or talk. The vast majority of the adoptees in the ERA Project experienced extreme early global deprivation as a consequence of this early placement in Romanian institutions. Many of these children faced physical, emotional, and sexual abuse as well as a number of diseases and malnutrition (Gloviczki, 2004; Holden, 1996). The ERA Project has followed the development of 165 adoptees from Romania who entered the United Kingdom between 0 and 42 months of age and a comparison sample of 52 nondeprived U.K. children adopted within the United Kingdom before 6 months of age. Both groups of children were assessed at 4, 6, 11, and 15 years of age. At each time point, developmental assessments have been carried out with the children, focusing on behavioral/emotional, cognitive, academic, social relationship, and health outcomes. Parental interviews have also been carried out at each time point. These have been concerned with the adoptive parents' perspectives regarding the children's development and behavior and also information about their own views of the adoption experience. A third source of information comes from teachers, who have provided further data regarding the children's educational achievements and behavior at school. The findings from the assessments at 4 and 6 years were striking in showing that there was a dramatic degree of cognitive catch-up but that significant deficits remained in a substantial minority (Beckett et al., 2006).

Previous results evidenced a negative effect of these early privations on cognition. Analysis of significant associations between the age at which the children were adopted and their cognitive performance at 6 years of age were included. Thus, the Romanian children adopted at age 6 years exhibited lower cognitive scores (perception, language, memory) and anthropomorphic developmental impairment compared with Romanian children adopted between ages 6 months and 24 months (O'Connor et al., 2000). Findings also included assessments of 4- and 6-year-old children with normal profiles, suggesting a modulation of resilience-related factors. More recently, Beckett et al. (2006) compared cognitive performance on the Wechsler Intelligence Scale for Children (3rd ed.) from a subsample of 11-year-old English and Romanian adoptees. They found persistent effects of privations on cognitive development, but also found a significant improvement over time in children who had evidenced the lowest IQ scores when they were 6 years old. Additionally, in a recent study Nelson et al. (2007) showed that cognitive performance in the same children who remained in institutions was significantly below that of never-institutionalized children and those taken out of the institutions and placed into foster care.

Richards and Wadsworth (2004) also studied the long-term effect of early adverse circumstances on cognitive function, using multiple linear regressions and including gender, birth order, and family SES. As expected, they found that once early adverse circumstances in terms of material home conditions, maternal care, and the experience of parental divorce had been analyzed, such factors were strongly associated with lower cognitive ability during both childhood and adolescence. They also observed that these associations were detectable on measures of verbal ability, memory, processing speed, and concentration in midlife. However, these long-term effects were mostly explained by the effects of adversity on either child or adolescent cognitive ability or by differences in educational attainment and adult socio-economic conditions. These results also support the idea that child poverty effects persist, affecting adult cognitive functions.

MEDIATOR MECHANISMS OF POVERTY IMPACTS

Inasmuch as poverty and child development are both multifactorial, it is difficult for researchers to determine and analyze poverty's underlying effects (Hoff, Laursen, & Tardif, 2002). Exploring mediator mechanisms is important not only for a better understanding of the basic processes involved in these effects but also for the development of effective interventions, especially when increases in family income are not possible (Brooks-Gunn & Duncan, 1997).

Bradley and Corwyn (2002) proposed—using the principles of parallel, convergent, and reciprocal causation—that results be interpreted in terms of effects and mediators. The principle of *parallel causation* holds that several processes or factors should be sufficient, but not necessary, to produce a significant impact on development. The *convergent causation* concept outlines that a particular process should be necessary but not sufficient to produce a particular result—that is, its effect depends on the presence of a second factor. Additionally, the principle of *reciprocal causation* holds that bidirectional influences are required between processes and interactive factors over time to produce a significant impact on development. For example, Bradley, Corwyn, McAdoo, and Garcia Coll (2001) used a hierarchical linear model to examine relationships among three home environment factors: learning stimulation, maternal sensitivity, and physical punishment. They found that each factor contributed to reading skills irrespective of the other skills, whereas mother sensitivity and physical punishment contributed more significantly to the development of behavioral disorders.

In a recent review, Conger and Donnellan (2007) described three general, theoretical approaches likely to provide possible explanations for the associations between SES and individual development: social causation, social selection, and twin interaction. According to these authors, empirical evidence supports the first perspective on the basis of studies showing that SES affects both family and child development in terms of the quality of emotional home environment and family investments in child health and education. At the same time, evidence has also been found supporting the fact that individual characteristics lead to SES-related differences in development. Finally, Conger and Donnellan (2007) noted that recent research is consistent with an interactionist approach, which proposes a dynamic relationship between SES and changes over time in several developmental trends, where links between SES, parenting behaviors, and child development remain the most important target variables to be included in further studies.

In general, mediators included in reviews are (a) peri- and postnatal physical health and nutrition, (b) home environment, (c) parent–child interactions, (d) parent mental health, and (e) neighborhood social and material resources (Bradley & Corwyn, 2002; Guo & Harris, 2000; Walker et al., 2007). However, further research is necessary on other potential mediators, such as access to and use of prenatal and pediatric care systems, exposure to environmental toxic agents, stability of home socioemotional interactions, community learning experiences, and quality of community schools (Adler & Newman, 2002; Brooks-Gunn & Duncan, 1997; McLoyd, 1998).

Common obstacles in the study of mediators are associated with their appropriate exploration, especially in terms of their applicability to different cultural groups (Bradley & Corwyn, 2002). In addition, many of them have not been integrated into child development models, which results in lack of information on complex ecological processes. Furthermore, when poverty is conceptualized within SES, accurately determining the potential mediators involved is not that simple because this construct is concomitant with other conditions, also likely to influence child cognitive development. Examples of the latter are being part of an ethnic minority, living in a single-parent home, having family members with either disabilities or serious mental illness, and exposure to teratogenic agents as well as other environmental risk factors. Therefore, it is difficult to disentangle SES effects from cofactor effects. Besides, any direct biological damage also contributes to SES differences—for example, brain disorders caused by either injury or exposure to environmental toxic agents—and both circumstances are more likely to occur within socially vulnerable environments.

One of the main limitations of the studies discussed here is the difficulty of considering simultaneously how a particular process could influence a given aspect of development. For instance, a child suffering from nutritional deficiency is at a higher risk for being exposed to environmental toxic agents at pre- and postnatal stages, or subject to a family context wherein inadequate rearing patterns are favored (Pollit, 2000). Prenatal exposure to either legal substances such as alcohol and tobacco (Korkman, Kettunen, & Autti-Ramo, 2003) or illegal drugs such as cocaine has been associated with long-term effects on cognitive control skills (Espy, Kaufmann, & Glisky, 1999). Finally, studying mediators requires the use of specific statistical techniques, such as structural equation modeling (Brody, Dorsey, Forehand, & Armistead, 2002; Bull, Espy, & Wiebe, 2008; Dodge et al., 2003). However, a lack of model specificity remains an obstacle to fully understanding the underlying mechanisms involved.

Pre- and Perinatal Health

Both physical and mental health disorders in early childhood have been repeatedly associated with inadequate prenatal care as well as a broad range of other parental and community factors. The most widely reported risk factors in literature are parent education and lifestyle behaviors (e.g., legal and illegal drug abuse, lack of home hygiene, and poor routine parenting practices), available information in the home, and care resources (Bradley & Corwyn, 2002; Brooks-Gunn & Duncan, 1997; Marmot, 2002; USDHHS, 2000a; Wassermann, Shaw, Selvin, & Gould, 1998). For instance, Ornoy (2003) has analyzed general verbal and achievement skills assessed with the Wechsler Intelligence Scale for Children—Revised among preschoolers born to heroin-dependent mothers. Lower IQs coupled with higher inattention rates compared with control rates have been found. This performance profile persisted at school, when higher attention-deficit/hyperactivity disorder rates were also verified. Children who had been adopted at a younger age and raised in mid- to high-SES homes showed average IQs but also persisting inattentive profiles, suggesting the continuity of a biological impact, a factor supporting recent findings on attention-deficit/hyperactivity disorder brain-retarded maturation (Shaw et al., 2007).

Mother smoking during pregnancy has been also associated with a higher risk of behavior problems in childhood (Wasserman, Liu, Pine, & Graziano, 2001). In a recent study, Buckhalt, El-Sheikh, and Keller (2007) assessed sleep, including actigraphy; sleep diaries; and self-report, and reaction time performance in a sample of African American, and European American schoolchildren from homes with variable SES backgrounds. They found that all children had similar cognitive performance when sleep was optimal, but after controlling for SES, children from low-income homes showed lower performances.

Family SES has been found to predict different health outcomes throughout the life span. Specifically, SES has been repeatedly related to higher risks for premature birth, low birth weight, and birth defects such as fetal alcoholic syndrome. In addition, children from low-SES families tend to suffer from more perinatal complications, postbirth infections, more days spent in the hospital after birth, and more days spent in the hospital during their first 3 years of life because of different injuries and illnesses. In turn, most of these factors have been associated with the development of neurological and developmental disorders, with impacts on both cognitive and academic performance (Bradley & Corwyn, 2002; Espy et al., 2002; Luciana, Lindeke, Georgieff, Mills, & Nelson, 1999; Marmot, 2002; McLoyd, 1998; USDHHS, 2000b). For instance, it has been found that prematurely born children's cognitive abilities measured by means of general intelligence standardized tasks (Ornoy, 2003) and neuropsychological tasks (Caravale, Tozzi, Albino, & Vicari, 2005) had been affected, a fact directly related to parental education levels.

Environmental Toxins

Children from low income or low-SES communities are more likely to suffer from the impact of environmental toxic agents on their physical and mental health because of the higher presence of agents such as lead, methyl mercury, polychlorinated biphenyls, dioxins, and pesticides (Hubbs-Tait, Nation, Krebs, & Bellinger, 2005; Mendola, Selevan, Gutter, & Rice, 2002; Ornoy, 2003; Wassermann et al., 1998, 2001; Wilkinson, 1999). For instance, lead exposure has been associated with underweight, hair loss, vitamin D metabolic dysfunctions, blood cell genesis dysfunctions, renal disorders (Ornoy, 2003), behavior problems (Wasserman et al., 2001), less self-regulated attention (Winders Davis, Chang, Burns, Robinson, & Dossett, 2004), and poor executive functioning (which includes focused attention, attention switching, working memory, inhibitory control, and poor learning in early childhood; Canfield, Creer, Cornwell, & Henderson, 2003).

Malnutrition

Underweight according to child age is one of the most prevalent factors among children living in poor homes. As a unique risk factor, it is associated with a probability for developing physical illness as well as cognitive and socioemotional disorders, which in turn are likely to persist throughout childhood and adolescence (Brooks-Gunn & Duncan, 1997; McLoyd, 1998). Although macro- and micronutrients are necessary for brain functioning throughout all the developmental stages, some nutrients have a deeper effect than others. For example, children from either poor or nonpoor homes suffering from iron anemia, are more likely to evidence retardation in their motor and cognitive development. This impact is increased by poverty because of the existence of many other cumulative risks (Pollit, 2000). Effects of the same type have been suggested in connection with other micronutrient deficits such as zinc, iodine, and selenium as well as a lack of vitamins (e.g., B6), carbohydrates, and proteins (Bhatnagar & Taneja, 2001; Georgieff & Rao, 2001; Grigorenko, 2003).

Using nutrition as a mediator, research has revealed that lower SES is associated with (a) impacts on physical growth (Brooks-Gunn & Duncan, 1997); (b) a higher probability for neural tube defects because of an inadequate incorporation of folic acid during pregnancy (Wassermann et al., 1998, 2001); (c) a prevalence of iron anemia because of inadequate nourishment, lacking iron-rich vegetables and meat (Pollit, 2000; USDHHS, 2000a); and (d) poor performance in tasks tapping long-term memory processes after long poor nutrition episodes (Brooks-Gunn & Duncan, 1997). Moreover, Valenzuela (1997) offered evidence that lethargy resulting from chronic malnutrition is likely to reduce children's energy in their interactions with adults resulting in less adult attention and care and leading to a higher probability for insecure attachments, negative affections, and limited motivation.

Several authors have agreed that assessing the extent to which nutritional deficits contribute to the alteration of aspects of child development is a most complex task, inasmuch as children deprived of adequate nutrition are also deprived of access to other resources, such as medical and social care.

Thus, it is difficult to determine whether any condition related to poor nutrition status also reflects inadequate prenatal and preventive care or any increase of infections because of poor personal hygiene (Adler & Newman, 2002; USDHHS, 2000a, 2000b).

In addition, because many poor families cannot afford health services, they usually resort to emergency services for either chronic or advanced illnesses, a habit bound to increase both comorbidity and mortality risks. In addition, adult lack of information because of poor education as well as the nonstandard treatment for medical problems that is often applied within certain cultures can deeply hinder any possible search for appropriate medical services when a child faces symptoms of illness (Adler & Newman, 2002; Guo & Harris, 2000; Marmot, 2002; Rutter, 2003).

Having access to material and social resources is one of the most well-known associations between socioeconomic level and child well-being. For instance, Klerman (1991) suggested an association pattern uniting low income and worse physical health with no access to goods, health services, clean drinking water, and waste elimination facilities. Schroeder, Martorell, Rivera, Ruel, and Habicht (1995) proposed a model in which nutrition is identified as a key for health development. In accordance with this model, absorption disorders and inadequate incorporation of micro- and macronutrients are associated with alterations in immunological response against infections. In turn, a poor nutritional status in pregnant women contributes to a higher morbidity and mortality incidence. Gorman and Pollit (1996) offered a similar formulation, with complementary evidence that poor nutritional status affects prenatal brain growth, a fact that further contributes to poor school achievement in childhood. Such an impact could also be modulated by the accumulation of risk factors, as these same researchers reported in a study performed on adolescents from Guatemala.

Housing

Housing conditions are also factors associated with deleterious effects on child health (Bradley & Corwyn, 2002; Brooks-Gunn & Duncan, 1997; McLoyd, 1998). Children living in homes with dwelling problems due to lack of maintenance are usually exposed to a large number of risk factors—for example, either floors in very poor condition or plain hard-packed soil surfaces, excessive heat and humidity, infestations of insects and vermin, open stoves, stairs without rails, walls painted with toxic materials (e.g., lead), cracked roofs, and precarious electric installations (Adler & Newman, 2002; Bradley & Corwyn, 2002; Guo & Harris, 2000; Marmot, 2002). These housing conditions are not only associated with an increase in morbidity but also with different injuries from home-located accidents. Any functional household organization should include not only physical but also organizational order—for instance, in addition to a safe play area, cleanliness, safe light and gas installations, and so on, it would include routines regarding medical control—inasmuch as household organization has also been associated with the intellectual and social well-being of children (Bradley & Corwyn, 2002; Brooks-Gunn & Duncan, 1997; Evans, 2004; Guo & Harris, 2000).

Home Physical and Stimulating Environments

Chronic poverty influences on child cognitive and socioemotional development have been repeatedly associated with an increase in family exposure to negative life events and stressors—and those in turn generate a psychological distress that reduces parents' ability to provide their children with sensitive, responsive care while increasing the likelihood for punitive, coercive parenting styles (McLoyd, 1998).

Family relationships play a key role in explaining the development of problem behaviors across most theoretical models. Specifically, social learning, cognitive–behavioral family systems, and biobehavioral models provide significant explanations for family processes. Although experimental evidence suggests that family dysfunctional interactions and lack of resources are consistent across a wide range of behavior disorders, a majority of studies are limited inasmuch as they only focus on single symptoms or disorders. Given the high rate of comorbidity across childhood disorders, scrutinizing those family environmental features is warranted.

Whether family environments are adaptive may also depend on contextual factors, such as family socioeconomic background. For instance, Carrie, Herma, and Ostrander (2006) analyzed the associations among depression symptoms, behavior disorders, inattention, and family environment, with a cross-sectional design comprising parents and teachers in a sample of more than 350 first to fourth graders from different SES backgrounds. They found that depression alone was related to a family milieu not conducive to child expressiveness, independence, and activity and favoring higher control levels. Furthermore, lower SES was significantly and negatively associated with intellectual activity and family environments, showing a socioeconomic modulation.

The HOME Inventory (Bradley, 1994) has been widely used in a number of societies—in Africa, Asia, Australia, Europe, Latin America, and the Caribbean—to identify positive, significant correlations between home environment rearing conditions and motor, mental–verbal, and achievement quotients in infants and preschoolers. Evidence confirms that despite several cultural differences, more parental stimulation, such as availability of learning materials, parental involvement, and responsiveness, significantly correlates with children's cognitive development (Bradley & Corwyn, 2005; Bradley, Corwyn, & Whiteside-Mansell, 1996; Farah et al., 2008). In addition, several studies have suggested that variations with regard to parents' completed years of education, mother's verbal skill levels during a child's first 3 years of life, and type of rearing practices all correlate significantly with the emergence of executive processing (Gauvain, Fagot, Leve, & Kavanagh, 2002; Landry, Millar-Loncar, Smith, & Swank, 2002).

Regarding language development, a recent review of SES and parenting by Hoff et al. (2002) has shown that higher SES mothers from varying cultures talk more with their children and more frequently elicit pleasant conversation with their children, whereas lower SES mothers do not really converse with their children and instead speak to them only for the purpose of directing behavior. As one of the same authors stated in another study (Hoff, 2003), relationship between SES and language development could be the result of several factors—both biological and environmental—such as parenting, home environment, and learning experiences. To determine whether children from variable SES backgrounds differ in their productive vocabulary rates because of their different learning experiences, Hart and Risley (1995) analyzed interactions between high- and low-SES mothers and their 2-year-old children. Findings showed that mother speech was the mediating variable. Specifically, SES-related differences in growth and productive vocabulary were fully explained in terms of differences in the mother's way of speech. Hart and Risley addressed the importance of these findings, which not only identified children's living environments as the source of SES-related differences in their language development but also argued for the principle of environmental specificity rather than proposing a global environmental influence.

Parenting and Stress

A response to stress is one of the most significantly cited mediators in the impact of SES on cognitive and socioemotional development (McLoyd, 1998; Shonkoff & Phillips, 2002). Threats, exposure to environmental dangers, family and community violence and abuse, family dissolution, moving, unemployment, labor uncertainty, and persistent economic privation are among the most frequent stressful circumstances to which people living in poverty are exposed (Bradley & Corwyn, 2002). This set of risk factors is significantly associated with socioemotional, self-regulatory alterations and dysfunctions in both adults and children. Low self-esteem and self-regulation processes are also involved (Brooks-Gunn & Duncan, 1997; McLoyd, 1998; Shonkoff & Phillips, 2000).

Physiologically, any chronic exposure to stressful conditions elicits a number of possible reaction patterns. Some researchers have proposed the *allostatic loading* concept to analyze the impact of stress on adaptive behaviors. This concept refers to the capacity of different body systems adapt and adjust to environmental demands. The activation and constant deactivation of physiologic responses toward stressful conditions are related to the allostatic load, which causes long-term effects—for example, persistent high blood pressure. Research carried out in nonhuman primates also has suggested that allostatic loading involved in biological as well as metabolic adaptive and adjusting processes throughout development could modulate the susceptibility to acquire illnesses, such as changes in cardiovascular activity and a persistent elevation in blood pressure (Bradley & Corwyn, 2002).

Parenting practices could also be related to stress impact on allostatic loading. For instance, uncertainty caused by economic privations could increase the probability for negative emotional responses such as anxiety, depression, anger, which in turn could modulate interactions among family members while inducing people to resort to negative control strategies, less sensitivity, and more negligence (McLoyd, 1998; Mistry, Lowe, Benner, & Chien, 2008). It is significant that some studies verified that even under social risk conditions, the maintenance of a pattern of adequate parenting practices could represent a protective factor (Brody et al., 1994, 2002).

Adult Expectations

Another significant mediator mechanism between a given socioeconomic level and stimulating cognitive experiences could be found in either parents' attitudes or children's expectations. With regard to populations from diverse SES backgrounds, studies on differences in parent–child interactions identified several patterns—for example, emphasis placed on verbal abilities, independence, and creativity. In addition, several cross-cultural studies have disclosed that parents from higher SES homes use more verbal communication and provide more learning opportunities to their children (Bradley et al., 2001). Other studies have shown that parents from higher SES homes also establish richer conversations in terms of linguistic content, sensitive answers, and involvement (Hoff et al., 2002), and their teaching style includes more support and complex verbal strategies (Bradley & Corwyn, 2002).

Attitudes and expectations of teachers were also proposed as mediators for the poverty impact on cognitive development (McLoyd, 1998). Perceptions of students from low-SES backgrounds was associated with negative prejudices in terms of their potential and their cognitive and self-regulatory skills (Pretzlik, Olsson, Nabuco, & Cruz, 2003). In turn, such perceptions cause teachers to both pay less attention to pupils and provide them with less positive reinforcement. This interaction style is most likely to increase feelings of frustration in children, which in turn could be associated with difficulties in their cognitive and behavioral responses to multiple school demands (Bradley & Corwyn, 2002).

Ecological Perspectives

When studying cognitive development, an analysis of community and cultural factors should also be considered because evidence has been found that neighborhoods are related to child health and behavior, even when family income and parental education are statistically controlled (Brooks-Gunn & Duncan, 1997; Wassermann et al., 1998). Specifically, children growing up in low-income urban environments are exposed to more social risk factors. For instance, some studies have found associations between these conditions and the development of behavioral stress—for example, posttraumatic stress— as well as cognitive alterations (Garbarino, Bradshaw, & Vorrasi, 2002).

As per several theories of child development, when the number of stress factors in a neighborhood increase and social support resources decrease, allostatic loading also increases (Bradley & Corwyn, 2002). In neighborhoods where the unemployment rate is high and single-parent families are commonplace, feelings of social isolation also increase (Narayan, Chambers, Shah, & Petesch, 2000). Positive effects of higher SES communities on cognitive performance have been related to adjusted adult models and monitoring practices as the main mediators (Brooks-Gunn & Duncan, 1997). As expected, institutional resources (e.g., schools, child care and medical services, employment opportunities, family social support, and effective community norms) have been identified as the main mediators related to the impact on child well-being caused by low-income neighborhoods (Leventhal & Brooks-Gunn, 2000). In an another study on the relationship between family conflict, community violence, and young children's socioemotional functioning, Farver, Xu, Eppe, Fernandez, and Schwartz (2005) explored how children's social cognition and mothers' psychological functioning are likely to mediate the outcomes associated with such exposure. They observed that whenever mothers mentioned that their children had witnessed violent acts in their community, this occurrence was related to the children's distress symptoms; teachers' reports on aggression among pupils; and, obviously, police crime rates. A path analysis also disclosed that children's social awareness and mothers' depressive symptoms partially mediated the effects of community violence and family conflicts on children's mental outcomes.

Keegan Eamon (2001) has applied the Bronfenbrenner model (see the section "Conceptual and Methodological Issues Related to the Impacts of Poverty and the Accumulation of Risk Factors" earlier in this chapter) to the analysis of the impact of poverty on socioemotional development. The first systemic level, *microsystems*, includes immediate environment proximal processes, such as home environment, peer group, and school resources and quality, which could either make easier or hinder development. For example, from the stress-coping theory point of view, chronic poverty in a home environment may have a strong influence on children's adjustment inasmuch as multiple life stressors have cumulative effects (Shaw, Vondra, Hommerding, Keenan, & Dunn, 1994). Specifically, economic privation can affect coping behaviors, causing a sense of powerlessness, which in turn affects the sense of control and efficacy (Kaplan, Roberts, Camacho, & Coyne, 1987). Stress-coping models also suggest that adverse economic conditions affect family interactions by creating economic pressure or daily strains, which are also likely to cause mental health disorders (Conger & Brent-Donnellan, 2007), a situation caused by the alteration of children's socioemotional functioning that leads directly to low nurture levels, uninvolved and inconsistent parenting, and harsh discipline.

Peer groups and school are also involved in the microsystems level of analysis, inasmuch as children from poor homes are more likely to go to schools that are in need of resources, fail to expect achievements from their pupils, and whose classroom behavior setting leaves much to be desired (Bradley & Corwyn, 2002; Brooks-Gunn & Duncan, 1997). Finally, gender, temperament, chronic medical problems, malnutrition, and exposure to environmental toxic agents are frequently scrutinized when assessing the relationship between poverty and child socioemotional development. Those factors cause an impact on development because they affect the regular quality of proximal processes operating within the microsystems structure (Keegan-Eamon, 2001). For instance, child temperament could have either independent or moderating effects on parenting practices, which in turn influence socioemotional development (McLoyd, 1998).

Interactions between two or more microsystems that have been designed to offer material, cognitive, and emotional support to the children involved are considered *mesosystems*. Relations between teachers or peer groups and parents are good examples of mesosystems. A significant issue of this analysis level is that experiences observed within one microsystem are most likely to influence processes and interactions in the other microsystem. For example, mothers who are not involved with their child's school achievement may also use less skilled parenting practices at home.

Exosystems encompass connections and processes between two or more settings, but only one setting contains the child involved. For example, events that occur at parents' work could have consequences for their child at home. Exosystems that mediate between poverty and socioemotional development act as parents' social support network within the overall neighborhood context as well (Brooks-Gunn & Duncan, 1997). Specifically, social support networks involve a family in activities and exchanges of either an affective or a material nature that in turn could mitigate the impact of stress while enhancing parenting practices. Indeed, poor communities' needs are most affected by the lack of social contacts, besides receiving lower levels of material and social support (Narayan et al., 2000). In turn, a lower quality of community environment is likely to affect child socioemotional development by either undermining parenting practices or providing fewer economic and social opportunities, inappropriate role models, inadequate adult supervision, or detrimental peer influences (Keegan Eamon, 2001).

Macrosystems are basically made up of cultural values, customs, and laws. The effects of principles defined by these systems have a cascading influence throughout the interactions of all the other systems (Bronfenbrenner & Ceci,

1994). For example, if it is the belief of the culture that parents should be solely responsible for raising their children, that culture is less likely to provide resources to help parents develop child-rearing skills.

Finally, *chronosystems* are based on a time dimension, including either steadiness or change over time. Specifically, timing, duration, and frequency of exposure to poverty are important facts for understanding the effects of poverty. For instance, children from poor homes evidence a higher incidence of health problems throughout their 1st year of life. Their childhood health disorders have also been related to a higher rate of adjustment difficulties in adulthood than rates found in nonpoor populations. Some studies suggest that either recent financial difficulties or transitions create more distress and damage to an individual's capacity for adapting himself or herself than chronic poverty status does (Keegan Eamon, 2001). However, other studies suggest that either a transitory job loss or a transitory poverty condition do not contribute to the development of long-term consequences on behavior (McLoyd, Jayaratne, Ceballo, & Borquez, 1994).

CONCLUSION

After reviewing the literature devoted to the poverty-related impact on childhood development, it could be said that (a) effects have been observed at biological, psychological, and social levels and (b) such impact begins even before a person is born. Privations also include factors and cofactors, the cumulative action of which is likely to expand over time in a variable fashion, thus modulating both impact levels and future consequences on development. This also implies that any early impact on child physical and mental health creates risk conditions such that disorders and diseases are likely to appear—hence, child development opportunities are jeopardized, in some cases into adult life. Of course, such a situation depends on both when privations start and their persistence.

Considering the phases of both the biological and psychological systems, poverty impact analysis is essential for any type of action aimed at improving people's development opportunities. Such a program should also include a careful consideration of the many ways privation impacts may take place. In this sense, the family and community contexts not only should be taken into account but also should be approached comprehensively—that is, considering poverty impact in terms of lack of food and material goods as well as in terms of having access to social life. As a complement, if one considers childhood development as an interactive biological and social construct, an analysis performed on the mediator mechanisms of the poverty impact on children would also be required, taking into consideration the childhood poverty conceptual and operational definitions that have been dealt with in chapter 1 of this volume.

In summary, (a) social vulnerability involves several risks, accumulation of which implies higher impacts, and (b) the multidimensional nature of poverty and development imply the need to design and apply multidisciplinary approaches to analyze the covariation of multiple factors over time. Specifically, this chapter has only considered the psychometric-, and educational-related approaches to the poverty impact on cognitive development. The literature demonstrates the importance of the socioeconomic modulation of children's cognitive and school performances, which can be assessed by means of standardized intelligence and academic tests. Nonetheless, at some developmental stages, some measurements seem to be losing sensitivity when it comes to assessing the socioeconomic modulation of child performance. Experimental research as well as the inclusion of approaches capable of observing cognitive development in terms of basic operations are not only valid but also necessary to deepen both basic and applied knowledge in the area of developmental cognitive neuroscience.

4

EFFECTS OF POVERTY ON DEVELOPMENT II: COGNITIVE NEUROSCIENCE PERSPECTIVES

Cognitive neuroscience and cognitive psychology have developed tools that allow researchers to analyze performance in terms of basic operations or computations. In turn, these tools are interesting candidates for attempting to scrutinize the involved neural substrates. This approach would allow more specific studies than plainly psychometric ones and would allow researchers to investigate how neural networks organize thought processes and how poverty modulates such processes. This chapter reviews recent studies on poverty modulation of infant, preschooler, school-age, and adolescent cognitive performance from both cognitive and neuroscientific perspectives. First, evidence is presented regarding how poverty modulates performance in tasks demanding attention, inhibitory control, working memory, self-monitoring, and linguistic processing. Next, comments are issued on studies wherein socioeconomic status (SES) and early deprivation (e.g., orphanage experience) have been analyzed in terms of their effects on neural activation patterns.

Effects of poverty on cognitive performance usually have been characterized in terms of standardized tests results, school readiness, and sociological variables. Although recent studies have associated brain volume with IQ

(Haier, Jung, Yeo, Head, & Alkire, 2004) and intelligence test performance with specific neural networks (Duncan et al., 2000), the dependent variables used in studies dealing with the influence of poverty on cognition tend to measure the combined functioning of multiple cognitive systems, such as memory, language, executive function, perceptual function, and spatial ability. Even though some of these processes, such as memory, are commonly included in intelligence tests, and basic abilities are included in theories of intelligence, a linkage between those processes has not been assessed comprehensively (Ackerman, Beier, & Boyle, 2005). Furthermore, standardized tests have not yet been designed to analyze either the underlying basic mental operations involved or poverty-caused modulations.

Viewing cognition as consisting of component codes computed in various ways and programmed to perform complex everyday tasks leads to new proposals on how the brain organizes thought processes (Posner & Raichle, 1994). Basic processes involved in early cognitive control and language development, such as the attention subsystems, working memory, flexibility, and phonological processing, are fundamental to all forms of cognitive activity and social behavior throughout the life span. A growing body of studies describes the relevance of these processes for child development and social adaptation, including school achievement (Blair, 2002), self-regulation (Posner & Rothbart, 2000), resiliency (Buckner, Mezzacappa, & Beardslee, 2003), and psychopathology (Pennington & Ozonoff, 1996). Impacts on the development of these basic processes has negative repercussions on both learning and the internalization of needed socialization rules (Mezzacappa, 2004).

As described in chapter 3 of this volume, children growing up in low-SES environments evidence lower performance levels on a broad range of cognitive measures and school readiness. Therefore, given the multiplicity of factors influencing and modulating brain development, the impact of poverty on cognition is most likely to have a neurocognitive basis. Hence, a number of other basic cognitive functions, such as attention-related components and executive functions, also could be modulated by socioeconomic background (Farah et al., 2006).

Only recently have preliminary studies begun to evaluate associations among forms of poverty and the basic, underlying processes involved in cognitive performance. Although most of these studies have addressed behavioral issues, and inferences regarding brain function are indirect (Cacioppo, Berntson, & Nusbaum), they have contributed significantly to a better knowledge of poverty modulation on cognition from a basic processes standpoint. For example, studies by the National Institute of Child Health and Human Development and Early Child Care Research Network (2003, 2005) showed that the quality of home environment (e.g., availability of stimulating toys and learning materials, parental efforts to provide stimulation, mother sensitivity, and child care characteristics) could predict child performance in sustaining attention, inhibitory control, and planning. The studies also showed that there is a need to assess the role of dimensions and mediators through which environment could exert an influence on these and other basic cognitive processes involved in school and social functioning. For instance, data from a sample of 700 first graders showed that the cumulative quality factors of a given child-rearing environment were significantly related to attention and memory but not to planning. Moreover, researchers have verified that home environment quality was more strongly associated with outcomes than either child care or school qualities. It was also observed that the quality of both environments, at either an early or a later time, predicted child performance on attention- and memory-related tasks.

POVERTY-CAUSED MODULATION OF CHILD NEUROCOGNITIVE PERFORMANCE: BEHAVIORAL EVIDENCE

In the context of the scientific literature on poverty and cognitive performance in both healthy children and those suffering from various disorders, neurocognitive approaches usually evaluate the impact of deprivations on performance at the level of basic components or operations. Several such studies have evaluated a wide range of specific prenatal and perinatal conditions associated with mothers' exposure to toxins, either from environmental causes or from substance abuse. For example, Luciana, Lindeke, Gerogieff, Mills, and Nelson (1999) compared the cognitive performances of 7- to 9-year-old survivors of preterm neonatal intensive care and age-matched control children. Results showed that neonatal intensive-care survivors demonstrated more memory errors on a spatial working memory task, more planning latencies, poorer pattern recognition, and shorter spatial memory span than children from the control groups. In turn, children living in poverty are at greater risk for exposure to multiple agents because of their communities being too close to industrial areas or from toxic building materials in the home. For example, prenatal and postnatal exposure to polychlorinated biphenyls (Cichetti, Kaufman, & Sparrow, 2004), prenatal exposure to alcohol (Korkman, Kettunen, & Autti-Ramo, 2003), and postnatal exposure to lead (Hubbs-Tait, Nation, Krebs, & Bellinger, 2005) have been associated with specific neurocognitive deficits in neonates, developing infants, children, and adolescents. Furthermore, prenatal cocaine exposure, alone or in combination with exposure to other drugs, has been associated with deficits in executive functioning such as visual–motor set-shifting and inhibitory control in childhood. Presence of brain microstructural changes suggesting less mature development of frontal white matter pathways has also been observed (Warner et al., 2006).

INFLUENCES OF POVERTY ON CONTROL, MONITORING, AND LANGUAGE PROCESSING

Mezzacappa (2004) assessed alerting, orienting, and executive attentional processes in a sample of 249 children between 5 years and 7 years old who had been recruited from the Project on Human Development in Chicago Neighborhoods. This study was aimed at assessing correlations among sociodemographic characteristics (e.g., ethnicity, highest educational and occupational status, and highest income ever achieved by the primary caregiver) as well as attention component processes. Mezzacappa found that older, socially advantaged children performed more proficiently under attentional demand conditions in terms of overall accuracy and in reaction times to alerting, orienting, and executive attention processes.

Lipina, Martelli, Vuelta, and Colombo (2005) assessed the executive performance of 280 healthy infants aged 6 months to 14 months who lived in both poor and nonpoor homes in either the City of Buenos Aires, Argentina, or the greater Buenos Aires area. The poverty criterion used was the Unsatisfied Basic Needs (UBN) index described in chapter 1 of this volume. Infants were administered the A-not-B task (Diamond, 1985), which taps working memory and inhibitory control processes. The authors hypothesized that as usually occurs with standardized tests administrated to older children, infants from poor homes would perform less efficiently than children from nonpoor homes in terms of maintaining information online and control of interferences from irrelevant stimuli. It is interesting to note that comparisons of several prenatal and perinatal variables between groups showed that mothers in the UBN group had had more previous deliveries, fewer previous abortions and cesareans, more smoking, and more pregnancy-related hypertensive episodes, indicating the presence of several poverty-related risk factors in the developmental prenatal stage. Cognitive performance comparisons between groups showed that the UBN group made fewer consecutive correct responses and more perseverative responses, an indication that poverty had modulated infant performance (Figure 4.1).

Lipina, Martelli, Vuelta, Injoque Ricle, and Colombo (2004) also assessed the executive performance of 247 healthy children between 3 years and 5 years old from a broad range of UBN schools and satisfied basic needs schools from the same Argentine districts. Children were administered a battery of executive tasks aimed at tapping working memory, inhibitory control, flexibility, and planning processes. Results showed that children from UBN homes had fewer correct trials and more perseverative errors in tasks tapping working memory, inhibitory control, and set-shifting processing. Furthermore, they obtained lower scores in visuospatial and planning tasks. It is interesting that children from both groups evidenced similar performances in the Stroop-like day–night test, a fact that could be associated with an earlier maturation of the underlying processes, as other researchers have sug-

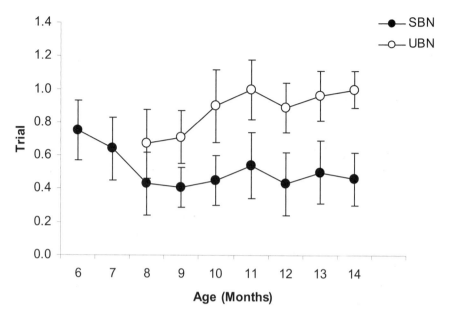

Figure 4.1. Perseverative error performance in the A-not-B task (delay: 5 seconds) in infants from UBN (unsatisfied basic needs) and SBN (satisfied basic needs) homes.

gested with regard to inhibitory control processes (Luciana & Nelson, 1998; Noble, Farah, & McCandliss, 2006).

In a recent study, Blair and Razza (2007) examined the role of self-regulation in emerging school abilities among 141 children between 3 years and 5 years of age from low-income homes attending Head Start programs. Measurements of effortful control, false belief understanding, inhibitory control, and attention-shifting aspects of executive function were related to both arithmetical and literacy measurements. Results indicated that although child self-regulatory competencies were moderately correlated, each one tended to account for a unique variance in arithmetical and literacy measurements. Specifically, teacher-reported effortful control and inhibitory control were positively associated with arithmetical ability and letter knowledge. False belief understanding was significantly related to letter knowledge and marginally significant with both arithmetical knowledge and phonological awareness. According to the authors, these findings suggest that preschool curricula designed to improve self-regulation skills as well as enhance early school abilities may be most effective in helping children succeed when they start elementary school (see chap. 5, this volume).

In a recent series of preliminary seminal cross-sectional studies, Noble, Farah, McCandliss, and colleagues have assessed neurocognitive systems of preschool children (Noble, Norman, & Farah, 2005), school-aged children (Noble, Farah, & McCandliss, 2006; Noble, McCandliss, & Farah, 2007; Noble, Wolmetz, et al., 2006), and preadolescents (Farah et al., 2006). Assessment was aimed at determining socioeconomic contributions to prediction of variances in performance and neural activation.

In the majority of such studies (Noble et al., 2007; Noble, Farah, & McCandliss, 2006; Noble, Norman, & Farah, 2005; Noble, Wolmetz, et al., 2006), authors have conceptualized poverty as a composite based on an SES that includes the following three variables: parental education, parental occupation, and parental income in terms of the income-to-needs ratio criterion. The income-to-needs ratio was estimated by the researchers for each family and defined as the total family income divided by the official poverty threshold for a family of a specific size. Finally, an SES index score was determined for each child by entering the three variables into a factor analysis that explained 73.5% of the variance with a single factor. This factor loading was then used as the SES index score for each child. As authors have mentioned, this approach is a proxy that fails to include most of the other risk factors found in populations of children living in poverty.

Three studies (Farah et al., 2006; Noble et al., 2007; Noble, Norman, & Farah, 2005) assessed seven systems related to neurocognitive functioning among preschoolers, school-aged children, and preadolescents from varied ethnic and socioeconomic backgrounds, using tasks drawn from the cognitive neuroscience literature (see Table 4.1). In all cases, tasks were aimed at determining how SES predicts variances in behavioral performances. Authors selected each set of systems on the basis of (a) the fact that each system featured relatively mutual independence and (b) the role of cognitive development and school achievement in these sets.

The following systems were included: (a) left perisylvian language system, associated with language processes, such as lexical–semantic knowledge, grammar reception, and phonological awareness; (b) parietal–spatial cognition system, associated with spatial cognition processing; (c) medial temporal declarative memory system, related to the ability to form new memories without any strategic effort to learn; (d) lateral–orbital–medial prefrontal systems, associated with attention, spatial working memory, inhibitory control, theory of mind, set-shifting, and reward processing; and (e) occipitotemporal–pattern vision system, involved in pattern perception and visualization from memory.

The first study (Noble, Norman, & Farah, 2005), involved a sample of 30 middle- and 30 low-SES-background healthy kindergarten children from Philadelphia, Pennsylvania. Findings suggest that socioeconomic background differences were associated with performance disparities in both language and executive function systems, with fewer disparities in visual cognition and visuospatial skills. Group means were on the order of 1 standard deviation apart on composites of language skills, and on the order of 0.5 standard deviation apart on executive function tasks. Furthermore, no SES-related differences were found in either memory ability or spatial ability, the associations between SES and the executive function being statistically mediated.

The authors argued that language and executive systems showed the greatest performance gaps across SES because both cognitive mechanisms are involved in processes that have been shown to undergo a more protracted course of maturation than has been observed in other neural areas. Thus, it is possible that as a result of a longer development period, both the language and the executive systems were more susceptible to environmental influences, as other studies have shown about parenting influences (Landry, Millar-Loncar, Smith, & Swank, 2002) and parents' educational level (Ardilla, Rosselli, Matute, & Guajardo, 2005) on the development of executive functions in children from various cultures. Environmental influences have also been observed in the socioeconomic modulations of mother speech on early vocabulary development (Hoff, 2003). In addition, Noble, Norman, and Farah (2005) hypothesized that such relationships hint at a possible causal pathway, inasmuch as both socioeconomic background and executive function performance have independently predicted child language ability. However, socioeconomic background cannot account for any variance in executive function ability. Another variable correlated with socioeconomic background—for example, proacademic activities in the home, home literacy environment, or parental disciplinary style—could drive both performances because the researchers have constrained socioeconomic factors that potentially correlate with SES to a small number of simple, parent-reported aspects of child experience.

Farah et al. (2006) conducted a second study involving a sample of 60 children between the ages of 10 years and 13 years from low- and middle-SES healthy African American homes. This study was aimed at characterizing the neurocognitive profile of socioeconomic background by using a more fine-grained analysis of neurocognitive systems, particularly involving prefrontal circuits. At the same time, any medical conditions likely to account for socioeconomic disparities in cognitive performance were avoided. In this study, the authors pointed out a fact that is usually unclear—namely, which specific prefrontal system is involved in SES, inasmuch as the prefrontal cortex is a complex, highly interactive structure associated with different neurocognitive systems (E. K. Miller & Cohen, 2001). In the present study, Farah et al. used a heterogenous set of tasks, including working memory, cognitive control, set-shifting, theory of mind, and delay gratification in an attempt to discern more accurately how the prefrontal system correlates with SES by assessing separately the dorsolateral prefrontal (working memory), the anterior cingulate (cognitive control), and the ventromedial (reward processing) prefrontal systems. The authors also included an analysis of the medial temporal memory system, which underlies the learning of academic school demands and a broad range of everyday activities. With regard to poverty-related criteria, this study only assessed them in terms of SES—that is, parental occupation and education status—without taking income records into account.

Results showed disparities between SES groups regarding working memory, cognitive control, and especially language and memory. By con-

TABLE 4.1
Studies on Poverty Modulation of Neurocognitive Systems

Neurocognitive system	Study		
	Noble, Norman, and Farah (2005)	Farah et al. (2006)	Noble, McCandliss, and Farah (2007)
Left perisylvian (language)	PPVT	PPVT	PPVT
	TROG (Bishop, 1983)	TROG (Bishop, 1983)	CTOPP
	TOPA		
Parietal (spatial cognition)	Line orientation (Benton, Varney, & Hamsher, 1978)	Line orientation (Benton et al., 1978)	Line orientation (NEPSY, Korkman, Kira, & Kemp, 1998)
	Mental rotation	Mental rotation	Mental rotation
Medial temporal (declarative memory)	Incidental face learning	Incidental face learning	Delayed memory for faces (NEPSY)
	Incidental picture learning	Incidental word learning	Incidental picture pair learning
Lateral prefrontal (working memory)	Spatial working memory (Hughes, 1998)	Spatial working memory (CANTAB)	Spatial working memory (Klingberg, Forssberg, & Westerberg, 2002)
	Go/no go	Two-back (Casey et al., 1995)	Delayed nonmatch to sample (Marks et al., 2001)
	False alarms DCCS (Zelazo, Frye, & Rapus, 1996)		
	Theory of mind (Frye, Zelazo, & Tibor, 1995)		
	Delay of gratification		
Anterior cingulate (cognitive control)		Go/no go	Go/no go
		Number Stroop	Auditory attention and response (NEPSY)
Orbitofrontal/ventromedial (reward processing)		Reversal learning (CANTAB)	Reversal learning (Fellows and Farah, 2003)

		Delay (Gordon, McClure, & Aylward, 1996)	Delay of gratification (Carlson and Moses, 2001)
Occipitotemporal (pattern vision)	Shape detection (VOSP)	Shape detection (VOSP)	
	Color imagery	Face perception (Mooney, 1957)***	

Note. Each study explanation includes information on what tasks and tests were administered by each neurocognitive system. PPTV = Peabody Picture Vocabulary Test; TROG = Test of Reception of Grammar; CTOPP = Comprehensive Test of Phonological Processing; TOPA = Test of Phonological Awareness; NEPSY = Developmental Neuropsychological Assessment; CANTAB = Cambridge Neuropsychological Testing Automated Battery; DCCS = Dimensional Change Card Sort Test ; VOSP = Visual Object and Space Perception Battery.

trast, reward processing and visual cognition did not differ significantly. More specifically, in the prefrontal system, two of the three assessed dimensions—working memory and cognitive control—seemed to be more developed in middle-SES children. Contrary to a previous study (Noble, Norman, & Farah, 2005), a substantial difference (0.66 standard deviation) was observed in memory-related abilities, but in the earlier study, both groups performed at the same level with regard to the reward-processing dimension. The authors considered that this fact could be related to the earlier maturation of the ventromedial prefrontal networks. More recently, Smith and Farah (2008) assessed memory and habit-learning performance among adolescents from low- and middle-SES families to find out whether SES-related modulation on declarative memory was driven by a stress-related impairment of the hippocampus but not by striatally mediating learning networks. Results suggested that habit-learning performance is not SES-modulated.

In a third study, Noble et al. (2007) analyzed SES as a continuous variable across the broad range represented in their sample of 168 first graders recruited from nine New York City public schools (see Table 4.1). The hypothesis tested in the study performed by Noble, Norman, and Farah (2005) included the extent to which SES accounts for individual differences in the above-mentioned neurocognitive systems, including a finer grained analysis of prefrontal executive function than has been previously reported, additional assessments on visual–spatial and memory functions, as well as on the relationships among parent-reported aspects of children's home behavior and their neurocognitive development. With an exception made for reward processing, results showed that SES statistically accounted for a portion of variance in each system: 32.0% in the language composite, 16.7% in the visuospatial composite, 10.2% in the memory composite, 5.5% in the working memory composite, and 5.5% in the cognitive control composite. The authors also found that controlling for language ability eliminated the association between SES and cognitive control and reduced the association between SES and all the other systems. This pattern of results suggests that language could mediate the association between SES and cognitive control and could partially mediate the associations between SES and visuospatial skills, memory, and working memory. In addition, SES associations with cognitive control were accounted for by semantic rather than by phonological abilities.

To investigate relationships between home and school as mediator factors between SES and neurocognitive performance, two component analyses were carried out by Noble et al. (2007) with a set of variables based on parent and school reports: (a) home literacy environment (parental reading of newspapers and books, reading with the child, and practicing writing letters or words with the child) and (b) frequency of physical punishment. Several factors have been identified as loading on home literacy environment, aspects of the school environment, and time spent at either day care center or preschool. All factors involved were entered into a single regression step, followed by the SES index for each neurocognitive system composite. Results suggest that school environment accounted for variance in language, memory, and working memory performance. Attendance at either day care center or preschool accounted for variance in visuospatial skills. Finally, home literacy environment accounted for additional variance in working memory.

In a fourth study, Noble, Farah, and McCandliss (2006) scrutinized how SES is likely to influence the association between the understanding of language sounds and the ability to map them in letters. They argued that although this association is likely to be multifactorial, a major determinant is the SES gradients in reading-related experiences, such as home literacy environment; the degree to which a child has been in early contact with printed material; and the quality of early schooling. In addition, they pointed out that phonological awareness (PA) is necessary for the acquisition of reading skills because preliterate children who have acquired better phonological skills at home learn to read more quickly than their peers when they are in school (Wagner & Torgesen, 1987). Some researchers have also observed that the absolute level and the acquisition rate of the same skills predict elementary reading skills (Byrne, Fielding-Barnesley, & Ashley, 2000; Share, Jorm, MacLean, & Mathews, 1984). They have hypothesized that the predictive relationship between child experience and reading skills varies in terms of the function of child access to these resources. Thus, children with higher phonological skills are likely to succeed in reading regardless of their SES. However, with regard to children with lower skills, socioeconomic differences may matter.

A battery of reading and receptive vocabulary tests was administered to 168 first graders recruited from the previously mentioned New York City public schools (Noble et al., 2007; Noble, Farah, & McCandliss, 2006). Results first suggested that PA contributed to a unique variance in all the reading tasks, whereas SES contributed to a unique variance in single word reading and passage comprehension but not in *nonword reading* (i.e., the applying of grapheme–phoneme correspondences with letter strings that do not correspond to real words, such as *grall* instead of *ball*). To analyze an interaction between PA and SES, Noble and colleagues studied a subsample covering a broad range of SES because in the general sample, no children from the highest tercile of SES had performed at the lowest PA levels. The hierarchical regressions of this data subset showed that SES accounted for a unique variance in the second step dealing with the same tasks as in the previous analysis—single word reading and passage comprehension. They also found that a PA × SES interaction was significant for nonword reading (see Figure 4.2), suggesting that if they had not studied this interaction (determining that the effect of PA on reading ability differs across the SES spectrum), they would have mistakenly concluded that SES was not systematically associated with nonword decoding. More specifically, a PA major effect would be observed in all reading tasks because the higher the PA, the better the performance. In summary, this study not only replicated data from studies showing that SES is associated with reading abilities but also expanded such data by showing that SES interacts with PA to predict decoding.

Several biobehavioral markers, such as salivary cortisol, heart rate, and vagal tone, have been also related to self-regulatory skills and early school adjustment in preschoolers from low-income homes (Blair & Peters, 2003; Lupie, King, Meaney, & McEwen, 2001; A. L. Miller, Seifer, Stroud, Sheinkopf, & Dickstein, 2006). Recent studies have also extended those analyses to adolescent samples. For example, Hackman, Betancourt, Hurt, Gallop, and Farah (2008) analyzed whether SES predicts both baseline cortisol levels and reactivity to a social stressor in adolescents from low- and middle-SES families. Preliminary results did not show an SES modulation in their cortisol responses. However, the authors observed an interaction among time response to stressor, gender, and SES showing that males and low-SES females evidenced a larger response to the stressor than middle-SES females and that low-SES males showed a higher, though delayed, peak of cortisol response. This pattern suggests that SES indeed predicted cortisol reactivity to social stress, although modulated by gender.

On the basis of the research work that has been analyzed in this chapter, a first conclusion is that privations present in different forms of poverty modulate performance on tasks demanding basic cognitive control and monitoring operations and language. In particular, the series of studies by Noble and colleagues have also contributed to deepening some of those modulator aspects in the sense that there is no single significant modulation related to neurocognitive systems or age ranges. For example, findings have shown that SES modulated language and executive functions in preschoolers.

At the same time, these studies allowed for a deeper understanding of different mediation factors with regard to poverty modulation when analyzing performance in control and language-related tasks. For example, among preschoolers, it has been seen that the phonological processing level inter-

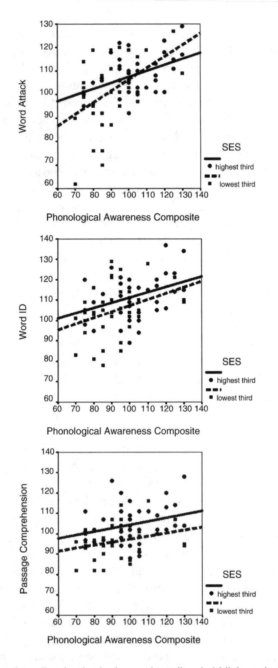

Figure 4.2. Nonword reading (top), single word reading (middle), and passage comprehension (bottom) plotted against phonological awareness. Main effects and interactions with the continuous variables of socioeconomic status (SES) are schematically rendered using the top and the bottom terciles of SES and plotting the regression lines (phonological awareness vs. reading measure) separately for each SES tercile, for each task. ID = identification. From "Socioeconomic Background Modulates Cognition-Achievement Relationships in reading," by K. G. Noble, M. J. Farah, and B. D. McCandliss, 2006, *Cognitive Development, 21,* p. 359. Copyright 2006 by Elsevier. Reproduced by permission.

acts with family's socioeconomic level, so children's reading decodification abilities can be predicted. In addition, school setting, attending a day care center, and the literacy environment are factors apt at mediating children's performance in tasks where language, working memory, and visuospatial processing skills are required.

EARLY EXTREME PRIVATION: ORPHANAGE EXPERIENCE

As mentioned in chapter 3 of this volume, low SES has been largely associated with a stressful lifestyle, and differences in home-located emotional support account for a significant portion of the variance in children's verbal, reading, and arithmetical skills (Brooks-Gunn & Duncan, 1997). In particular, children raised in chronically stressful or abusive circumstances also demonstrate an increased or irregular production of cortisol, which has low correlations with IQ and achievement test performance (Gunnar & Quevedo, 2007). Vasopressin and oxytocin neuropeptide systems that are critical in forging social bonds and regulating emotional behaviors proved to be altered in mistreated children (Wismer Fires, Ziegler, Kurian, Jacoris, & Pollak, 2005). Studies applying neurocognitive measurements and methods suggest that in children suffering from mistreatment-caused posttraumatic stress disorder, deficits in cognitive control also have been observed (Beers & De Bellis, 2002) as well as alterations in hippocampal brain areas, as evidenced by nueroimages obtained by magnetic resonance imaging (MRI; Carrion, Weems, & Reiss, 2007).

To identify potential causal relationships between mistreatment and brain changes, Noble, Tottenham, and Casey (2005) studied how the orphanage experience influences brain development. Regarding behavior, they found that most children's general cognitive ability scores fall within the average range. However, their estimated full-scale IQ scores negatively correlated with time spent at the orphanage. These authors also assessed cognitive control skills with a go–no go task tapping inhibitory control processing and found that adopted children's performance differed in accuracy from the age-matched controls. As in the case of IQ scores, performance also correlated negatively with age at adoption. When learning and hippocampal memory-related tasks were administered, a slower performance could be observed in terms of learning new stimulus–response associations.

POVERTY MODULATION OF NEURAL NETWORKS: NEUROIMAGING EVIDENCE

Neuroimaging has been used to examine brain mechanisms related to poverty. For example, at low levels of phonological awareness, children from high-SES homes, compared with low-SES homes, were more likely to evidence increased responses in the left fusiform gyrus. Noble, Wolmetz, et al.

(2006) concluded that these results suggest that SES could systematically influence brain–behavior relationships. Thus, children who lived within a lower SES environment evidenced below average phonological skill and a strong relationship between PA and activity in the fusiform gyrus, whereas the relationship was attenuated in children who lived in a higher SES environment, although these children had similar PA skills (see Figure 4.3).

These neuroimaging results provide an attractive and challenging insight into the potential mechanisms underlying the previously reported behavioral interactions among PA, reading, and SES (Noble et al., 2007; Noble, Farah, & McCandliss, 2006; Noble, Norman, & Farah, 2005). Noble et al. (2007) in particular suggested that the neural network involved in the observed interaction between PA and SES in reading skill lies in the left fusiform gyrus. Nonetheless, as the authors stated, mechanisms underlying the association between PA and those areas, as well as the computational processes performed therein remain to be investigated.

Neville and colleagues (Pakulak, Sanders, Paulsen, & Neville, 2005; Sabourin, Pakulak, Paulsen, Fanning, & Neville, 2007) have also studied neuroimaging SES modulation in search for language skills brain organization areas in children. For example, event-related brain potential records of spoken sentences including both semantic and phrase structure violation showed differences in an N400 amplitude and distribution among groups of children between 3 years and 5 years old. At the same time, syntactic violations have elicited a late positive component resembling a P600 in both groups. However, only children from higher SES families showed sustained, early negativity, suggesting that the associations between SES and language development may be reflected in differences in brain organization for language processing (Pakulak et al., 2005; Sabourin et al., 2007). Furthermore, researchers also found evidence that event related potential (ERP) records of selective auditory attention showed variation from 100 milliseconds to 300 milliseconds in poststimulus patterns in response to probes among low-SES children between 3 years and 8 years old (Laungier, Sanders, Stevens, & Neville, 2006).

Raizada et al. (2008) investigated the interactions between SES (parental education and occupation) and phonological awareness and the auditory processing of phonetic input in a sample of 5-year-old healthy children by administering a battery of standardized cognitive and linguistic tests and using functional magnetic resonance imaging to record neural activity during a rhyming task that predicts reading skills. Results showed significant correlations between SES and (a) the degree of hemispheric specialization in the left inferior or frontal gyrus and (b) grey and white matter volumes, even after controlling for language and cognitive test scores. Their findings suggest that the weaker language skills of low-SES children are related to reduced underlying neural specialization and show the importance of using neural–behavioral combined elevations in the analysis of SES modulation of cognitive development.

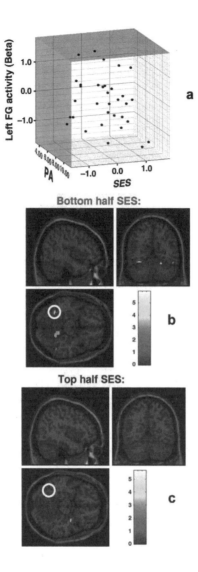

Figure 4.3. Relationship between activity in left fusiform gyrus (FG) regions of interest (ROI; centered at Montreal Neurological Institute coordinates −44, −58, −15) and phonological awareness (PA) across socioeconomic status (SES). Scatter plot (a) depicts the partial correlation of PA and left fusiform activity across SES, controlling for age, task accuracy, and run uses. A significant PA × SES interaction was found ($p < .006$), such that PA is more strongly associated with left fusiform activation at lower SES levels, whereas this association is attenuated as SES increases. This relationship is demonstrated in brain maps depicting correlations between PA and brain activity among subjects whose SES was below the median (b) and above the median (c). Correlations between PA and activity at the left fusiform ROI are circled in white ($p < .005$, uncorrected). Only the lower SES map shows a significant are of positive correlation. From "Brain–Behavior Relationships in Reading Acquisition Are Modulated by Socioeconomic Factors," by K. G. Noble, M. E. Wolmetz, L. G. Ochs, M. J. Farah, and B. D. McCandliss, 2006, *Developmental Science, 9*, p. 649. Copyright 2006 by Blackwell Publishing. Reproduced with permission.

Kishiyama et al. (2009) provided electrophysiological evidence indicating that prefrontal processing evaluated with executive functions measures is modeulated by SES (parental education, income, and income-to-needs ratio) in a sample of 7- to 12-year-old healthy children. The authors observed that early extrastriate (P1 and N1) and novelty-related (N2) ERP responses were reduced in children from the low-SES group compared with the high-SES group. As in Farah et al.'s 2006 study, cognitive performance indicated that the low-SES group was reduced compared with the high-SES group on measures of executive function (working memory, cognitive flexibility, and semantic fluency).

Noble, Tottenham, and Casey (2005) also examined the effects of institutionalization on brain development using the MRI technique. They replicated previously reported associations between total brain volume and IQ estimate as well as a moderate association between the lapse of time a child had spent in an orphanage and child's prefrontal and hippocampal volumes. They made the interesting observation that the hippocampal volume correlated with the time spent with the adoptive family, suggesting that the adoption experience has positive effects.

Finally, in a recent study, Sheridan, Khalea, D'Esposito, and Thomas (2008) measured cortisol reactivity to functional MRI scanning during a moderately stressful and novel experiment, requesting children from 8 years to 11 years old belonging to diverse SES backgrounds to learn certain rules. Results suggested that children from low-SES backgrounds learned the novel stimuli more slowly than children from higher SES households. Furthermore, performance was significantly correlated with income and cortisol reactivity during scanning.

The above-mentioned neuroimaging studies not only confirm findings observed at the performance level in cognitive tasks; more important, they contribute to the development of an integrated view and more soundly based understanding of how poverty-related privations modify the activation of different neural networks when children raised under different environmental conditions deal with specific demands. Nevertheless, this relatively new and attractive field is still at a preliminary stance and awaits further research.

CONCLUSION

Studies devoted to the analysis of poverty modulation of task performance involving specific neurocognitive demands and different neural networks allow researchers to confirm and expand previous knowledge on the basis of other theoretical and methodological approaches (see chap. 3, this volume). Even though they are still preliminary, these studies contribute to identification of the preferential sets of neural components and their dynamic changes underlying cognitive operations as well as their interactions involved in this modulation—that is, whether language modulates SES impact on cognitive control or SES modulates learning skills associated with preferential brain areas. Other cofactors also should be taken into account, such as school and home environments, that have been shown to modulate SES impact on basic cognitive operations. In addition to allowing better, more comprehensive knowledge regarding the impact of poverty conditions on cognitive performance and mediator mechanisms, the practical significance of understanding this preferential neural substrate involvement lies in its potential contribution to the design of learning-oriented specific activities demanding both literacy and numeracy skills. This and other interventions are discussed in chapter 5 of this volume.

5

INTERVENTION PROGRAMS

In this chapter, we present interventions aimed at improving both the cognitive and socioemotional development of child populations living in poverty. We first review programs based on the design, performance, and assessment of a number of multiple intervention modules that have been carried out during the past 4 decades among either industrialized or developing societies. This is followed by examples of general principles that are suggested for the design of efficient actions. Within this conceptual context, we present a brief discussion of several education programs applied by different countries as a part of their education policies. Finally, we include a detailed description of the main intervention studies to analyze possible contributions to the intervention area (see also chap. 6, this volume). Such studies, oriented to different child populations, were designed and applied during the past decade within the realm of cognitive neuroscience. Some examples deal with children living in disadvantaged socioeconomic conditions.

MULTIMODULAR INTERVENTION PROGRAMS

Within the context of this chapter, *early intervention program* refers to preventive educational, social, and health services provided during any of

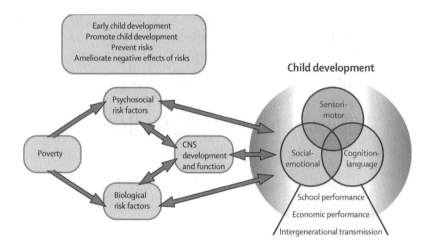

Figure 5.1. Conceptual model of how interventions can affect early child development. From "Strategies to Avoid the Loss of Developmental Potential in More Than 200 Million Children in the Developing World," by P. L. Engle, M. M. Black, J. R. Behrman, M. Cabral de Mello, P. J. Gertler, L. Kapiriri, R. Martorell, M. E. Young, and International Child Development Steering Group., 2007, *Lancet, 369,* p. 230, Copyright 2007 by Elsevier. Reproduced with permission.

the first 10 years in the lives of children living in disadvantaged socioeconomic environments (Reynolds, Wang, & Walberg, 2003b). The main objective of this type of program is the promotion of cognitive and socioemotional development in order to give children appropriate opportunities for school readiness and social inclusion (Aber, Jones, & Raver, 2007; C. T. Ramey & Ramey, 1998; Reynolds, 1994; Reynolds, Wang, & Walberg, 2003a; Zigler & Styfco, 2003; see also Figure 5.1). Although educational and social policymakers sustain a vigorous debate on these issues, most authors agree that objectives aimed at improving school readiness and social inclusion at the elementary school level are important with regard to reducing academic failure, grade repeating, and dropouts (Brooks-Gunn & Duncan, 1997; K. Johnson & Knitzer, 2006; Nation et al., 2003; Rutter, 2003).

At least five categories of early intervention programs can be identified according to their features (Barnett, 2006). The first category includes studies with randomized designs better at providing more accurate information than large nonexperimental studies or programs. Examples of these are the Abecederian Project (Campbell, Pungello, Miller-Johnson, Burchinal, & Ramey, 2001), the CARE Project (Wasik, Ramey, Bryant, & Sparling, 1990), the Infant Health and Development Program (IHDP; McCormick et al., 2006), the Milwaukee Project (Garber, 1988), and the Perry Preschool Program (Schweinhart et al., 2005). The second category includes studies with large-scale public programs, such as the Early Head Start (Love et al., 2005) and Head Start (Abbot-Shim, Lambert, & McCarty, 2003). Both categories involve appropriate randomized designs allowing adequate impact evaluations. A third category includes quasi-experimental studies such as the Chicago Child–Parent Centers (Reynolds, Temple, Robertson, & Mann, 2002) and the Tulsa, Oklahoma, study (Gormley, Gayer, Phillips, & Dawson, 2005). Although studies in this third category did not implement randomized trials, they did consider comparability of treatment and control groups, allowing researchers to distinguish family from program influences. A fourth category includes large statistical studies designed to analyze natural variations in programs and child participation, such as the Effective Provision of Pre-School Education Project (Sylva, Melhuish, Sammons, Siraj-Blatchford, & Taggart, 2004), the NICHD Project (Vandell, 2004), and the Northern Ireland Program (Melhuish et al., 2006). In these studies, data were collected directly from attending children as well as those not attending programs at the time they began kindergarten. The fifth category involves studies using survey data; child participation in the program was based on retrospective parental reports—for example, in the National Education Longitudinal Study (Ludwig & Miller, 2005).

The field of child development and social policy has acknowledged for nearly 50 years the vital role that ecological perspectives play in the development of children raised in disadvantaged conditions as well as in the interventions aimed at them. Now, after almost 40 years of research based on intervention programs—especially pertaining to the first and second categories described previously—several conceptual and methodological principles of program quality and efficiency have been identified (S. Ramey & Ramey, 2003; Zigler & Finn-Stevenson, 2007). In terms of child development, mechanisms involved in several behaviors, such as environmental exploration, expression of basic cognitive and social abilities, stimulation of language and communication, adult reinforcement regarding children's achievements, and avoidance of inappropriate punishments, have been addressed as primary targets (C. T. Ramey & Ramey, 1998). Regarding the key dimensions of interventions, positive impacts have been associated with the administration of a broad set of intensive, high-quality services involving education for children and parents alike and family supports—for example, links to social, health, and nutrition services. More specifically, efficiency has been identified as an important factor related to actions involving the following general principles: (a) a wide age range; (b) a high frequency of intervention activities in terms of number of hours per day, days per week, and weeks per year; (c) children receiving more direct than indirect interventions (indirect being, e.g., counseling or education of parents and teachers; however, the combination of both types of interventions—direct as well as indirect—has proven to be the best option); (d) involvement of the family and other mediating agents in the social environment to maintain the effects of interventions and to transfer their gains to other areas of development or achievement, such as school readiness; (e) beginning interventions at very early stages of development and maintaining them at least until adolescence; and (f) applying conceptual frameworks based on social and ecological approaches to child development in the design of any intervention module (Aber et al., 2007; Campbell et al., 2001; Huston et al., 2001; Karoly, Kilburn, & Cannon, 2005; C. T. Ramey & Ramey, 1998; S. Ramey & Ramey, 2003; Zigler & Finn-Stevenson, 2007).

A continuous analysis of program development not only allows updating of child and family information but also contributes to the ability to adjust future plans and actions at research and policy levels. This is a crucial practice because it allows the disclosure of accumulated environmental- and intervention-related effects of different factors on individual child health histories (e.g., pre- and postnatal health; parenting practices; community resources; home and school environments; quality and quantity of interactions between caregivers and children; and parents' beliefs, values, and routines; Aber et al., 2007; C. T. Ramey & Ramey, 1998; S. Ramey & Ramey, 2003). Most impact analyses performed on multimodular programs are based on experimental designs involving a random assignment of individuals to either experimental or control groups. In the past few decades, there has been a growing interest in and commitment to place-randomized trials (Aber et al., 2007; Boruch, 2005). That is, the delivery of actions at group level, for example, in either classrooms or neighborhoods, is a way to assess strictly the impact of the intervention. Recent examples of the group-randomized evaluation of a place-based program involving children and families in socioeconomically disadvantaged conditions include Success-for-All (Borman, Slavin, & Cheung, 2005) and the Progresa study in Mexico (Scott, 1999), which randomized schools and villages, respectively. Significant contributions to increase the efficiency of the programs are program staff training and commitment, the inclusion of community members into the staff, the consideration of community social and cultural practices, mobilization of the community on the basis of program goals, setting up and maintaining an open communication between staff and community, and an appropriate management plan allowing quality control and assessment of the program process (Maggi et al., 2005).

Principles described in previous paragraphs show that the success for any intervention depends on its being regularly applied over long time spans, as ecological child development theories suggest (Bronfenbrenner & Ceci, 1994). It is interesting to consider that inclusion of ecological perspectives on human development contribute to program and policy designs, generating strategies that address different contexts of development (Aber et al., 2007). However, not all children benefit in the same way from their participation in these types of programs. Individual differences are due to multiple interactive factors, crucial among them early risk accumulation and variation in quality of environments (Aber et al., 2007; Baker, Piotrkowski, & Brooks-Gunn, 1999; Campbell et al., 2001; Devaney, Ellwood, & Love, 1997;

National Institute of Child Health and Human Development & Early Child Care Research Network [NICHD], 2005; Reynolds, 1994; Reynolds et al., 2003a; C. T. Ramey & Ramey, 1998; S. Ramey & Ramey, 2003). Appropriate experimental designs allow researchers to explore alternative approaches and further contribute to the design and adjustment of intervention programs.

Children's participation in high-quality intervention programs has been consistently related to positive impacts on cognitive development—measured with general standardized tests, motivation, and school achievement in the short run and on lower rates of repeaters and need for special education during elementary school in the mid-run (Reynolds et al., 2003b). In the long run, programs endowed with extensive longitudinal designs, including cases with random assignments, have had an effect on the number of completed school years and on employment rates (Boocock, 1995; 2003).

INTERVENTION PROGRAMS

Detailed descriptions of some of the intervention programs mentioned in the previous section are presented here. We provide some parameters for an analysis of the potential contributions of neuroscience to this field (see chap. 6, this volume). In addition to including specific studies dealing with each program and details of their components and activities, we also discuss complementary revision studies (e.g., Karoly et al., 2005; Reynolds et al., 2003a; Ripple & Zigler, 2003) as well as meta-analyses (e.g., Anderson et al., 2003) that are necessary for an analysis of the more important issues.

Because of their high financial requirements, multimodular intervention programs have been designed and applied mainly in industrialized countries. Examples of this trend are Head Start and Early Head Start, Abecederian, Milwaukee, CARE, IHDP, Perry Preschool, and the Longitudinal Study of Chicago that have been carried out in the United States; the Victoria Day Project in Canada; and the Study of Early Childhood in Australia (Barnett, 2006; Boocock, 1995; Boocock & Larner, 1998).

Curricula in both Early Head Start and Head Start consist of written documents for implementing a quality child development and education program. As far as curriculum determination is concerned, two basic approaches have been proposed: Staff and parents at each center either base a curriculum on an already-developed model and adapt it for the group of children being served or develop a local curriculum. Either way, the curriculum must be in accordance with all Head Start program performance standards (Currie, 2001) in addition to being based on universal principles of child development. First, when it comes to serving infants, toddlers or preschoolers, including children with disabilities, the standards require that the curriculum must include the following four aspects: (a) goals for children's development and learning, (b) experiences through which they shall achieve these goals, (c) roles of staff and parents in helping children to achieve these goals, and (d) materials needed to support the implementation of the curriculum.

Child development principles are applied to all children regardless of their gender, race, culture, or country of origin. The following three main concepts are included: patterns of growth and development are orderly and sequential, human growth and development proceed from simple to complex organization, and learning is influenced by the child's social and cultural context. Although each child is considered unique, there are general goals, such as developing positive, nurturing relationships with adults and peers. For every identified goal, developmentally appropriate experiences are selected from the curriculum, planned, and presented to the children. For example, one goal for children lies in achieving an increasing competence in numeracy. Because children need active experiences to develop an age-appropriate arithmetical understanding, teachers are encouraged to take advantage of everyday materials, daily routines, and child interests to foster an emergent arithmetical ability within the curriculum limits. Staff members create environments and select materials that support an arithmetic-oriented thinking. They engage children in meaningful conversations about the work they are doing. Finally, throughout the year, both staff and parents take time to discuss the ways the curriculum seems to be working for both the children as a group and for individual children. On the basis of discussion about the children's progress, changes are made to try and keep curriculum responsive and supportive of the children as they grow and learn, as their interests expand, and as their skills and knowledge change (Office of Human Development Services, 2008; Taylor, 2000).

Studies evaluating the impact of Head Start have been conducted by a number of research groups during the 40 years the program has been in force. During the 1st decade (1965–1975), attention was focused on cognitive improvements through changes in IQ scores. The first reports showed a rapid increase of up to 10 points in a number of participants. However, once children left the program, this effect was not necessarily sustained during elementary school. Within the same decade, studies that showed the same tendency in other achievement tests were questioned because of methods used for sampling. In the following decade, a study carried out by the Consortium of Longitudinal Studies confirmed an increase in child IQ during the first phases, an increase that disappeared progressively during elementary school. At the same time, however, in other areas, long-term positive effects, such as less special education and lower grade-repeating rates, were verified (Boocock, 2003; Boocock & Larner, 1998).

Of particular interest is a recent study about the effectiveness of the Early Head Start program based on the evaluation of 17 research programs administered in different areas of the United States (Love et al., 2005). Research questions focused on the impacts on child and parenting outcomes when programs had come to an end, the adherence of centers to the Head Start standards, and the effects of offering both center- and home-based services rather than only one or the other. Results showed significant impacts on child and parent outcomes when children were 3 years old at the end of the program. Specifically, children exposed to the Early Head Start program scored higher on the Bayley Mental Development Index; a reduction in the proportion of children scoring below 85 was verified, and there was more than 1 standard deviation difference on the Peabody Picture Vocabulary Test among Head Start subjects than among control groups. Furthermore, children in the intervention group were rated higher on parents' commitment and on sustained attention to objects. Regarding parenting behavior, Early Head Start programs produced positive impacts on emotional support, such as reductions in aggressive behavior, on the basis of the Child Behavior Checklist and on parental support for language and learning abilities, on the basis of the corresponding HOME Inventory (Bradley, 1994) measures for these dimensions. Programs that fit better with Head Start standards in addition to adopting a mixed approach—that is, combination of home- and center-based services—produced a greater impact range.

One of the most important contributions of this study was the systematic measuring of program implementation and the assessment of its role in producing intervention impacts (Love et al., 2005). Results are significant not only in terms of their consistency with previous evaluations of early childhood programs for infants and toddlers (Brooks-Gunn, Klebanov, Liaw, & Spiker, 1993; Campbell & Ramey, 1994) but also for the use of a large number of variables across which significant effects have been found. As Love et al. (2005) addressed, however, two important points must be taken into account: A variety of cognitive–emotional assessment instruments are not available for those age ranges, and many times parents' reports are the only available assessment tools. Within these contextual difficulties, the mentioned study by Love et al. becomes even more important because it addresses the need to improve the assessment methods for infants and toddlers. Finally, taking into account that cognitive and emotional development are continuous phenomena, the results of intervention programs based on age-range criteria should be included as a contribution to intervention designs.

The trends for reduction of short-term gains found in Head Start and Early Head Start have not been checked in intervention programs designed for experimental exploration goals. Five of these studies are particularly informative: Perry Preschool, Milwaukee, Abecedarian, CARE, and IHDP. All these projects showed improvement in IQ and a reduction of cases with mental retardation during the preschool years. In all these studies, with the exception of the IHDP, effects persisted until mid- or more advanced childhood, although the IQ differences either declined or stopped in adolescence. However, positive impacts have appeared at a later age in other indicators, such as the reduction of grade repeating and special education rates, with the exception of the Milwaukee Project.

Abecederian Project, Project CARE, and the IHDP were multidisciplinary programs, contextually embedded in local service delivery systems and organized around the key concepts of efficiency described in the previous section. Programmatic features involved nutritional supplements, family support through social services, pediatric care and referral, and early childhood education at a center. Educational services involved children from 6 weeks to 5 years of age and operated 8 hours per day, 5 days a week. Efforts were made to involve families. Parents served on the day care center's advisory board and were offered a series of voluntary programs covering such topics as family nutrition, legal matters, behavior management, and toy making. Supportive social services were available to families facing problems with housing, food, and transportation. In addition, social meetings were held at centers for families of treated children—that is, intervention groups. Control groups were provided with nutritional supplements for the first 15 months of life to ensure comparable 1st-year nutrition in intervention and control groups. In addition, control group families were given disposable diapers until the child was toilet trained. Supportive social work services and pediatric care were also available to these families (Campbell & Ramey, 1994; C. T. Ramey, Campbell, & Ramey, 1999).

Educational activities were based on Early Partners and Partner for Learning curricula, plus other documented approaches to enhance cognitive, language, perceptual motor, and social development (Sparling & Lewis, 1991). Partners, a curriculum emphasizing adult–child interactions, was developed in the 1980s and was first used in the IHDP. The first part of the curriculum (Early Partners) emphasizes factors that are of particular salience in the development of low-birth-weight children, focusing on early specific behaviors—that is, cues from the baby, sleep–wake states, calming, levels of stimulation, interaction and communication, muscle tone, eye–hand coordination, and independent handling and manipulation. The goals of the activities are to free the parent to relax, notice, and enjoy their child. Careful observation helps parents become more effective partners who accept and understand infant behaviors and know how to respond in ways that meet children's needs. To reach this and other goals, the curriculum uses the technique of showing cartoon illustrations of adults who are experiencing the joys and frustrations of parenting a low-birth-weight child, including the adult's thoughts, language, and decisions. The second part of the curriculum (Partners for Learning) supports adult–child interactions both at home and within day care programs. The cards that present the curriculum contain simple text and cartoons that are color coded to indicate specific developmental age periods. The curriculum was designed to be delivered either at the family home by a home visitor or to be used by a teacher or caregiver at a day care center.

This curriculum has four basic features: (a) Gamelike learning activities enable easy assimilation by day care staff members, home visitors, and parents. Each game is presented on one of the curriculum activities. (b) Two-week use cycles help either parents or teachers use several games to allow for all aspects of good practice—that is, observation, implementation, and assessment. (c) Curriculum activities, as well as enriched care routines (i.e., diapering, feeding, and dressing), are integrated into daily life either at home or at the day care center. (d) Specific skills for children provide for clarity and immediate utility, and general principles gradually enable parents or teachers to gain a deeper understanding of an instructional model for early education.

Games and activities for children cover a full spectrum of 23 developmental skill areas, organized into four broad themes: cognitive, motor, social, and language. Skill areas are further divided into skill goals, each goal related to one of the 26 specific learning activities of Early Partners or to one of the 200 learning activities of Partners for Learning. Finally, an instructional model is included in the curriculum, organized around seven principles regarding adult skills: (a) preparing materials and ideas needed for children's learning activities; (b) observing children's behaviors that disclose their learning status; (c) modeling, through adult behavior, appropriate language, and problem-solving abilities; (d) supporting steps children take toward skill improvement; (e) prompting children's most appropriate behavior; (f) helping children by revising tasks that are too difficult for them; and (g) building new skills by adding challenging elements to tasks children have previously completed.

The Perry Preschool study was a scientific experiment that identified both the short- and long-term effects of a high-quality preschool education program for socially disadvantaged children. From 1962 to 1967, this project was aimed at avoiding school failure. Researchers identified 123 low-income African American children with school failure risks and randomly assigned 58 of them to a program group that received a high-quality preschool program at ages 3 and 4 and the other 65 to a group receiving no preschool program. Data on both groups were collected annually from ages 3 through 11 and again at ages 14, 15, 19, 27, and 40, with a 6% attrition rate across all measures. Findings on program effects through age 40 showed positive impacts, including more long-term financial independence, better academic achievements, and significantly fewer legal problems (Figure 5.2; Schweinhart et al., 2005).

In the Perry Preschool Program, researchers applied the High/Scope curriculum, which focuses on the promotion of reading, writing, and arithmetic skills. In this curriculum, reading and writing are considered interdependent components of literacy, which opens opportunities to academic advances. Consequently, the curriculum prepares children for reading and writing through each daily routine, using literacy-related materials included in every area of either the classroom, center, or home setting. This frame-

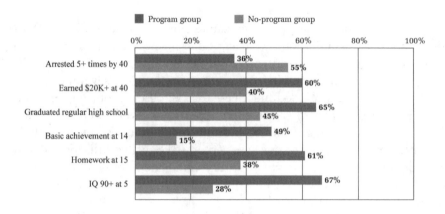

Figure 5.2. Intervention impacts of the High/Scope Perry Preschool Study at 40. From *Lifetime Effects: The High/Scope Perry Preschool Study Through Age 40* (p. 2), by L. J. Schweinhart, J. Montie, Z. Xiang, W. S. Barnett, C. R. Belfield, and M. Nores, 2005, Ypsilanti, MI: High Scope Educational Research Foundation. Copyright 2005 by High/Scope Press. Reproduced with permission.

work is based on five main principles: (a) Learning to read and write begins as early as possible and builds on children's basic need to communicate; (b) children learn to read and write at different rates and in different ways; (c) children acquire literacy through key experiences in speaking, listening, and reading; (d) reading and writing are best learned in contexts wherein literacy skills are tied to meaning and comprehension; and (e) children learn to read and write because they enjoy it and want to emulate adults. At all levels, High/Scope teachers and caregivers receive systematic training to learn specific strategies for promoting literacy in partnership with parents. Teachers and caregivers share control of the learning process with children by embracing the following intentional methods of teaching as they promote literacy experiences in each setting (classroom, center, or home): (a) creating a print-rich environment (e.g., a reading area with a wide variety of age-appropriate books and reading materials), (b) making reading a team effort and part of daily routines, (c) exploring oral language sounds, (d) providing an array of writing materials and reasons to write, (e) introducing early in childhood the idea of letters and words as written symbols, and (f) planning for and supporting children's learning processes by assessing their literacy development (High/Scope Educational Foundation, 2003).

Regarding arithmetic, the High/Scope curriculum is based on the Preschool Child Observation Record, which promotes learning in classification, seriation, number, space, and time. Classification is one way children organize objects and interactions, and this is promoted by High/Scope through such thought processes as (a) exploring and describing similarities, differences, and attributes of objects; (b) distinguishing and describing shapes; (c) sorting and matching; (d) using and describing something in several ways;

(e) holding more than one attribute in mind at a time; and (f) describing characteristics something does not possess or what class it does not belong to. Seriation objects are placed in order on the basis of either differences (e.g., in size) or a repeating sequence or pattern. High/Scope provides three experiences in seriation: (a) comparing attributes (e.g., longer–shorter, bigger–smaller), (b) arranging several elements and objects one after another in a series or pattern and then describing the relationships (e.g., big–bigger–biggest, red–blue–red–blue), and (c) fitting one ordered set of objects to another through trial and error (e.g., small cup and small saucer–medium cup and medium saucer–big cup and big saucer). This curriculum promotes number concepts through three key activities: (a) comparing the numbers of elements in different sets to determine "more," "fewer," or "same"; (b) arranging sets of objects in one-to-one type correspondence; and (c) counting objects. High/Scope key experiences in space include (a) filling and emptying; (b) fitting objects together and taking them apart; (c) changing the shape and arrangement of objects and elements; (d) observing people, places, and things from various space viewpoints; (e) experiencing and describing positions, directions, and distances in the play space, building, and neighborhood; and (f) interpreting space relationships in drawings, pictures, and photos. Finally, time learning is approached through four key experiences: (a) starting and stopping an action on signal; (b) experiencing and describing rates of movement; (c) experiencing and comparing time intervals; and (d) anticipating, remembering, and describing sequences of events (Epstein, 2003).

In a recent study, Belsky et al. (2007) examined the impact of early child care on school achievement and socioemotional functioning from preschool to sixth grade, and their results showed that although parenting was a stronger and more consistent predictor than early child care experience, as was observed in the NICHD (2005) study, higher quality care predicted higher vocabulary scores, and more time spent in day care predicted more teacher-reported externalizing problems. These types of studies, because they include intervention impact predictions from an assessment of various mediating factors (see chap. 2, this volume), contribute significantly by helping design interventions on the basis of an ecological approach to child development.

In developing countries, there are few examples of these types of programs. Those that exist fulfill only partially some of the efficiency requirements. Examples are the Progresa program in Mexico, the Cali Project in Colombia, the Village Preschool Study in India, the Integrated Service for Child Development in India, the Program of Preschool Instruction at Home in Turkey, and the Programa de Intervención Escolar (Program of School Intervention) in Argentina. Finally, the Portage Project is an interesting example of a multicenter intervention program applied in the United States of America, India, Bangladesh, Jamaica, and England with an age-appropriate curriculum based on the main developmental cores in cognition, language, and socialization development (Andersson, 1992; Baker et al., 1999; Boanida,

Espe-Sherwinot, & Borges, 2000; Boocock, 1995, 2003; Colombo & Lipina, 2005; Devaney et al., 1997; Huston et al., 2001; C. T. Ramey & Ramey, 1998; Reynolds, 1994; Scott, 1999; Sturney et al., 1992).

On the basis of these and other community programs in Colombia, India, Kenya, Mozambique, Peru, the Philippines, and Portugal, Maggi et al. (2005) outlined a set of components related to program effectiveness. Most of these components are similar to those based on the assessment process of high-quality programs, such as the Abecederian (discussed previously and in the next section, "Preschool Curricula"). However, the following are more specifically related to needs and resource availability present in developing countries: (a) involving parent participation in terms of parent education and home visiting; (b) designing early childhood care and stimulation modules as a complement to existing health or community programs; (c) integrating traditional caregivers into quality child care practices; (d) using media to transfer information on programs and child needs; (e) including older siblings when they are the primary caregivers; (f) promoting a transition from community programs to school contexts; (g) integrating child programs into general community programs, especially programs aimed at helping women; and (h) making use of existing community, social, and governmental networks.

In summary, *intervention* means something more than just an experimental design aimed at testing hypotheses dealing with socioeconomic backgrounds and cognitive development (Noble, McCandliss, & Farah, 2007). As previously described, a number of randomized controlled trials have shown that educational interventions are endowed with the potential to narrow the performance gap across socioeconomic continuum. For example, the IQs of socioeconomically disadvantaged children who have participated in the Abecederian Project are between 0.5 and 1.0 standard deviation higher than those of children in socioeconomically disadvantaged control groups (C. T. Ramey & Ramey, 1998). A meta-analysis of the long-term effects of early childhood programs showed that early childhood education produces persistent, cost-effective effects on academic achievement (Barnett, 1998).

With regard to the identification of specific needs, training, or education related to cognitive stimulation for target samples according to their initial risk factors profile, some of these programs (e.g., Abecederian and CARE) have been based on a framework assuming differences in accordance to the impact of biological and environmental factors on the central nervous system (C. T. Ramey & Ramey, 1998). Cognitive stimulation or training modules applied in a majority of these programs have had a positive impact on language, achievement, and emotional development, improving school readiness at the same time (Baker et al., 1999; Boocock, 2003; C. T. Ramey & Ramey, 1998; Reynolds, 1994).

In general, as we have seen, cognitive training modules consist of curricular adaptations adopted by preschool and school official systems of each district. However, impacts of those modules have not been assessed with regard to specific approaches, such as those recently developed by cognitive neuroscience (see the "Cognitive Neuroscience Contributions to Intervention" section later in this chapter). Instead, they have been assessed by means of standardized tests (Boocock, 2003; C. T. Ramey & Ramey, 1998) based on traditional child development theories and psychometric tools. In this analysis context, it is important to consider that historically speaking, the evolution of programs and policies has been influenced much more by ideological debates, political negotiations, fiscal realities, the public's and policymakers' perception of needs, and the history of program and policy results than they have been influenced by theory and research (Aber et al., 2007). However, to maximize the potential of impacts on cognitive and socioemotional achievement across socioeconomic status (SES) samples, increasing the precision of the interventions is necessary. Thus, research is likely to influence programs and policies by means of the design and conduct of strict evaluations.

PRESCHOOL CURRICULA

Education-related public policies do not conceptualize education curricula in terms of intervention programs such as those that have just been described. Nevertheless, from an ecological perspective of child development, school context is a critical modulator of both poverty-caused impact and education practices (see chap. 2, this volume). Studies have shown that children living in poverty attend schools where both human and material resources are lacking, and usually by the end of their school cycles, such children demonstrate poor or below average skills—a fact hindering any aspiration for a higher education (Murname, 2007).

Nevertheless, in some of the intervention programs described previously, such as Head Start, practices based on curriculum activities have been included in cognitive development stimulation modules. Because impact assessment of these programs has shown an improvement in child cognitive, socioaffective, and school performance, analysis of such curricular activities is an interesting aspect to be taken into account whenever the design and application of interventions and public policies are considered. The opposite is equally important—that is, an analysis of school practices considered as potential activities to be included in the design of intervention programs for socially disadvantaged children. It has been possible to check this aspect recently from an assessment of school experiences that led to the improvement of school performance on the basis of a cognitive control framework from neurocognitive (Diamond, Barnett, Thomas, & Munro, 2007; see "Cognitive Neuroscience Contributions to Intervention" later in this chapter) and socioaffective (Rogoff, Goodman Turkanis, & Bartlett, 2001) perspectives.

In the field of intervention designs aimed at disadvantaged children, some approaches are based on deepening both school activities design and teacher training through the application of efficiency principles as mentioned previously—for example, instruction based on proven academic and behavioral curricula and classrooms staffed by teachers receiving specific training based on child development frameworks (Duncan, Ludwig, & Magnuson, 2007).

As in the case for intervention programs, only a few impact assessment studies have used experimental designs with random assignment in the field of preschool and school curriculum. For example, the European experience with preschool education programs has produced recommendation guidelines similar to those found in the intervention program framework (Boocock, 2003). Moreover, some educational programs fulfilling these criteria have had positive impacts on cognitive and socioemotional development as well as on school achievement at the elementary level.

PRESCHOOL PROGRAMS OUTSIDE THE UNITED STATES

In France, where the state fully supports preschool education and provides a full-day program, both the curriculum and the teacher training procedure have been designed by the Ministry of Education. This program is applied in the whole country: 100% of children from 3 years to 5 years old are included, and the program is gradually being extended to the 2-year-old population. To assess impact, the French government examines elementary grade repeaters. In the 1990s, the Ministry of Education conducted a survey among 20,000 sixth graders, comparing pupils who had attended preschool programs for 1, 2, or 3 years. Results indicated that every year of participation in the education program reduced the probability of academic failure, especially in children with low socioeconomic backgrounds. However, effectiveness levels were lower than levels attained in some intervention programs applied in the United States of America, such as the Abecederian (Barnett, 1998; Hurless, 2004).

In England, public investment in full-day preschool programs is limited, and many middle- and high-SES families hire nannies, which also occurs in many Latin American countries. In addition, fewer than half the children between 3 years and 4 years old attend schools in either the public or the private sectors. However, many children whose mothers or fathers are at home meet game groups with other children several times a week at school. In the 1990s, the British government carried out a survey on 9,000 families (Centre for Longitudinal Studies, 2005) aimed at analyzing the effects of preschool and other programs on children's cognitive and socioemotional skills as well as school achievements when children were between 5 years and 10 years old. Results showed that any public or private preschool program participation was associated with positive impacts only on cognitive development (Boocock, 2003; Centre for Longitudinal Studies, 2005).

Before 1991, 65% to 70% of children between 3 years and 6 years old in West Germany attended half-day public schools. Evaluation studies indicated that attending this system reduced rates of grade retention and assignment to special education, suggesting that preschool experience improved children's readiness for school (Boocock, 2003; Boocock & Larner, 1998).

The Swedish system is probably one of the most complete in terms of services and conditions offered to its citizens. Local governments support the care of all children and their families and provide careful supervision. Parents can choose between a preschool program and a home care system from birth until the child is 7 years old, when children begin elementary school. The Swedish government has carried out longitudinal studies systematically since 1965, the design of which have complied with the quality standards needed to analyze the impact of preschool and home programs on home environment as well as child development and well-being. Conceptually, the Swedish system is based on a model of dual socialization, assuming that in contemporary society, children spend their time in two different social universes—home and school—therefore requiring the integration of the educational and social systems (Dencik, 1995).

Before the year 2000, the Hungarian kindergarten system was strongly oriented toward classroom activities focusing on cognitive and social skill demands. Specifically, preschool and primary school curricula involved training in basic cognitive demands (e.g., attention, inhibitory control, and working memory), which are related to reductions of cognitive gaps associated with socioeconomic background and developmental disorders (Mills & Mills, 2000).

Bodrova and Leong (1996, 2001) designed a series of tools and strategies based on a constructivist educational framework (i.e., Vygotskian) to support the development of early literacy, including metacognitive and metalinguistic skills as well as other foundational literacy skills. These authors designed an intensive, teacher-focused training module using child assessment and technology transfers. During the first stage of project development, they worked with an expert in the mathematical modeling of psychological processes and design of artificial intelligence systems, aiming at developing a diagnostic–prescriptive computerized assessment system. This system acts like an expert teacher capable of giving advice on how to meet the specific instructional needs of an individual student (Bodrova & Leong, 2001). Tutor supervision—which has been proven to be more sustainable—can substitute for this approach. Results of an empirical evaluation involving different American urban school districts disclosed that those strategies had a positive effect on literacy achievement in young children, including those living in socioeconomically disadvantaged homes. Recently, Diamond et al. (2007), in the context of an interdisciplinary effort involving education and cognitive neuroscience, reported that this curriculum improved cognitive control performance in preschoolers attending regular classrooms with their regular teachers. Specifically, they showed that 4- to 5-year-old children from Tools of the Mind classrooms obtained higher scores than controls in tasks tapping inhibitory control and working memory demands.

Finally, results of studies carried out in industrialized countries of East Asia are consistent with the pattern of results obtained by some American and European researchers. In Japan, Hong Kong, Taiwan, South Korea, and Singapore, birth rates have fallen significantly, so many children grow up in families with only one or two siblings. In this social context, preschool programs are seen by families as alternative socialization. For example, in Singapore, it has been seen that children between 3 years and 6 years old who attended some type of preschool program improved their language and socioemotional skills significantly (Boocock, 2003).

COGNITIVE NEUROSCIENCE CONTRIBUTIONS TO INTERVENTION

The potential contribution of cognitive neuroscience to promotion of child development and education is not only at its early stages but also remains a matter of great controversy among neuroscientists. Recently, however, there has been growing interest in potential contributions to education and learning (Ansari & Coch, 2006; Goswami, 2006; Posner & Rothbart, 2005; see also chap. 6, this volume), raised by results obtained from laboratory studies on behavioral training as well as the remediation of basic cognitive processes in either healthy children (Rueda, Rothbart, McCandliss, Saccomanno, & Posner, 2005; Thorell, Lundqvist, Bergman Nutley, Bohlin, & Klingberg, 2009), children with attention-deficit/hyperactivity disorder (ADHD; Klingberg et al., 2006; Klingberg, Forssberg, & Westerberg, 2006), children with dyslexia (McCandliss, Beck, Sandak, & Perfetti, 2003; Shaywitz et al., 2004.; Temple et al., 2003), and children with dyscalculia (Wilson, Dehaene, et al., 2006).

On the basis of previous studies showing that attentional networks follow a specific developmental course and genetic associations, Rueda et al. (2005) designed and applied an executive attention training program for healthy children. They assessed executive attention and intelligence before and after the intervention among 49 children ages 4 and 6 years. They also assessed a dopamine-related gene (DAT1) associated with attentional network test performance and other conflict resolution tests (Diamond, Briand, Fossella, & Gehlbach, 2004; Fossella et al., 2002), recorded scalp electrical activity generated by neuronal function (event-related brain potential), and administered a child temperament questionnaire to parents (Child Behavior Questionnaire; Rothbart, Ahadi, & Hershey, 1994).

Rueda et al.'s (2005) training program covered 5 training days divided into 9 or 10 exercises that included anticipation, stimulus discrimination, conflict resolution, and inhibitory control demands, depending on the experiment. Exercises were aimed at achieving a specific type of training that the researchers thought would be related to executive attention and were divided into seven or eight levels based on task difficulty, with children progressing through by making a number of correct responses in a row. The first three exercises taught children to track a cartoon cat on a computer screen by using a joystick. Then children were asked to move the cat to a grassy area and avoid muddy ones. Grassy areas grew progressively smaller, while the muddy areas expanded, thus increasing control demands. In a chase exercise, children had to catch a moving umbrella to keep the cat dry. In a maze exercise, they moved the cat through a maze to obtain food. The anticipation exercises taught children how to anticipate the movements of a duck plunging at random into a pond by moving the cat to where children thought the duck would be. Difficulty was modulated with changes on the visibility of the duck route. In the stimulus discrimination exercises, children were required to remember a multiattribute item—cartoon portraits—to pick out an array. Difficulty was modulated by introducing delays requiring children to memorize the attributes. For the conflict resolution exercises, children had to match Arabic digits with quantities. In a Stroop-like exercise, they had to move their joystick to pick out the larger of two arrays. Difficulty was modulated by introducing numbers instead of cartoons. Finally, 6-year-old children performed an inhibitory control exercise where they were told to help a farmer bring sheep inside a pen. Children were to click as fast as possible when there was a sheep but to withhold the response if there was a wolf.

Results showed that both 4- and 6-year-olds showed more mature performance in terms of less difficulty in solving conflict after they had been trained than the control groups did in an attentional network test. The overall training effect was about half as large as the effect obtained after the 2 development years from 4 to 6 years old (Figure 5.3a). Results also evidenced a generalization of training in certain aspects of intelligence because a child IQ test showed a small overall gain in intelligence, strongest in the matrices subscale (Figure 5.3b). Event related potential (ERP) data suggest that the impact of training was similar to that of development, thus confirming the direction of behavioral data in showing more adultlike performance after training. Specifically, trained 4-year-old children showed a prefrontal effect in which more negative amplitudes were observed for incongruent than for congruent trials. Whereas nontrained 6-year-old children showed the same effect as trained 4-year-olds, trained 6-year-olds showed the more dorsal frontal effect found in adult data. Finally, regarding examination of differences in temperament and genotype, Rueda et al. (2005) found that the long form allele of the DAT1 dopamine gene was associated with stronger, more effortful

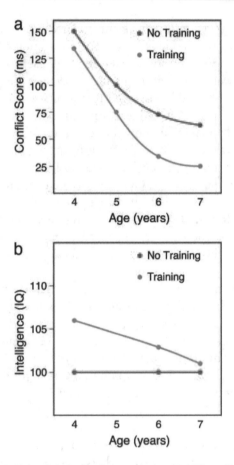

Figure 5.3. Differential training effects across age. (a) The effect of training versus no training (baseline) on executive attention performance. (b) The effect of training versus no training on intelligence performance. Data points at ages 4 and 6 and the data point at age 7 for the average conflict score of the untrained group are based on data from Rueda et al. (2005). All other data points are hypothesized because no data are available for these ages. ms = milliseconds. From "Educating Executive Attention," by K. Holmboe and M. Johnson, 2005, *Proceedings of the National Academy of Sciences USA, 102*, p. 14820. Copyright 2005 by the National Academy of Sciences, USA. Reproduced with permission.

control but less extraversion, suggesting that less outgoing, more controlled children may require less attention training.

In summary, Rueda et al.'s (2005) study shows that both genotype and training influence performance on attentional and intelligence specific tasks in 4- and 6-year-old healthy, middle-SES children. Although more research is required to comprehend the complex interactions involved, this study presents a promising perspective in terms of cognitive neuroscience contributions to practical proposals (Holmboe & Johnson, 2005). Recently, Rueda, Chueca, and Santoja (2008) replicated these findings—namely, the beneficial effect of attention training on brain activation while subjects deal with the conflict task and scores obtained on the abstract reasoning subscale of the K-BIT. Furthermore, they observed that trained children increased their postintervention performance in the Child Gambling Task, a task involving affective regulation, whereas children in the control group did not.

Klingberg et al. (2002, 2006) designed a working memory training paradigm, assessing the effects in a sample of 7- to 15-year-old children with ADHD. These children represent a group of subjects with working memory deficit due to an impairment of frontal lobe functioning (Shaw et al., 2007). Because working memory skills help to retain and manipulate information during short periods, they underlie everyday behaviors as well as school-related complex reasoning, which is a characteristic of populations suffering from this specific deficit.

Pre- and posttraining evaluation in the Klingberg et al. (2002, 2006) studies included either computerized or manual versions of a trained visuospatial working memory task, the Corsi block tapping task, the Stroop task, the Raven Coloured Progressive Matrices test (Raven, 1995), and a choice reaction time task. The computerized training program included four subtests to be presented during each training session. First, children were administered the same visuospatial working memory task used for testing. The task presented circles one at a time in a 4 × 4 grid. Immediately afterward, children had to indicate the circles' positions in the same order as they had appeared. Second, children were presented a keyboard with numbers and digits while a voice in the computer read those numbers and digits aloud. Children were asked to mark the digits in a backward way. Third, letters were read aloud one at a time, and children were asked to remember their name and order. A row of lamps was then visible, and a flashing lamp cued children as to which letter should be reported back. Fourth, two grey circles were presented on the screen, and children were told to press a spatially congruent key when one of the circles became green and to avoid responding when one of the circles became red. Although the latter was not a working memory task, the authors included it on the basis of evidence that children with ADHD are impaired in reaction-time and go–no go demands. For all tasks, difficulty was modulated by changing the number of stimuli to be remembered. Children completed 30 trials on each task, 25 minutes per day, for 25 days. It is interesting that a placebo/low-dose version was administered involving 10 trials per task, with two stimuli to remember in the visuospatial and digit span task and three stimuli in the letter-span task. This set of exercises was intended to control (a) the effect of taking the assessment test repeatedly, (b) the spontaneous improvement in the training period of 5 to 6 weeks, and (c) the effects of what was expected from subjects.

Results showed that intensive and adaptive computerized working memory training gradually increased the amount of information that subjects could maintain on line. In addition, some improvement was observed after 5 to 6 weeks of training. Increased performance was seen in both trained and nontrained visuospatial working memory tasks, suggesting a generalization of the effect on other skills. A main, ADHD-specific finding was that training significantly reduced the number of head movements, which was also correlated with performance improvements.

In a recent study, Thorell et al. (2009) administered two computerized training programs of visuospatial working memory and inhibitory control to a sample of healthy 5-year-old children. Both training programs included an algorithm for continuously adapting the difficulty level on the basis of performance and had an identical interface regarding rewards and feedback. Each program included five different tasks (only three were administered). Each task took 5 minutes to complete, which means that the children were trained for 15 minutes each day during 5 weeks. The working memory program was based on previous versions (Klingberg et al., 2002, 2006).

Results showed that working memory training was effective at improving both the spatial and verbal domains as well as having significicatn transfer effects on laboratory measures of attention but not on inhibitory control tasks and problem solving. Although inihibitory training improved performance significantly on several trained tasks, it did not generalize to nontrained tasks of eitehr inhibition or other executive functions. The findings suggest that this type of working memory training could be effective in early interventions for children with working memory difficulties and that more research is necessary to evaluated which cognitive functions can be trained and to what extent the effects of training can be generalized to other functions.

McCandliss et al. (2003) examined the reading skills of 38 children ages 7 years to 10 years with deficient decoding skills assessed through the Woodcock Reading Mastery Test—Revised (Woodcock, 1998), before and after an intervention called Word Building in the context of a controlled randomized design. First, they classified children on the basis of their reading-related skills, word recognition, passage comprehension, and phonological awareness skills. Half the children were randomly assigned to engage in a laboratory-based tutorial program, the focus of which was the participants' decoding skills, whereas the other half joined a waiting-list group to receive the same intervention the following semester.

The intervention program included 77 lessons. Each lesson presented a set of 5 to 16 letter cards, instructions on how to form a chain of words that differed by a single letter transformation, a set of flashcards containing each word formed during the lesson, and a set of sentences consisting mostly of words formed there. Lessons were grouped into 23 units, each of them containing three to five lessons preceded and followed by a short test. The lessons progressively advanced in grapheme–phoneme units and word forms, incorporating more difficulty. The first 10 units focused on short vowels; the next 5 introduced long vowel sounds controlled by silent *e*; the next 4 included changes in vowel diagraphs; and the final 4 involved changes in vowel sound in varying environments. During each lesson, children were given a set of letter cards and asked to build words after receiving tutor instructions. Once children had formed and successfully read a word, they had to insert, delete, or change a specific letter card, which transformed the previous word into the next one during the lesson. Letter changes had been designed to require the child's attention when positioning changes within a word and to ensure that the same letters appeared at different positions. Children in the intervention group were administered 20 sessions three times a week, each one 50 minutes long, and completed 4 additional sessions for testing purposes.

Findings indicated that participation in the program resulted in gains in decoding, phonemic awareness, and passage comprehension skills. The largest gains appeared in measures directly assessing decoding skills, and within that context, the greatest gains occurred for grapheme units within middle and final positions of word forms. The second and third largest gains appeared in an elision task and passage comprehension, respectively. Further research shall be required to better understand the underlying process regarding the program's successful impact. However, McCandliss et al. (2003) addressed the importance of (a) using the same protocol in future studies to achieve more than gross comparisons of school curricula and (b) identifying specific activities likely to lead to improvements in targeted reading skills.

Shaywitz et al. (2004) designed and applied a phonologically mediated reading intervention combining behavioral and imaging approaches, aimed at improving reading fluency as well as the development of the fast-paced occipitotemporal systems related to skilled reading in a sample of 77 children ages 6 to 9 years with and without reading disabilities. The children were assigned to three experimental groups: experimental intervention from schools; community intervention; and community control. Criteria for reading disability had been set up with a Woodcock and Johnson battery. The community intervention group met the criteria for reading disability and received a variety of interventions provided by the school involved rather than the intervention protocol. Children in the intervention group were provided with 50 minutes of daily, individual, explicit, and systematic tutoring, focused on helping them understand the alphabetic principle—that is, how letters and their combination represent segments of speech or phonemes. Each lesson covered the following five steps: (a) a review of sound–symbol associations, (b) practice in phoneme analysis and blending by manipulating letter cards or scrabble tiles to make new words, (c) timed reading of previously learned words to develop fluency, (d) oral reading of stories, and (e) dictation of words with phonetically regular spelling–sound patterns. In addition, during the last step, children were stimulated to say words slowly before spelling, aiming at emphasizing phonologic and orthographic connections. As children became more proficient, they progressed from reading single-syllable words to reading multisyllabic ones made from those learned previously. Moreover, as reading proficiency increased, a wider variety of narrative and expository texts were introduced instead of devoting time to control reading phonetically, so that fluency, comprehension, and enjoyment were promoted. Children received an 8-month intervention–an average of 105 hours—between pre- and posttests. During this period, although children continued receiving regular classroom reading instruction, they were administered neither remedial reading protocol nor assistance. Children in all groups were imaged before and after intervention so researchers could examine brain activation patterns while the children engaged in a cross-modal letter identification task.

Results showed that children who had participated in the intervention protocol made more significant gains in reading and fluency skills than children in control groups. Moreover, increased activation in left inferior frontal gyrus and middle temporal gyrus proved to be associated with behavioral gains. These findings suggest that the intervention was critical to successful outcomes in children with reading disabilities and that the use of an evidence-based phonologic reading intervention facilitates the development of the involved neural networks underlying skilled reading. Thus, these findings not only suggest neural system plasticity for reading in children but also, and more specifically, that an intervention promoting proficiency in reading had been a key factor in the functional organization of the underlying neural networks involved.

Temple et al. (2003) studied whether behavioral remediation has positive effects on the dysfunctional neural mechanisms underlying developmental dyslexia. They applied the Fast ForWord, a computerized intervention program from Scientific Learning Corporation, to 20 children ages 8 to 12 years old with dyslexia and to 12 controls. The intervention program involves seven adaptive exercises designed to improve auditory and language processing by using nonlinguistic as well as acoustically modified linguistic speech. The program is aimed at (a) discriminating between sequences of two brief, successive, acoustic sweeps; (b) sorting sound changes from individual phonemes; (c) identifying specific phonemes from a series of consonant–vowel and vowel–consonant–vowel stimulus pairs; (d) matching consonants and vowels within simple word structures; (e) distinguishing between words that differ only in an initial or a final consonant by identifying which of two pictures represents a target word; (f) following instructions of increasing length and/or grammatical complexity; and (g) distinguishing 40 classes of grammatical structures and rules. Children were trained in the exercises during 100 minutes a day, 5 days a week, for 28 days. Before and after training, functional magnetic resonance imaging scans taken during identical tasks for both groups were obtained. Children were administered three tasks in a block design for phonological and nonphonological processing and a nonletter baseline task.

Results showed that children with dyslexia improved so much in reading ability (real word reading, pseudoword decoding, and passage comprehension) that they were raised to the normal range. These children also improved in oral language ability and rapid naming. However, Temple et al. (2003) observed individual variability in the extent of improvement. More research is needed to predict which children are likely to be helped by the intervention. Functional magnetic resonance imaging results showed that in children with dyslexia, activity increased in the left hemisphere temporoparietal cortex and inferior frontal gyrus: Both showed activity in children with normal reading ability performing the task for rhyming versus matching. In these children, increases were also seen in other nonactive brain areas from frontal, temporal, parietal, and occipital lobes as well as in the anterior thalamus. Thus, neural effects of remediation occurred both in brain areas that are normally involved in phonological processing but are dysfunctional in dyslexia and in other regions that are not normally activated during phonological processing.

Stevens, Fanning, Coch, Sanders, and Neville (2008) examined whether 6 weeks of high-intensity training with the Fast ForWord program (100 minutes a day) would also influence neural mechanisms of selective auditory attention previously shown to be deficient in school-age children with specific language impairment (Stevens, Sanders, & Neville, 2006). They administered the training program to 20 children ages 6 to 8 years old with and without this impairment. Additionally, 13 children whose language was developing typically received no specialized training but were tested and retested after a comparable time span for a maturation and test–retest effects control (control group was not subject to intervention). Before and after training, all children completed standardized language assessments, and an ERP measure of selective auditory attention was taken. In comparison with the control group, children receiving training showed increases in standardized measures of receptive language and larger increases in the effects of attention on neural processing after training. The enhanced effect of attention on neural processing represented a large effect size specific to changes in signal enhancement of attended stimuli. Findings suggest that the neural mechanisms of selective auditory attention are likely to be modified, improved, and generalized to language via a specific training.

More recently, Stevens, Currin, et al. (2008) examined whether 4- to 5-year-old children at risk for reading difficulty evidence similar deficits in the early neural mechanisms of selective attention and, if so, whether such deficits could be ameliorated by means of training with a variant of a previously validated, interpersonally delivered reading intervention (Early Reading Intervention). Results suggest that children at risk for reading show reduced effects of selective attention on early stimuli processing if compared to their peers. After an 8-week training with Early Reading Intervention, results suggested that at-risk children (a) either approached or achieved the levels for basic early literacy skills, which are predictive of later reading skills and (b) showed larger attention effects on stimuli processing, a fact suggest-

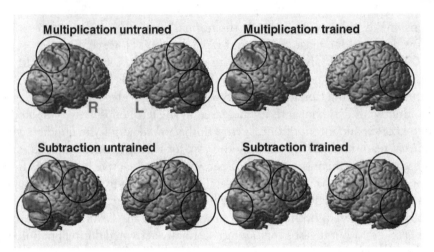

Figure 5.4. Contrasts of the four calculation conditions (multiplication untrained, multiplication trained, subtraction untrained, and subtraction trained) against baseline (number matching). The contrast trained minus untrained subtraction did not yield any significant activation. L = left; R = right. From "How Specifically Do We Learn? Imaging the Learning of Multiplication and Subtraction," by A. Ischebeck, L. Zamarian, C. Siedentopf, F. Koppelstätter, T. Benke, S. Felber, and M. Delazer, 2006, *NeuroImage, 30,* p. 1372. Copyright 2006 by Elsevier. Adapted with permission.

ing that effective reading and language intervention may work partially by training selective attention.

Wilson and colleagues (Wilson, Dehaene, et al., 2006; Wilson, Revkin, Cohen, Cohen, & Dehaene, 2006) designed an adaptive computerized game for remediation of dyscalculia, inspired by cognitive neuroscience research, specifically on the current understanding of brain representation of number, and the hypothesis that dyscalculia is caused by a core deficit in number sense or in the association between number sense and symbolic number representations (Feigenson, Dehaene, & Spelke, 2004). Studies aimed at analyzing modifications of brain activation patterns related to the training of multiplication and subtraction among healthy young adults have shown contrasts between trained and untrained individuals (Ischebeck et al., 2006; Figure 5.4). Wilson and colleagues carried out both mathematical simulations (Wilson, Dehaene, et al., 2006) and a trial with nine 7- to 9-year-old children with arithmetic difficulties (Wilson, Revkin, et al., 2006). Software (The Number Race) has been designed to train children with an entertaining comparison task that presents numerical problems adapted to individual performance. The major contribution of this software is the algorithm specifications used, which are based on an internal model of the child's knowledge in a multidimensional learning space. The latter consists of three difficulty dimensions, numerical distance, response deadline, and conceptual complexity, which represent a continuum from nonsymbolic number processing to increasingly complex symbolic operations. Child performance in core numerical tasks—counting, transcoding, base-10 comprehension, enumeration, addition, subtraction, and symbolic and nonsymbolic numerical comparison—was assessed pre- and posttraining. The training protocol involved sessions on numerical comparison for half an hour a day, 4 days a week, over a 5-week period.

Results from arithmetical simulations suggest that the software adapts well to varying levels of initial knowledge and learning speeds. Children showed specific increases in performance on core number sense tasks. In addition, speed of subitizing and numerical comparison increased, as did subtraction accuracy (23%). Performance on addition and base-10 comprehension tasks did not improve over the study period. Results suggest that the software application has been successful in increasing number sense over the short study period. However, as expected, Wilson, Revkin et al. (2006) pointed out that further research with larger and controlled groups is needed to examine both transfer to higher level tasks and developmental time windows for intervention. Because the software is open source and freely available online, other researchers are applying it in other studies, including one researcher who works with low-income preschool children (see http://www.unicog.org).

The studies described here analyzed basic processes in either normal populations or populations with specific neurological disorders. The application of cognitive neuroscience frameworks to intervention programs aimed at improving low-income or SES populations' cognitive development is even more preliminary.

On the basis of the studies described in chapter 4 of this volume (Colombo & Lipina, 2005; Lipina et al., 2004; Lipina, Martell, Vuelta, & Colombo, 2005), we and our colleagues designed a multimodular intervention program that included cognitive exercises, nutritional supplements, teacher training, and health and social counseling for parents. This program has been applied to a sample that includes approximately 250 healthy 3- to 5-year-old children from unsatisfied basic needs homes enrolled in three public schools located in the city of Buenos Aires, Argentina. This program was designed as a controlled, randomized trial, before and after cognitive intervention. Children were administered a battery of tasks requiring use of executive processes, namely Tower of London (Shallice, 1982), Corsi Blocks, Three and Four Colors (Balamore & Wozniak, 1984), and a set of tasks from the Delayed Response Paradigm (A-not-B, Color Reversal, Spatial Reversal; Espy, Kaufmann, & Glisky, 1999). Moreover, in the posttest of the 1st year of the program, Flexible Item Selection Task (Jacques & Zelazo, 2001) and the Attention subtest of the NEPSY battery (Korkman, Kettunen, & Autti-Ramo, 2003) were added. Both groups were in contact with all the program modules except for the cognitive module, which was reserved for the intervention group. Instead, children in the control group were exposed to activities lack-

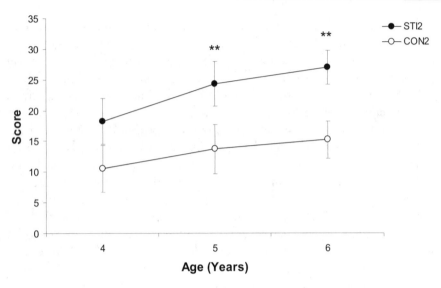

Figure 5.5. Posttraining scores in the Flexible Item Selection Task of trained (STI2: two runs of exercises) and control (CON2) groups. ****p* < .01.

ing executive demands but with the same intensity and time span as the executive-demand activities. Based on Klingberg et al.'s (2002) framework, the cognitive training module includes the individual administration of exercises with executive demands, the difficulty of which are progressively increased depending on the child's performance. Exercises were similar to those used in pretraining testing but with a difficulty modulation. Activities were carried out at schools in well-equipped rooms. Each session took approximately 30 to 40 minutes. In each session, motivation and instruction comprehension were assessed before cognitive exercises were administered. In other words, cognitive training was administered only to children whose motivation and instruction comprehension was adequate.

Three training schedules were used: 16, 25, or 32 weekly sessions during 16 weeks for 1 or 2 school years. Results suggested that participation in the 32-session schedule, in combination with iron and folic acid supplementation, was most effective at improving cognitive performance in healthy children from unsatisfied basic needs homes in the Tower of London, Three and Four Colors, and Corsi Blocks tasks (exercising effect). The same pattern was observed in Attention and FIST performances (Figure 5.5), suggesting a generalization effect. These results strongly suggest the presence of efficient levels of plasticity, which help to modify the performance of children from low socioeconomic backgrounds.

Recently, Neville et al. (2008) tested the hypothesis that after 40 minutes per school day over 8 weeks of either music or attention training in a small group, Head Start preschoolers would display gains in a number of cognitive domains, including language, preliteracy and visual–spatial skills, numeracy, and nonverbal IQ, and that these gains would be larger than those observed among control subjects in either large or small groups. In these interventions, children were randomly assigned to one of the four groups, besides being matched on different variables associated with cognitive performance. Children in the music training group received 8 weeks of small group classes (5 students and 2 teachers), focused on musical activities including listening, moving, singing, and playing music. Classes ran for 40 minutes each day, 4 days a week, during the regular Head Start school day. Control groups included two classes receiving regular Head Start instruction but with different student:teacher ratios (i.e., 5:2 and 18:2) and a small class (i.e., 5:2) receiving attention training. Results showed that children in the music training group displayed significant improvements on (a) receptive and expressive language scores, (b) the object assembly subtest of the Wechsler Intelligence Test, (c) overall Stanford–Binet nonverbal IQ test (including fluid and quantitative reasoning and the critical thinking subtests), and (d) the Developmental Numeracy Assessment. Results from the attention-trained group showed comparable gains in similar domains. However, large and small control groups have also displayed similar improvements in receptive and expressive language as well as in phonological awareness scores. Furthermore, the small control group has also evidenced an improvement in the object assembly test and in overall nonverbal IQ. As a whole, these results suggest that gains in language may have been due to either Head Start itself or to test–retest effects. Specific effects observed in both the music and attention training groups suggest that being individually tutored or taught in a small group is likely to improve the effects of training.

CONCLUSION

The studies described in this chapter are among the first demonstrating the possibility of changing basic cognitive processes associated with preferential neural networks involved in learning acquisition—a crucial fact as far as literacy and numeracy are concerned, given that it is at the first stages of development that children learn basic cognitive operations. This neural circuit preference also contributes to the design of activities to be adjusted in terms of different cognitive demands at individual levels. Specifically, with regard to interventions aimed at socioeconomically disadvantaged children, studies that have been carried out in the field of cognitive neuroscience confirm that cognitive performance in these children is likely to be optimized. At the same time, the studies have contributed new methodologies that potentially can be integrated into education as well as social development–related curricula.

However, authors in the field have pointed out that beyond these promising findings, more experiments must be carried on so that design and methodological issues are improved to determine associations that are likely to contribute to the understanding of causal, underlying mechanisms and applied features. In this sense, further studies are required in order to examine the potential generalization of intervention beyond a specific domain of instruction should any training in a general domain competence, such as visual attention, be transferred to a specific domain, such as numerical cognition, reading, or emotional development (Posner & Rothbart, 2005). These efforts may also reduce the gaps that are hindering the current possibilities for building bridges between cognitive neuroscience and other disciplines, including intervention and policy designs (see chap. 6, this volume).

6

CONTRIBUTIONS TO PUBLIC POLICY

> The urge for social justice can only develop properly and be effective
> when it grows out of man's sense of freedom and responsibility, and is
> based upon it.
>
> —Rudolf Rocker

As we have discussed in the preceding chapters, studies carried out in a number of societies over the past 80 years repeatedly illustrate how poverty affects children's physical and mental health during their earliest years, thus conditioning their cognitive and socioemotional development and, consequently, their opportunities for educational and social inclusion. The main risk factors involved that have been identified are child physical and nutritional health, whether the child experiences prenatal and postnatal exposure to environmental toxic agents, home environment and whether there is adult provision of stimulating learning experiences, parents' and caregivers' mental health, quality of human and material resources in neighborhoods, quality of school education, and quality of relationships with peers and adults (Adler & Newman, 2002; Brooks-Gunn & Duncan, 1997; Corcoran & Chaudry, 1997; Evans, 2004; Grigorenko, 2003; Guo & Harris, 2000; Johnson & Knitzer, 2006; McLoyd, 1998).

The realm of cognitive neuroscience could add new and important insights into the improvement of policies dealing with brain development and poverty in terms of specific approaches to the analysis of impacts and potential contributions to intervention efforts. This chapter provides a series of suggestions with the aim of contributing to both the analysis and the design of policies aimed at children from economically disadvantaged families. Of course, many of these suggestions are likely to coincide with advice from other disciplines linked to child development (e.g. early childhood intervention).

Development-related areas such as health, education, and social competence are necessarily involved in any discussion of analysis and intervention in childhood poverty. However, recommendations from the field of cognitive neuroscience are of particular interest in such discussions because (a) its conceptual and methodological models provide a scientific basis for intervention and suggest ways in which different interventions might be combined and (b) interest in the brain provides a vehicle for communication with the general public via the mass media.

Thus, we comment here on policy-related features to illustrate several issues relevant to neuroscience research, particularly in the evidence raised from cognitive neuroscience, as described in previous chapters. However, such recommendations must take into consideration the cultural idiosyncrasies of each society and its own particular problems and resource limitations.

COMPREHENSIVE FRAMEWORKS FOR ANALYZING THE COMPLEXITY OF CHILD DEVELOPMENT

Given the multidimensional nature of the complex phenomena of poverty and child development, any intervention-related program or policy intended to either optimize or improve child life conditions and opportunities also requires action-linked designs at a number of levels, including children; parents; teachers; and nongovernmental, governmental, and international organizations. Such interventions require not only an appropriate integration of several conceptual and methodological frameworks (S. Ramey & Ramey, 2003) but also the consideration of the complexity of the various levels of analysis.

During the past few years, the disciplines of developmental psychology and developmental cognitive neuroscience have contributed to such frameworks. The modern field of child development can be considered an attempt to analyze a set of fundamental questions about children involving analysis levels such as nature–nurture relationships, how children contribute to their own development, which developmental phenomena are continuous or discontinuous and which are development-producing mechanisms, how social and cultural contexts influence development, why some children differ from others, and how both society and policymakers use research to improve child welfare (Siegler, DeLoache, & Eisenberg, 2003). In turn, current theoretical frameworks from developmental cognitive neuroscience contribute concepts on the construction of complex neural representation levels in the developing brain. Thus, neural development takes place in the context of multiple constraints, interacting on various levels of organization or analysis from the individual cell to external environment, such as probabilistic epigenesis; experience-dependent elaboration of small-scale neural structures; interactions between brain regions in functional brain development; the role of proactive acquisition of knowledge; and the interaction between mind and body, which is itself embedded in a physical and social environment (Mareschal et al., 2007; Sirois et al., 2008; Westermann et al., 2007).

In this theoretical context, cognitive development can be understood as a trajectory originating from constraints on the underlying neural structures, contributing an integrated view of normal and abnormal development (Westermann et al., 2007). Even the maturational and skill-learning perspectives on brain and behavioral development (M. H. Johnson, 2006) assume a view of interacting developmental systems. Furthermore, these neurocognitive frameworks are also likely to be articulated within approaches aimed at scrutinizing development in a broader context, conceptualizing the environment children develop into as a set of nested layers, including the broader society and even the historical time (Bronfenbrenner & Ceci, 1994).

The conceptualizations and neurocognitive methodologies described in chapters 4 and 5 of this volume are still at a preliminary phase with regard to their potential applications to public policies and require more basic as well as applied research. However, the amount and quality of current knowledge in this field could initiate the design and application of multimodel interventions aimed at improving development opportunities for socioeconomically disadvantaged children. If an environmental perspective is sustained, not only children but also parents; teachers; and developmental contexts such as home, school, and neighborhood should be involved. Taking an integrated approach into account, this contribution could function as a complement to interventions dealing with either children, parents, or teachers by including specific training (a) on basic and critical cognitive activities intended to improve school learning and (b) for adult caregivers and members from social organizations so that brain development–related needs are better understood. In the latter case, contributions could include child care training from conception to school years covering the multiple biological and psychological needs that are specific to each stage of cognitive and emotional development—that is, pollution control, nutritional supplements, and access to prenatal medical controls.

As an example of a preliminary integrative contribution at a policy level, a recent advocacy project developed by the Organisation for Economic Co-operation and Development (OECD) was aimed at establishing a link between brain researchers and learning scholars to (a) promote new approaches on brain and education, (b) explore research data sources, (c) synthesize either already existing or new findings from cognitive and brain science, (d) work out popular misunderstandings regarding the brain and its relationships with learning and teaching, and (e) make the results of the project widely accessible to nonspecialists (OECD, 2007). The OECD has also created a Web site (http://www.oecd.org) where the general public can find and download literature and software as well as participate in online forums dealing with related topics.

Abadzi (2006) recently reviewed the cognitive research on basic skills and their poverty-caused modulations as well as several resources available for effective learning focused on teachers' and educational systems' performances, specifically in developing countries. It is of note that this book was published by the World Bank and also offers some policy guidelines based on cognitive neuroscience frameworks for socioeconomically disadvantaged educational settings in developing countries. For example, students are offered enough time to learn the small units that are required before higher functions—for example, analysis and comprehension—are achieved. In addition, materials are included that deal with basic cognitive operations (e.g., attention and memory) needed for the training curricula of both teachers and school administrators.

OTHER ASSESSMENT TRENDS IN CHILD POVERTY MEASUREMENT

As mentioned in chapter 1 of this volume, poverty measurement methods do not all assess the same dimensions or consider in a similar way variables and mechanisms involved in cognitive functioning and other developmental processes (Hill & Michael, 2001; Minujin, Delamonica, Davidziuk, & González, 2006). However, studies that analyze the effects of poverty and mediators usually apply either income-based or stratification methods (Bradley & Corwyn, 2002; Brooks-Gunn & Duncan, 1997; Corcoran & Chaudry, 1997; Guo & Harris, 2000; McLoyd, 1998). A similar trend is observed in recruitment criteria applied in some intervention programs (Roosa, Deng, Nair, & Lockhart Burrell, 2005), which sometimes contribute with obstacles rather than solutions, such as in the case of participant selection based on poverty definitions that are likely to exclude some portions of the low-income, but not necessarily poor, population. At the same time, new trends in child poverty measurements that address the need for identification of direct predictors and dimensions so that more appropriate actions can be taken against child poverty are being developed and assessed in a number of countries, especially in developing countries (Gordon, Nandy, Pantazis, Pemberton, & Townsend, 2003; Roosa et al., 2005). For example, stress-related measures of economic pressure in combination with timing, frequency, and duration could be linked to an extensive theoretical as well as empirical literature on poverty-related stress and coping. At the same time, measurements dealing with collective poverty, neighborhood disadvantage, and school poverty could provide a framework for developmental ecological approaches applied to an understanding of poverty-related experiences, although significant issues in conceptual definition remain to be solved.

Thus, there is a need for child poverty measurements to be reconsidered so that they can be applied to either studies dealing with poverty effects on child development or intervention programs likely to allow researchers and policymakers to design more efficient actions oriented toward children. Within this context, the following should be considered: (a) findings from experimental studies based on animal models showing how early material and sensory deprivation as well as exposure to environmental neurotoxic agents alter brain developmental aspects (see chap. 2, this volume) and (b) the short-, medium-, and long-term impacts on cognitive performance and social behavior caused by living in poverty conditions (see chaps. 3 and 4, this volume).

One possibility could be to incorporate those factors that directly or indirectly modulate the development of cognitive and social skills into the design of instruments that measure child poverty. In doing so, a series of items could be included involving variables linked to the nature of risk factors and the length of time that children were exposed. Among such factors, environmental toxins, parenting practices, and home-related characteristics (particularly the degree of stimulation in the home offered) could be included. Another potential application could involve examining how certain poverty-linked factors affect brain and cognitive development and how this relates to economic costs. This would allow a decision about whether investing in risk factor elimination is advisable rather than facing social costs in the long run (e.g., exposure to lead and methyl mercury; Trasande, Landrigan, & Schechter, 2005). Implementing adequate methodological designs aimed at developing new policy measures, fighting government corruption, struggling against the lack of adequate human resources for designing and administering surveys, and taking cultural diversity into account are among the main challenges for these types of interdisciplinary research efforts (CROP/Childwatch, 2007).

In this context, policies should guarantee that studies aimed at developing better child poverty measuring instruments, coupled with intervention-oriented goals, are offered more sound financial support. Meanwhile, the use of income-based, stratified methods requires that limitations be better understood on the basis of a combination of available indicators.

IDENTIFYING THE IMPACT OF POVERTY ON SPECIFIC COGNITIVE PROCESSES FOR INTERVENTION PURPOSES

Cognitive neuroscience studies, as described in chapter 4 of this volume, have been useful to identify effects of poverty on specific, basic cognitive processes, strongly associated with (a) early development of crucial literacy and numeracy skills and (b) individual differences in temperament (Posner & Rothbart, 2007b). A potential contribution in this context could be an application of cognitive performance assessment instruments to find the precise impact of poverty in terms of basic cognitive processes. Because of costs and logistics, applying laboratory image technology to group studies and community locations is likely to be difficult (Varma, McCandliss, & Schwartz, 2008), but it is a useful technology for identifying aspects of cognitive performance such as alertness, orientation, and control attentional processes (Posner & Rothbart, 2007a) and for integrating intervention. In turn, those behavioral instruments (e.g., the attention network task) could be used as cognitive markers in population-related surveys, which would require some standardization as well as contribute to the settlement of periodic performance lines in longitudinal interventions. Finally, the inclusion of performance-related variables based on basic processing paradigms could also help studies dealing with cognitive improvement prediction profiles within intervention programs (Burchinal, Roberts, Hooper, & Zeisel, 2000; Segretin, Lipina, Benarós, Hermida, & Colombo, 2008).

Beyond the ethical and ideological debate involved in the behavioral genetics area, findings over the past 5 years support the need for a follow-up process aimed at analyzing both interactions and methodological approaches (Mareschal et al., 2007). In a context of public policy discussion, as suggested by some studies on candidate genes associated with cognitive operations (Posner, 2008; Posner & Rothbart, 2007a; Sheese, Voelker, Rothbart, & Posner, 2007), genotyping could also serve as a tool in identifying specific intervention needs in child subsamples. As research continues to make steady progress in this field, there is a growing possibility of identifying subpopulations of children endowed with varying cognitive and social characteristics. Data like these could be of utmost importance in designing interventions and activities based on those characteristics.

CONTRIBUTIONS OF COGNITIVE NEUROSCIENCE TO INTERVENTION EFFORTS

International organizations have stated that answers to child poverty depend on political and economic decisions emanating from both the international community and local governments. Those organizations have stressed the importance of supporting the design of policies that take into account economic, health, educational, social development, and security frameworks. The objectives of such policies should be oriented toward increasing family income, allowing people to have access to basic social services, increasing the protection of child rights, and designing locally conceived interventions instead of using generic programs and formulas (CROP/Childwatch, 2007; K. Johnson & Knitzer, 2006; Maggi et al., 2005; United Nations Children's Fund, 2005). Thus, policies may focus primarily on monetary and cultural underlying processes that link social determinations to child outcomes in order to minimize the effects of low income. This means that child poverty elimination is necessary to equalize children's educational opportunities, a fact requiring substantial investments to obtain positive returns over many years (Esping-Andersen, 2005). This brings up another issue that ought to be stated, though it is beyond the scope of this book. To put it bluntly, poverty is not a matter that pertains only to children but to entire families and communities. Hence, no public policy can substitute for the elimination of poverty conditions—uneven distribution of income, lack of well-paid labor, limited access to culture, and so on. However, even if these conditions were corrected, optimization of child-bearing, socioemotional, and cognitive development conditions would still be needed.

Even though suggestions, answers, and actions abound worldwide, such as those described elsewhere in this volume (see chap. 5), certain immediate actions should be taken. The multimodal programming framework seems to be an appropriate answer to build actions aimed at giving opportunities to socioeconomically disadvantaged children and their families (e.g., Bronfenbrenner & Ceci, 1994). However, despite the evidence showing that high-quality programs improve poor children's cognitive and socioemotional outcomes (Belsky et al., 2007; Esping-Andersen, 2005), experiences cannot be compared easily because information on impact assessment and comparability between alternative programs includes only a few studies and data provided only by some governments (Boocock, 1995, 2003). In addition, a serious common problem with regard to many countries, especially developing countries, is the lack of coordination and integration in implementing activity programs coupled with financial discontinuity due to cyclic, political changes and lack of impact evaluation (K. Johnson & Knitzer, 2006). Currently, great variability is still to be found among programs in terms of specific objectives, design, methodology, contents, and impact assessment (Boocock, 2003; Brooks-Gunn & Duncan, 1997; Reynolds, Wang, & Walberg, 2003a).

To face some of these obstacles and challenges, several research groups have designed and applied projects aimed at promoting appropriate research activities and policy advocacy. For instance, the Young Lives project (Attawell, 2004), partially supported by the U.K. Department for International Development, is aimed at analyzing the nature of childhood poverty over time in some developing countries. The Young Lives project's main objectives are the promotion of research activities, which include data collection on a set of core child well-being outcomes and determinants, and changes in public policies. This project also develops activities such as media coverage and promotes links between researchers, governments, and civil societies to support an effective dissemination and use of findings.

Both basic and applied research in the field of cognitive neuroscience—especially research activities during the past decade—have reinforced recommendations that were put forward by early interventions some time ago. Initial recommendations concerned both prenatal and postnatal health nutrition and exposure to different toxic agents and drugs. More recently, studies on training programs for children with or without developmental disorders have also suggested the possibility of contributing to the design of cognitive interventions implementing learning methods and to the improvement of preschool and elementary school curricula. It should be noted that such proposals can be addressed within multimodular programs.

PRENATAL AND POSTNATAL HEALTH: NEUROTOXINS, SUBSTANCE ABUSE, MALNUTRITION, AND INFECTIOUS DISEASES

As described in chapters 2 and 3 of this volume, the experimental evidence of the past 2 decades shows that any exposure to neurotoxic agents, legal or illegal drugs, and lack of elemental nutrients required for normal brain development—especially during the embryonic and fetal developmental stages—are linked directly to brain structural and functional disorders, taking into account that in some cases, such disorders are likely to appear in later stages of child development (e.g., Espy, Kaufmann, & Glisky, 1999; Luciana, Lindeke, Georgieff, Mills, & Nelson, 1999). Such risks contribute to a significant increase of economic, social, and psychological costs because of an impressive range of physical and functional disorders (e.g., Trasande et al., 2005).

In developing societies, the interdisciplinary work among researchers, lawmakers, civil servants, and industrialists must be furthered to improve conditions for child development. The required actions need to integrate accurate, reliable demographic analyses, endowed with accessible and efficient medical and social services for mothers and children. Sound public policies also require the commitment of those involved with pollution control and industrial waste disposal systems because all of those facts bear on economic interests.

In spite of the accumulated knowledge regarding the health hazards of exposure to environmental toxins and legal or illegal drugs, lack of adequate nutrients and energy sources, and infections suffered at various stages of brain development, these are issues that have been only partially taken into account by administrators and public policymakers. Such omissions could be corrected through active participation in activities involving lawmaking; design of adult education plans; campaigns to disseminate mass information; and activities in which parents, health professionals, social workers, teachers, industrialists, and journalists could be included.

INTEGRATION OF NEUROCOGNITIVE FRAMEWORKS INTO MULTIMODULAR INTERVENTIONS

In general, intervention programs and trials based on a cognitive neuroscience framework described in chapter 5 of this volume have been designed without including modules that could affect either developmental dimensions or mediator mechanisms. One exception is a program we implemented (Colombo & Lipina, 2005) that integrated the cognitive intervention as a module with modules on health examination and monitoring, nutrition supplements, and teacher training and parent support. Thus, applications of brain-based intervention for children at social risk due to poverty could be integrated as a module within an even more comprehensive intervention approach.

Potential cognitive neuroscience contributions could be the provision of materials useful for school activities, software packages using algorithms so that they could be adapted to individual abilities, and the offer of an intensive training program within an appropriate developmental context (Temple et al., 2003; Wilson, Revkin, Cohen, Cohen, & Dehaene, 2006). One main issue that needs to be considered is the training of people involved in such activities—teachers, assistants, and parents—in terms of the motivational and other socioemotional specifications required (e.g., Murnane & Steele, 2007). Because social and geographical development contexts appear to mediate the impacts of socioeconomic disadvantages on children's basic cognitive processes (National Institute of Child Health and Human Development & Early Child Care Research Network, 2005), some effective community programs (Maggi et al., 2005) and high-quality intervention programs (S. Ramey & Ramey, 2003) have already addressed the importance of involving parents. Hence, cognitive neuroscience interventions should also design technologies that can be applied in either community or home settings (P. A. Fisher & Kim, 2007).

The use of computers concentrates children's interest and improves methodological application issues, thus reducing financial implementation costs. Some researchers' training programs are freely available on the Web— for example, the attentional training program from Rueda et al. (2005; http:// www.teach-the-brain.org), and The Number Race from Wilson and colleagues (Wilson, Dehaene, et al., 2006; Wilson, Revkin, et al., 2006; http:// www.unicog.org).

However, aside from the unquestionable contribution of such tools and methodologies, economic inequalities between geographic regions in both developed and developing countries would hinder access to this useful material. Poverty gaps in most developing countries include differences in knowledge of basic computer operations, not only in terms of having a computer but also access to the Internet. Therefore, computer-related aspects remain an issue to be solved by local governments. In this sense, a transitory solution could be the transfer of discarded business computers to schools located in poor or economically depressed areas, coupled with the use of appropriate free programming software (Eckersley et al., 2003) in order to adapt existing educational brain-based software. Projects such as One Laptop Per Child (see http://wiki.laptop.org/go/The_OLPC_Wiki) could also be a potential implementation setting. Consequently, such a project needs policy supports in both economic and local government areas. It would be wonderful indeed if the computer industry could be encouraged—by appealing to their social responsibility or encouraged by public policies—to offer their contribution so that the technological gap could be narrowed in developing countries.

However, just as the crucial socioemotional dimension involving tutor–child interactions must be taken care of when any complementary technology or combined interventions are used, researchers' assessments would also be needed. Educational software could also contribute to parental training to include parents in a comprehensive intervention such as those designed by P. A. Fisher and Kim (2007) for foster children. Automated control of activities at home and information collection would also be two issues for policymakers' consideration; such issues could contribute to both remote supervision and impact analysis.

This approach could also contribute to evaluation efforts by considering the inclusion of behavioral measures in the design of programs and policies in order to evaluate more specific cognitive processes (e.g. attention, working memory, inhibitory control). Financial support for the development and application of this type of tool could be a specific target for policymakers because of the fact that such tools could improve comparability conditions among geographical areas as well as longitudinal efforts. In addition, it would be useful to promote the formation of expert committees for supervising and collecting information from different geographical regions via the Internet, an activity that in turn requires the participation of interdisciplinary teams to solve legal and ethical issues. The experience of OECD expert teams should constitute a valuable source of information for future efforts aimed at each of these topics (e.g., Eckersley et al., 2003)

As already mentioned, one of the main challenges facing investment in design and implementation of intervention programs is fragmentation (K. Johnson & Knitzer, 2006; Reynolds et al., 2003a). Because of the fact that intervention effectiveness results from the comprehension and quality of services, the way investments should be made is crucial for establishing the best cost–benefit formula. Potential issues regarding investment in brain-based intervention involve computing technology and software development, staff training, implementation of new technologies (e.g., genotyping), and interdisciplinary efforts such as those involved in the new field of educational neuroscience (see next section, "Educational Neuroscience"). Obtaining financial support could represent a complementary objective because this technology could be applied in research settings. Future development of low-cost technology is likely to change the way researchers and policymakers use imaging technology to evaluate the impact of interventions.

Beyond the specific questions that cognitive neuroscience raises in terms of both basic and applied research in the field of intervention (e.g., which contents and procedures are effective for achieving generalized improvement in basic processes as well as in academic achievement, and how long it takes for an intervention to succeed in altering networks; Posner & Rothbart, 2005), more applied studies must be designed and implemented. This would allow an adjustment to be performed from laboratory to community settings on multiple conceptual and methodological issues. Because several study designs are correlational, and causal inferences can only be drawn with caution, confusing variables inherent to poverty conditions need to be controlled. Therefore, designs and analyses must be improved before the research community considers the modulation of the causal role of underlying mediation mechanisms and the effects of generalization to cognitive- and socioemotional-specific domains.

EDUCATIONAL NEUROSCIENCE

For more than a decade, researchers in the neuroscience field, educators, and policymakers have progressively been involved in debates about the potential role and application of neuroscience research to education (e.g., Battro, Fischer, & Lena, 2008; Education Commission of the States, 1996; Posner & Rothbart, 2007b). Despite extreme viewpoints that present neuroscience as either a reforming field of education or a field with no values to transfer, several neuroscientists have addressed the importance of focusing on adequate conceptual and methodological discussions aimed at establishing productive interactions between both fields (McCandliss, Beck, Sandak, & Perfetti, 2003; Szucs & Goswami, 2007). An important education-related aspect is the systematic shaping of neurocognitive networks and the dependence of the structure and function of brain on cognitive development (Dehaene & Cohen, 2007; Mareschal et al., 2007; Szucs & Goswami, 2007; Westermann et al., 2007). Consequently, education involves the shaping of individual brains through the experiences that children gather in classrooms. Recent cognitive neuroscience research described in chapter 5 of this volume (e.g., cognitive training interventions) would significantly contribute to these processes in several ways.

With regard to teaching and learning procedures to be included in brain-based interventions for disadvantaged children, one preliminary alternative effort would deal with either applying or adapting procedures used in recent studies on cognitive neuroscience concerning literacy, numeracy, and temperament (Ansari & Coch, 2006; Blair & Razza, 2007; Dehaene & Cohen, 2007; Desoete, Roeyers, & De Clerq, 2003; Goswami, 2006; Posner & Rothbart, 2005, 2007b). For example, computerized algorithms used in some studies (e.g., Rueda et al., 2005; Wilson et al., 2006a, 2006b) could be adjusted to school activities together with analyses of curricula such as Tools of the Mind (Bodrova & Leong, 1996, 2001; Diamond, Barnett, Thomas, & Munro, 2007), Montessori (Lillard & Else-Quest, 2006) or Successful Intelligence (Sternberg & Grigorenko, 2004). In the context of these types of efforts, two complementary policy issues are (a) promoting meetings for the exchange of ideas (epistemological, ethical, and methodological) among neuroscientists and educators and (b) reconsidering financial supports for both basic and applied research (McCandliss et al., 2003; Varma et al., 2008).

These types of interdisciplinary integrations would also require qualified teachers (Murnane & Steele, 2007). Authors have suggested that one crucial issue in the bridge-building process between cognitive neuroscience and education should be a teacher training process in neuroscience (Ansari & Coch, 2006; Goswami, 2006). It is interesting to take into consideration recent studies suggesting that policies focused solely on increasing teachers' education are not enough to either improve classroom quality or maximize children's academic gains (Early et al., 2007). Moreover, any classroom application of brain-based interventions requires more than mere knowledge of concepts because those activities feature a specific type of exercises and methodologies. Furthermore, training processes face specific interdisciplinary obstacles in terms of theoretical resistance based on dogmatic conceptual views of child development processes (e.g., knowledge construction vs. social world, or introspectionism vs. behaviorism).

ETHICS AND RESPONSIBILITY IN THE COMMUNICATION OF NEUROSCIENCE FINDINGS

Among the political implications for neuroscience in relation to child development in general, and possible improvement with regard to children living in poverty, an important aspect should be taken into account, namely the way scientific knowledge is disseminated and used by politicians, journalists, and researchers. Another serious problem still arises in spite of some researchers making their best effort to counteract it (e.g. Bruer, 2006; OECD, 2007; Thompson & Nelson, 2001). This problem deals with the maintenance of several myths, such as those holding that the first 3 years of life constitute the only period of rapid synapse formation, the critical period in brain development, during which learning is easiest and most efficient and during which environmental enrichment or deprivation has necessarily irreversible effects on the brain.

These mistaken beliefs have a serious impact on policies because they make it difficult for educators and policymakers to distinguish fact from fiction and cause them to promote interventions that are both ineffective and expensive. For example, on the basis of results both from animal experiments as described in chapter 2 of this volume (i.e., enriched vs. deprived rodents) and results from the study by Rauscher, Shaw, and Ky (1993) showing a temporary enhancement of spatial–temporal reasoning in a few college students after listening to the first 10 minutes of Mozart's Sonata for Two Pianos in D Major (K. 448), the governors of both the State of Tennessee and the State of Georgia in the United States have started programs giving Mozart

CDs to every newborn's mother (Sack, 1998). In addition, in the State of Florida, a law has been enacted requiring that classical music be played daily in state-funded child care and educational programs, and hundreds of hospitals were given free CDs of classical music by the National Academy of Recording Arts and Sciences Foundation in May 1999 (Florida Legislature, 1999).

In turn, these same types of myths also create unrealistic, unfounded expectations and incorrect policy recommendations (Bruer, 2006), such as financial concentration on programs for children until they are 3 years old or focusing on only a few intervention issues (e.g., nutrition) instead of using a multimodular framework based on an integrative viewpoint dealing with child development. With regard to child poverty, it could be said that such ideas are at the same level as the feeble evidence (amounting to myths) described in the preceding paragraph and in chapters 2 and 5 of this volume.

Myths also overemphasize developmental neurobiology at the expense of other disciplines such as cognitive psychology and cognitive neuroscience, contributing to a confusion of scientific interest, especially with educational relevance (Bruer, 2006). In this context, researchers' social commitment should contribute to halting the dissemination of incorrect information or political practices that are not based on scientific evidence.

Other areas that policymakers should consider are (a) including specific contents within training programs for any future professionals who will be dealing with child development and education—journalism included—and (b) promoting discussion and dissemination forums, either online or personally, such as forums suggested for the general public, mass media, and educators by the Dana Foundation (see http://www.dana.org); through activities and publications (such as Brain Awareness Week) and the Society for Neuroscience (see http://www.sfn.org); and through several publications such as *Brain Briefings* (available at http://www.sfn.org) and *Brain Facts* (Society for Neuroscience, 2008). Finally, both the United Nations Children's Fund (2005) and the Society for Neuroscience have free guides aimed at orienting the press on how, when covering news related to either brain development or child poverty, they should delve more deeply into this worldwide problem by fostering the work of lawmakers and ethics and child-rights specialists.

REFERENCES

Abadzi, H. (2006). *Efficient learning of the poor. Insights from the frontier of cognitive neuroscience.* Washington, DC: International Bank for Reconstruction and Development/The World Bank.

Aber, J. L., Jones, S. M., & Raver, C. C. (2007). Poverty and child development: New perspectives on a defining issue. In J. L. Aber, S. J. Bishop-Josef, S. M. Jones, K. T. McLearn, & D. A. Phillips (Eds.), *Child development and social policy* (pp. 149–166). Washington, DC: American Psychological Association.

Abbott, M. L., Joireman, J., & Stroh, H. R. (2002). *The influence of district size, school size, and socioeconomic status on student achievement in Washington: A replication study using hierarchical linear modeling* (Technical Rep. No. 3). Seattle, WA: School Research Center.

Abbott-Shim, M., Lambert, R., & McCarty, F. (2003). A comparison of school readiness outcomes for children randomly assigned to a Head Start program and the program's wait list. *Journal of Education for Students Placed at Risk, 8,* 191–214.

Ackerman, P. L., Beier, M. E., & Boyle, M. O. (2005). Working memory and intelligence: The same or different constructs? *Psychological Bulletin, 131,* 30–60.

Adler, N. E., & Newman, K. (2002). Socioeconomic disparities in health: Pathways and policies. *Health Affairs, 21,* 60–76.

Altman, J., & Das, G. D. (1965, August 28). Post-natal origin of microneurones in the rat brain. *Nature, 207,* 953–956.

Andersen, S. L. (2003). Trajectories of brain development: Point of vulnerability or window of opportunity? *Neuroscience and Biobehavioral Reviews, 27*(1–2), 3–18.

Anderson, L. M., Shinn, C., Fullilove, M. T., Scrimshaw, S. C., Fielding, J. E., Normand, J., & Carande-Kulis, V. G. (2003). The effectiveness of early childhood development programs. A systematic review. *American Journal of Preventive Medicine, 24,* 32–46.

Andersson, B. E. (1992). Effects of day-care on cognitive and socioemotional competence of thirteen-year-old Swedish schoolchildren. *Child Development, 63,* 20–36.

Ansari, D., & Coch, D. (2006). Bridges over troubled waters: Education and cognitive neuroscience. *Trends in Cognitive Sciences, 10,* 146–151.

Appleyard, K., Egeland, B., Van Dulmen, M. H. M., & Sroufe, L. A. (2005). When more is not better: The role of cumulative risk in child behavior outcomes. *Journal of Child Psychology and Psychiatry, 46,* 235–245.

Ardilla, A., Rosselli, M., Matute, E., & Guajardo, S. (2005). The influence of the parents' educational level on the development of executive functions. *Developmental Neuropsychology, 28,* 539–560.

Attawell, K. (2004). *International longitudinal research on childhood poverty: Practical guidelines and lessons learned from Young Lives* (Working Paper No. 11). London: Young Lives.

Baker, A. J. L., Piotrkowski, C. S., & Brooks-Gunn, J. (1999). The Home Instruction Program for Preschool Youngsters (HIPPY). *The Future of Children, 9*, 116–133.

Balamore, U., & Wozniak, R. H. (1984). Speech–action coordination in young children. *Developmental Psychology, 20*, 850–858.

Barnett, W. S. (1998). Long-term effects on cognitive development and school success. In W. S. Barnett & S. S. Boocock (Eds.), *Early care and education for children in poverty: Promises, programs, and long-term results* (pp. 11–44). Albany: State University of New York.

Barnett, W. S. (2006). *Preschool education studies: A bibliography organized by research strengths*. New Brunswick: National Institute for Early Education Research, Rutgers, The State University of New Jersey.

Barrera, M., Caples H., & Tein, J. Y. (2001). The psychological sense of economic hardship: Measurement models, validity, and cross-ethnic equivalent for urban families. *American Journal of Community Psychology, 29*, 493–508.

Bartels, M., Rietveld, M. J. H., Van Baal, G. C. M., & Boomsma, D. I. (2002). Genetic and environmental influences on the development of intelligence. *Behavior Genetics, 32*, 237–249.

Battro, A. M., Fischer, K. W., & Lena, P. J. (2008). *The educated brain. Essays in Neuroeducation*. Cambridge, MA: Cambridge University Press.

Beccaria, L., & Minujin, A. (1991). *Sobre la medición de la pobreza: Enseñanzas a partir de la experiencia argentina* [About poverty measurement: Learning from Argentine experience] (Working Paper No. 8). Buenos Aires: UNICEF—Argentina.

Beckett, C., Maughan, B., Rutter, M., Castle, J., Colvert, E., Goothues, C., et al. (2006). Do the effects of early severe deprivation on cognition persist into early adolescence? Findings from the English and Romanian adoptees study. *Child Development, 77*, 696–711.

Beddington, J., Cooper, C. L., Field, J., Goswami, U., Huppert, F. A., Jenkins, R., et al. (2008, October 23). The mental wealth of nations. *Nature, 455*, 1057–1060.

Beers, S. R., & De Bellis, M. D. (2002). Neuropsychological function in children with maltreatment-related posttraumatic stress disorder. *American Journal of Psychiatry, 159*, 483–486.

Belsky, J., Burchinal, M., McCartney, K., Vandell, D. L., Clarke-Stewart, K .A., Owen, M. T., & NICHD Early Child Care Research Network. (2007). Are there long-term effects of early child care? *Child Development, 78*, 681–701.

Bennett, A. J., Lesch, K. P., Heils, A., Long, J. C., Lorenz, J. G., Shoaf, S. E., et al. (2002). Early experience and serotonin transporter gene variation interact to influence primate CNS function. *Molecular Psychiatry, 7*, 118–122.

Bennett, E. L., Diamond, M. C., Krech, D., & Rosenzweig, M. R. (1964, October 30). Chemical and anatomical plasticity brain. *Science, 146*, 610–619.

Benton, A. L., Varney, N. R., & Hamsher, K. D. (1978). Visuo-spatial judgement: a clinical test. *Archives of Neurology, 35*, 364–367.

Bezard, E., Dovero, S., Belin, D., Duconger, S., Jackson-Lewis, V. Przedborski, S., et al. (2003). Enriched environment confers resistance to 1-Methyl-4-Phenyl-1,2,3,6-Tetrahydropyridine and cocaine: Involvement of dopamine transporter and trophic factors. *Journal of Neuroscience, 23,* 11007–10999.

Bhardwaj, R. D., Curtis, M. A., Spalding, K. L., Buchlolz, B. A., Find, D., Björk-Ericsson, T., et al. (2006). Neocortical neurogenesis in humans is restricted to development. *Proceedings of the National Academy of Sciences USA, 103,* 12564–12568.

Bhargava, A. (1998). A dynamic model for the cognitive development of Kenyan schoolchildren. *Journal of Educational Psychology, 90,* 162–166.

Bhatnagar, S., & Taneja, S. (2001). Zinc and cognitive development. *British Journal of Nutrition, 85,* 139–145.

Bishop, D. V. M. (1983). *The Test for Reception of Grammar.* University of Manchester, Manchester, England: Age and Cognitive Performance Research Centre.

Blair, C. (2002). School readiness: Integrating cognition and emotion in a neurobiological conceptualization of children's functioning at school entry. *American Psychologist, 57,* 111–127.

Blair, C., & Peters, R. (2003). Physiological and neurocognitive correlates of adaptive behavior in preschool among children in Head Start. *Developmental Neuropsychology, 24,* 479–497.

Blair, C., & Razza, R. P. (2007). Relating effortful control, executive function, and false belief understanding to emerging math and literacy ability in kindergarten. *Child Development, 78,* 647–663.

Boanida, J., Espe-Sherwinot, M., & Borges, L. (2000). Community-based early intervention: The Coimbra Project (Portugal). *Child Care Dual Health Development, 26,* 343–354.

Bodrova, E., & Leong, D. J. (1996). *Tools of the mind. The Vygotskian approach to early childhood education.* Englewood Cliffs, NJ: Prentice Hall.

Bodrova, E., & Leong, D. J. (2001). *Tools of the mind: A case study of implementing the Vygotskian approach in American early childhood and primary classrooms.* Geneva, Switzerland: UNESCO, International Bureau of Education.

Boltvinik, J. (1995). *Poverty measurement methods—An overview.* Washington, DC: United Nations Population Division.

Boltvinik, J. (1999). Conceptos y medidas de pobreza [Poverty concepts and measurement]. In J. Boltvinik & E. Hernández (Eds.), *Pobreza y distribución del ingreso en México* (pp. 35–78). Mexico City, México: Siglo XXI Editores.

Boocock, S. S. (1995). Early childhood programs in other nations: goals and outcomes. *The Future of Children, 5,* 94–114.

Boocock, S. S. (2003). Lessons from Europe: European preschools revisited in a global age. In A. J. Reynolds, M. C. Wang, & H. J. Walberg (Eds.), *Early childhood programs for a new century* (pp. 121–138). Washington DC: Child Welfare League of America.

Boocock, S. S., & Larner, M. (1998). Long-term outcomes in other nations. In W. S. Barnett & S. S. Boocock (Eds.), *Early care and education for children in poverty: Promises, programs, and long-term results* (pp. 45–76). Albany: State University of New York.

Borman, G. D., Slavin, R. E., & Cheung, A. (2005). The national randomized field trial of Success for All: Second-year outcomes. *Educational Evaluation and Policy Analysis, 27*, 1–22.

Boruch, R. (2005). Better evaluation for evidence-based policy: Place randomized trials in education, criminology, welfare, and health. *Annals of the American Academy of Political and Social Sciences, 599*, 6–18.

Bradley, R. H. (1994). The HOME Inventory: Review and reflections. In H. W. Reese (Ed.), *Advances in child development and behavior* (Vol. 25, pp. 241–288). San Diego, CA: Academic Press.

Bradley, R. H., & Corwyn, R. F. (2002). Socioeconomic status and child development. *Annual Review of Psychology, 53*, 371–399.

Bradley, R. H., & Corwyn, R. F. (2005). Caring for children around the world: A view from HOME. *International Journal of Behavioral Development, 29*, 468–478.

Bradley, R. H., Corwyn, R. F., McAdoo, H. P., & Garcia Coll, C. (2001). The home environments of children in the United States Part I: Variations by age, ethnicity, and poverty status. *Child Development, 72*, 1844–1867.

Bradley, R. H., Corwyn, R. F., & Whiteside-Mansell, L. (1996). Life at home: Same time, different places—An examination of the HOME Inventory in different cultures. *Early Development and Parenting, 5*, 251–269.

Bradshaw, J. (2006). The use of indicators of child well-being in the United Kingdom and the European Union. In A. Ben-Aireh & R. M. Goerge (Eds.), *Indicators of children's well-being: Understanding their role, usage and policy influence* (Vol. 27, pp. 63–81). New York: Springer Science + Business Media.

Brady, D. (2003). Rethinking the sociological measurement of poverty. *Social Forces, 81*, 715–752.

Briones, T., Klintsova, A. Y., & Greenough, W. T. (2004). Stability of synaptic plasticity in the adult rat visual cortex induced by complex environment exposure. *Brain Research, 1018*, 130–135.

Brody, G. H., Dorsey, S., Forehand, R., & Armistead, L. (2002). Unique and protective contributions of parenting and classroom processes to the adjustment of African American children living in single-parent families. *Child Development, 73*, 274–286.

Brody, G. H., Stoneman, Z., Flor, D., McCrary, C., Hastings, L., & Conyers, O. (1994). Financial resources, parent psychological functioning, parent co-care giving, and early adolescent competence in rural two-parent African-American families. *Child Development, 65*, 590–605.

Bronfenbrenner, U., & Ceci, S. J. (1994). Nature–nurture reconceptualized in developmental perspective: A bioecological model. *Psychology Review, 101*, 568–86.

Brooks-Gunn, J., & Duncan, G. J. (1997). The effects of poverty on children. *The Future of Children, 7*, 55–71.

Brooks-Gunn, J., Klebanov, P., Liaw, F., & Duncan, G. (1995). Toward an understanding of the effect of poverty upon children. In H. E. Fitzgerald, B. M. Lester, & B. Zuckerman (Eds.), *Children of poverty: Research, health, and policy issues* (pp. 3–41). New York: Garland.

Brooks-Gunn, J., Klebanov, P., Liaw, F., & Spiker, D. (1993). Enhancing the development of low birthweight, premature infants: Changes in cognition and behaviour over the first three years. *Child Development, 64*, 736–753.

Bruer, J. T. (2006). Points of view: On the implications of neuroscience research for science teaching and learning: Are there any? A skeptical theme and variations: The primacy of psychology in the science of learning. *CBE Life Sciences Education, 5*, 104–110.

Buckhalt, J. A., El-Sheikh, M., & Keller, P. (2007). Children's sleep and cognitive functioning: Race and socioeconomic status as moderators of effects. *Child Development, 78*, 213–231.

Buckner, J. C., Mezzacappa, E., & Beardslee, W. R. (2003). Characteristics of resilient youths living in poverty: The role of self-regulatory processes. *Development and Psychopathology, 15*, 139–162.

Bull, R., Espy, K. A., & Wiebe, S. A. (2008). Short-term memory, working memory, and executive functioning in preschoolers: Longitudinal predictors of mathematical achievement at age 7 years. *Developmental Neuropsychology, 33*, 205–228.

Burchinal, M. R., Roberts, J., Hooper, S., & Zeisel, S. A. (2000). Cumulative risk and early cognitive development. A comparison of statistical risk models. *Developmental Psychology, 36*, 793–807.

Byrne, B., Fielding-Barnesley, R., & Ashley, L. (2000). Effects of preschool phoneme identity training after six years: Outcome level distinguished from rate of response. *Journal of Educational Psychology, 92*, 659–667.

Bystron, I., Blakemore, C., & Rakic, P. (2008). Development of the human cerebral cortex: Boulder Committee revisited. *Nature Reviews. Neuroscience, 9*, 110–122.

Cacioppo, J. T., Berntson, G. G., & Nusbaum, H. C. (2008). Neuroimaging as a new tool in the toolbox of psychological science. *Current Directions in Psychological Science, 17*, 62–67.

Caldji, C., Tannenbaum, B., Sharma, S., Francis, D., & Plotsky, P. M. (1998). Maternal care during infancy regulates the development of neural systems mediating the expression of fearfulness in the rat. *Proceedings of the National Academy of Sciences USA, 95*, 5335–5340.

Campbell, F. A., Pungello, E. P. Miller-Johnson, S., Burchinal, M., & Ramey, C. T. (2001). The development of cognitive and academic abilities: Growth curves from an early childhood educational experiment. *Developmental Psychology, 37*, 231–242.

Campbell, F. A., & Ramey, C. T. (1994). Effects of early intervention on intellectual and academic achievement: A follow-up study of children from low-income families. *Child Development, 65,* 684–698.

Canfield, R. L., Creer, D. A., Cornwell, C., & Henderson, C. R. (2003). Low-level lead exposure, executive functioning, and learning in early childhood. *Child Neuropsychology, 9,* 35–53.

Caravale, B., Tozzi, C., Albino, G., & Vicari, S. (2005). Cognitive development in low risk preterm infants at 3–4 years of life. *Archives of Disease in Childhood. Fetal and Neonatal Edition, 90,* F474–F479.

Carlson, S. M., & Moses, L. J. (2001). Individual differences in inhibitory control and children's theory of mind. *Child Development, 72,* 1032–1053.

Carrie, G., Herma, K. C., & Ostrander, R. (2006). The family environment and developmental psychopathology: The unique and interactive effects of depression, attention, and conduct problems. *Child Psychiatry and Human Development, 37,* 163–177.

Carrion, V. G., Weems, C. F., & Reiss, A. L. (2007). Stress predicts brain changes in children: A pilot longitudinal study on youth stress, posttraumatic stress disorder, and the hippocampus. *Pediatrics, 119,* 509–516.

Casey, B. J., Cohen, J. D., Jezzard, P., Turner, R., Noll, D. C., Trainor, R. J., et al. (1995). Activation of prefrontal cortex in children during a nonspatial working memory task with functional MRI. *Neuroimage, 2,* 221–229.

Centre for Longitudinal Studies. (2005). *Child health and education studies (CHES). The ten-year follow up, 1980.* London: Institute of Education, University of London.

Chen, E., Martin, A. D., & Matthews, K. A. (2006). Socioeconomic status and health: Do gradients differ within childhood and adolescence? *Social Science & Medicine, 62,* 2161–2170.

Chen, E., Matthews, K. A., & Boyce, W. T. (2002). Socioeconomic differences in children's health: How and why do these relationships change with age? *Psychological Bulletin, 128,* 295–329.

Chinapah, V. (2003). *Monitoring Learning Achievement (MLA) Project in Africa* (Working Document No. 2). Grand Bale, Mauritus: Association for the Development of Education in Africa.

Choi, B. H. (1989). The effects of methylmercury on the developing brain. *Progress in Neurobiology, 32,* 447–470.

Cichetti, D. V., Kaufman, A. S., & Sparrow, S. S. (2004). The relationship between prenatal and postnatal exposure to polychlorinated biphenyls (PCBs) and cognitive, neuropsychological, and behavioral deficits: A critical appraisal. *Psychology in the Schools, 41,* 589–594.

Colombo, J. A., & Lipina, S. J. (2005). *Hacia un programa público de estimulación cognitiva infantil. Fundamentos, métodos y resultados de una experiencia de intervención preescolar controlada* [Toward a cognitive stimulation public program. Foundations, methods and results from a controlled intervention in preschoolers]. Buenos Aires, Argentina: Editorial Paidós.

Colombo, J. A., Reisin, H. D., Miguel-Hidalgo, J. J., & Rajkowska, G. (2006). Cerebral cortex astroglia and the brain of a genius: A propos of A. Einstein's. *Brain Research Reviews, 52,* 257–263.

Conger, R. D., & Donnellan, M. B. (2007). An interactionist perspective on the socioeconomic context of human development. *Annual Review of Psychology, 58,* 175–199.

Corak, M. (Ed.). (1998). *Labour markets, social institutions, and the future of Canada's children* (Catalogue No. 89-553-XPB). Ottawa, Ontario, Canada: Statistics Canada

Corcoran, M. E., & Chaudry, A. (1997). The dynamics of childhood poverty. *The Future of Children, 7,* 40–54.

Corrie, B. P. (1994). The case for integrated child focused development strategies. *Community Development Journal, 29,* 251–256.

Corriveau, R. A., Huh, G. S., & Shatz, C. J. (1998). Regulation of Class I MHC gene expression in the developing and mature CNS by neural activity. *Neuron, 21,* 505–520.

Coss, R. G., & Globus, A. (1979). Social experience affects the development of dendritic spines and branches on tectal interneurons in the jewel fish. *Developmental Psychobiology, 12,* 347–358.

CROP/Childwatch. (2007). *Rethinking poverty and children in the new millennium: Linking research and policy.* CROP/Childwatch: Oslo, Norway.

Currie, J. (2001). Early childhood education programs. *Journal of Economic Perspectives, 15,* 213–238.

Dehaene, S., & Cohen, L. (2007). Cultural recycling of cortical maps. *Neuron, 56,* 384–398.

Dencik, L. (1995). Modern childhood in the Nordic countries: "Dual socialization" and its implications. In L. Chisholm, P. Buchnerm, H. H. Kruger, & P. Brown (Eds.), *Growing up in Europe: Contemporary horizons in childhood and youth* (pp. 231–249). New York: Garland.

Desoette, A., Roeyers, H., & De Clerq, A. (2003). Can offline metacognition enhance mathematical problem solving? *Journal of Educational Psychology, 95,* 188–200.

Devaney, B. L., Ellwood, M. R., & Love, J. M. (1997). Programs that mitigate the effects of poverty on children. *The Future of Children, 7,* pp. 88–112.

Diamond, A. (1985). Development of the ability to use recall to guide action, as indicated by infants' performance on AB. *Child Development, 56,* 863–883.

Diamond, A. (2007). Interrelated and interdependent. *Developmental Science, 10,* 152–158.

Diamond, A., Barnett, S. W., Thomas, J., & Munro, S. (2007, November 30). Preschool program improves cognitive control. *Science, 318,* 1387–1388.

Diamond, A., Briand, L., Fossella, J., & Gehlbach, L. (2004). Genetic and neurochemical modulation of prefrontal cognitive functions in children. *American Journal of Psychiatry, 161,* 125–132.

Dodge, K. A., Lansford, J. E., Salzer Burks, V., Bates, J. E., Pettit, G. S., Fontaine, R., & Price, J. M. (2003). Peer rejection and social information-processing factors in the development of aggressive behavior problems in children. *Child Development, 74*, 374–393.

Douglas-Hall, A., & Chau, M. (2007). *Basic facts about low-income children. National.* New York: Center for Children in Poverty, Columbia University Mailman School of Public Health.

Draganski, B., Gaser, C., Busch, V., Schuierer, G., Bogdahn, U., & May. A. (2004, January 22). Neuroplasticity: Changes in grey matter induced by training. *Nature, 427*, 311–312.

Duncan, G. J., & Brooks-Gunn, J. (2000). Family poverty, welfare reform, and child development. *Child Development, 71*, 188–196.

Duncan, G. J., Brooks-Gunn, J., & Klevanov, P. K. (1994). Economic deprivation and early childhood development. *Child Development, 65*, 296–318.

Duncan, G. J., Ludwig, J., & Magnuson, K. A. (2007). Reducing poverty through preschool interventions. *The Future of Children, 17*, 143–160.

Duncan, G. J., Yeung, W. J., Brooks-Gunn, J., & Smith, J. R. (1998). How much does childhood poverty affect the life chances of children? *American Sociological Review, 63*, 406–423.

Duncan, J., Seitz, R. J., Kolodny, J., Bor, D., Herzog, H., Ahmed, A., et al. (2000, July 21). A neural basis for general intelligence. *Science, 289*, 457–460.

Early, D. M., Maxwell, K. L., Burchinal, M., Bender, R. H., Ebanks, C., Henry, G., et al. (2007). Teachers' education, classroom quality, and young children's academic skills: Results from seven studies of preschool programs. *Child Development, 78*, 558–580.

Eckersley, P., Egan, G. F., Amari, S., Beltrame, F., Bennett, R., Bjaalie, J. G., et al. (2003). Neuroscience data and tool sharing. A legal and policy framework for neuroinformatics. *Neuroinformatics, 1*, 149–165.

Education Commission of the States. (1996). *Bridging the gap between Neuroscience and Education.* Denver, CO: Author.

Elliot, D. S., Wilson, W. J., Huizinga, D., Sampson, R. J., Elliott, A., & Rankin, B. (1996). The effects of neighbourhood disadvantage on adolescent development. *Journal of Research in Crime and Delinquency, 33*, 389–426.

Engle, P. L., Black, M. M., Behrman, J. R., Cabral de Mello, M., Gertler, P. J., Kapiriri, L., et al. (2007). Strategies to avoid the loss of developmental potential in more than 200 million children in the developing world. *Lancet, 369*, 229–242.

Epstein, A. S. (2003). Early math: The next big thing. *High/Scope ReSource for Educators, 2*, 5–10.

Esping-Andersen, G. (2005). *Children in the welfare state. A social investment approach* (DemoSoc Working Paper No. 10). Barcelona, Spain: Universitat Pompeu Fabbra.

Espy, K. A., Kaufmann, P. M., & Glisky, M. L. (1999). Neuropsychological function in toddlers exposed to cocaine in utero: A preliminary study. *Developmental Neuropsychology, 15*, 447–460.

Espy, K. A., Meade Stalets, M., McDiarmid, M. M., Senn, T. E., Cwik, M. F., & Hamby, A. (2002). Executive functions in preschool children born preterm: application of cognitive neuroscience paradigms. *Child Neuropsychology, 8,* 83–92.

Evans, G. W. (2004). The environment of childhood poverty. *American Psychologist, 59,* 77–92.

Evans, G. W., & English, K. (2002). The environment of poverty: Multiple stressor exposure, psychophysiological stress, and socioemotional adjustment. *Child Development, 73,* 1238–1248.

Faherty, C. J., Raviie Shepherd, K., Herasimtschuk, A., & Smeyne, R. J. (2005). Environmental enrichment in adulthood eliminates neuronal death in experimental Parkinsonism. *Brain Research Molecular Brain Research, 134,* 170–179.

Farah, M. J., Betancourt, L., Shera, D. M., Savage, J. H., Giannetta, J. M., Brodsky, N. L., et al. (2008). Environmental stimulation, parental nurturance and cognitive development in humans. *Developmental Science, 11,* 793–801.

Farah, M. J., Shera, D. M., Savage, J. H., Betancourt, L., Giannetta, J. M., Brodsky, N. L., et al. (2006). Childhood poverty: Specific associations with neurocognitive development. *Brain Research, 1110,* 166–174.

Farver, J. A. M., Xu, Y., Eppe, S., Fernandez, A., & Schwartz, D. (2005). Community violence, family conflict, and preschoolers' socioemotional functioning. *Developmental Psychology, 41,* 160–170.

Fatemi, S. H., Emamian, E. S., Kist, D., Sidwell, R., Nkajima, N., Akhter, P., et al. (1999). Defective corticogenesis and reduction in Reelin immunoreactivity in cortex and hippocampus of prenatally infected neonatal mice. *Molecular Psychiatry, 4,* 145–154.

Feigenson, L., Dehaene, S., & Spelke, E. (2004). Core systems of number. *Trends in Cognitive Sciences, 7,* 307–314.

Fellows, L. K., & Farah, M. J. (2003). Ventromedial frontal cortex mediates affective shifting in humans: evidence from a reversal learning paradigm. *Brain, 126,* 1830–1837.

Fisher, B. E., Petzinger, G. M., Nixon, K., Hogg, E., Bremner, S., Mwshul, C. K., & Jakowec, M. W. (2004). Exercise-induced behavioral recovery and neuroplasticity in the 1-methyl-4-phenyl-1, 2, 3, 6-tetrahydropyridine-lesioned mouse basal ganglia. *Journal of Neuroscience Research, 77,* 378–390.

Fisher, P. A., & Kim, H. K. (2007). Intervention effects on foster preschoolers' attachment-related behaviors from a randomized trial. *Prevention Science, 8,* 161–170.

Florida Legislature. (1999). Infants and toddlers in state-funded education and care programs; brain development activities. Title XXIX, Chapter 402, Article 25: Health and human services: Miscellaneuous provisions.

Fossella, J., Sommer, T., Fan, J., Wu, Y., Swanson, J. M., Pfaff, D. W., & Posner, M. I. (2002). Assessing the molecular genetics of attention networks. *BMC Neuroscience, 3,* 14.

Fotso, J. C., & Kuate-Defo, B. (2005). Socioeconomic inequalities in early childhood malnutrition and morbidity: modification of the household-level effects by the community SES. *Health Place, 11*, 205–225.

Fox, C., Merali, Z., & Harrison, C. (2006). Therapeutic and protective effect of environmental enrichment against psychogenic and neurogenic stress. *Behavioral Brain Research, 175*, 1–8.

Francis, D., Diorio, J., Liu, D., & Meaney, M. J. (1999, November 5). Nongenomic transmission across generations of maternal behavior and stress responses in the rat. *Science, 286*, 1155–1158.

Frye, D., Zelazo, P. D., & Tibor, P. (1995). Theory of mind and rule-based reasoning. *Cognitive Development, 10*, 483–527.

Galani, R., Coutureau, E., & Kelche, C. (1998). Effects of enriched postoperative housing conditions on spatial memory deficits in rats with selective lesions of either hippocampus, subiculum or entorhinal cortex. *Restorative Neurology Neuroscience, 13*, 173–184.

Galani, R., Jarrard, L. E., Will, B. E., & Kelche, C. (1997). Effects of postoperative housing conditions on functional recovery in rats with lesions of the hippocampus, subiculum, or entorhinal cortex. *Neurobiology of Learning and Memory, 67*, 43–56.

Garbarino, J., Bradshaw, C. P., & Vorrasi, J. A. (2002). Mitigating the effects of gun violence on children and youth. *The Future of Children, 12*, 72–85.

Garber, H. L., (1988). *The Milwaukee Project: Prevention of mental retardation in children at risk*. Washington, DC: American Association of Mental Retardation.

Garon, N., Bryson, S. E., & Smith, I. M. (2008). Executive function in preschoolers: A review using and integrative framework. *Psychological Bulletin, 134*, 31–60.

Garret, P., Ng'andu, N., & Ferron, J. (1994). Poverty experiences of young children and the quality of their home environments. *Child Development, 65*, 331–345.

Gaser, C., & Schlaug, G., (2003). Gray matter differences between musicians and nonmusicians. In G. Avanzini, C. Besta, C. Faienza, D. Minciacchi, L. Lopez, & M. Majno (Eds.), *Annals of the New York Academy of Sciences: Vol. 999. The neurosciences and music* (pp. 514–517). New York: New York Academy of Sciences

Gauvain, M., Fagot, B. I., Leve, C., & Kavanagh, K. (2002). Instruction by mothers and fathers during problem solving with their young children. *Family Psychology, 16*, 81–90.

Georgieff, M. K., & Rao, R. (2001). The role of nutrition in cognitive development. In C. A. Nelson & M. Luciana (Eds.), *Cognitive developmental neuroscience* (pp. 491–504). Cambridge, MA: MIT Press.

Gershoff, E. T., Aber, J. L., Raver, C. C., & Lennon, M. C. (2007). Income is not enough: Incorporating material hardship into models of income associations with parenting and child development. *Child Development, 78*, 70–95.

Giedd, J. N., Jeffries, N. O., Blumenthal, J., Castellanos, F. X., Vaituzis, A. C., Fernandez, T., et al. (1999). Brain development during childhood and adolescence: A longitudinal MRI study. *Nature Neuroscience, 2*, 861–873.

Gloviczki, P. J. (2004). Ceausescu's children: The process of democratization and the plight of Romania's orphans. *Critique, 3*, 116–125.

Gogtay, N., Giedd, J. N., Lusk, L., Hayashi, K. M., Greenstein, D., Vaituzis, A. C., et al. (2004). Dynamic mapping of human cortical development during childhood though early adulthood. *Proceedings of the National Academy of Sciences USA, 101*, 8174–8179.

Goldman, S. A., & Nottebohm, F. (1983). Neuronal production, migration, and differentiation in a vocal control nucleus of the adult female canary brain. *Proceedings of the National Academy of Sciences USA, 80*, 2390–2394.

Gordon, M., McClure, F. D., & Aylward, G. P. (1996). *The interpretive guide to the Gordon Diagnostic System (GDS)* (3rd ed.). Dewitt, NY: GSI Publications.

Gordon, D., Nandy, S., Pantazis, C., Pemberton, S., & Townsend, P. (2003). *Child poverty in the developing world.* Bristol, England: Policy Press.

Gorman, K. S., & Pollit, E. (1996). Does schooling buffer the effect of early risk? *Child Development, 67*, 314–326.

Gormley, W. T., Jr., Gayer, T., Phillips, D., & Dawson, B. (2005). The effects of universal pre-K on cognitive development. *Developmental Psychology, 41*, 872–884.

Goswami, U. (2006). Neuroscience and education: From research to practice? *Nature Reviews. Neuroscience, 7*, 1–6.

Gould, E., McEwen, B. S., Tanapat, P., Galea, L. A. M., & Fuchs, E. (1997). Neurogenesis in the dentate gyrus of the adult shrew is regulated by psychosocial stress and NMDA receptor activation. *Journal of Neuroscience, 17*, 2429–2498.

Gould, E., Reeves, A. J., Graziano, M. S., & Gross, C. G. (1999, October 15). Neurogenesis in the neocortex of adult primates. *Science, 286*, 548–552.

Gould, J. S. (1981). *The mismeasure of man.* New York: Norton.

Grantham-McGregor, S., Cheung, Y. B., Cueto, S. Glewwe, P., Richter, L., Struup, B., & the International Child Development Steering Group. (2007). Developmental potential in the first 5 years for children in developing countries. *Lancet, 369*, 60–70.

Greenough, W. T., West, R. W., & DeVoogd, T. J. (1978, December 8). Subsynaptic plate perforations: Changes with age and experience in the rat. *Science, 202*, 1096–1098.

Grigorenko, E. L. (2003). Intraindividual fluctuations in intellectual functioning: Selected links between nutrition and the mind. In J. R. Sternberg, J. Lautrey, & T. I. Lubart (Eds.), *Models of intelligence: International perspectives* (pp. 91–116). Washington, DC: American Psychological Association.

Grosh, M., & Glewwe, P. (1995). *A guide to living standards surveys and their data sets* (LSMS Working Paper No. 120). Washington, DC: World Bank.

Grossman, A. W., Churchill, J. D., McKinney, B. C., Kodish, I. M., Otte, S. L., & Greenough, W. T. (2003). Experience effects on brain development: Possible contributions to psychopathology. *Journal of Child Psychology and Psychiatry, and Allied Disciplines, 44*, 33–63.

Gunnar, M., & Quevedo, K. (2007). The neurobiology of stress and development. *Annual Review of Psychology, 58*, 145–173.

Guo, G., & Harris, M. K. (2000). The mechanisms mediating the effects of poverty on children's intellectual development. *Demography, 37*, 431–447.

Guralnik, J. M., Butterworth, S., Wadsworth, M. E., & Kuh, D. (2006). Childhood socioeconomic status predicts physical functioning a half century later. *The Journal of Gerontology: Series A. Biological Sciences and Medical Sciences, 61*, 694–701.

Hackman, D. A., Betancourt, L., Hurt, H., Gallop, R. J., & Farah, M. J. (2008, April). *Socioeconomic status and stress physiology: Acute cortisol response to a social stressor in adolescents*. Poster presented at the 15th Annual Meeting of the Cognitive Neuroscience Society, San Francisco.

Haier, R. J., Jung, R. E., Yeo, R. A., Head, K., & Alkire, M. T. (2004). Structural brain variation and general intelligence. *NeuroImage, 23*, 425–433.

Hamasha, A. A., Warren, J. J., Levy, S. M., Broffitt, B., & Kanellis, M. J. (2006). Oral health behaviors of children in low and high socioeconomic status families. *Pediatric Dentistry, 28*, 310–315.

Harpham, T. (2000). Measuring child poverty and health. A new international study. *Young Lives Working Papers, 2*, 1–11.

Hart, B., & Risley, T. R. (1995). *Meaningful differences in the everyday experiences of young American children*. Baltimore: Brookes.

Hebb, D. O. (1949). *The organization of behavior. A neuropsychological theory*. New York: Wiley.

Hernandez, D. J. (1996). *Trends in the well-being of America's children and youth: 1996*. Washington, DC: Child Trends, Inc.

High/Scope Educational Research Foundation. (2003). *How young children learn to read in High/Scope programs—A summary*. Ypsilanti, MI: Author.

Hill, C. J., & Michael, R. T. (2001). A new approach to measuring poverty. *Journal of Human Resources, 36*, 148–161.

Hoff, E. (2003). The specificity of environmental influence: Socioeconomic status affects early vocabulary development via maternal speech. *Child Development, 74*, 1368–1378.

Hoff, E. (2006). How social contexts support and shape language. *Developmental Review, 26*, 55–88.

Hoff, E., Laursen, B., & Tardif, T. (2002). Socioeconomic status and parenting. In M. Bornstein (Ed.), *Handbook of parenting: Vol. 2. Biology and ecology of parenting* (2nd ed., pp. 144–159). Mahwah, NJ: Erlbaum.

Holden, C. (1996, November 15). Small refugees suffer the effects of early neglect. *Science, 274*, 1076–1077.

Holmboe, K., & Johnson, M. H. (2005). Educating executive attention. *Proceedings of the National Academy of Sciences USA, 102*, 14479–14480.

Hubbs-Tait, L., Nation, J. R., Krebs, N. F., & Bellinger, D. C. (2005). Neurotoxicants, micronutrients, and social environments. *Psychological Science in the Public Interest, 6*, 57–121.

Hughes, C. (1998). Executive function in preschoolers: Links with theory of mind and verbal ability. *British Journal of Developmental Psychology, 16*, 167–178.

Hughes, C., & Graham, A. (2002). Measuring executive functions in childhood: Problems and solutions? *Child and Adolescent Mental Health, 7*, 131–142.

Hurless, B. R. (2004). Early childhood education in France. *Young Children, 59*, 20–24.

Huston, A. C., Duncan, G. J., Granger, R., Bos, J., McLoyd, V., Mistry, R., et al. (2001). Work-based antipoverty programs for parents can enhance the school performance and social behavior of children. *Child Development, 72*, 318–336.

Huston, A. C., McLoyd, V. C., & García Coll, C. (1994). Children and poverty: Issues in contemporary research. *Child Development, 65*, 275–282.

Huttenlocher, P. R. (1979). Synaptic density in human frontal cortex—Developmental changes and effects of aging. *Brain Research, 163*, 195–205.

Iceland, J. (2003). Measuring poverty: Theoretical and empirical considerations. *Measurement, 3*, 199 –235.

Iceland, J. (2003). *Poverty in America.* Berkeley: University of California Press.

Ichikawa, M., Matsuoka, M., & Mori, Y. (1993). Effect of differential rearing on synapses and soma size in rat medial amygdaloid nucleus. *Synapse, 13*, 50–56.

Ischebeck, A., Zamarian, L., Siedentopf, C., Koppelstätter, Benke, T., Felber, S., & Delazer, M. (2006). How specifically do we learn? Imaging the learning of multiplication and subtraction. *NeuroImage, 30*, 1365–1375.

Jacques, S., & Zelazo, P. D. (2001). The Flexible Item Selection Task (FIST): A measure of executive function in preschoolers. *Developmental Neuropsychology, 20*, 573–591.

Johnson, K., & Knitzer, J. (2006). *Early childhood comprehensive systems that spend smarter: Maximizing resources to serve vulnerable children* (Project THRIVE Issue Brief No. 1). New York: National Center for Children in Poverty, Columbia University.

Johnson, M. H. (2005). Sensitive periods in functional brain development: Problems and prospects. *Developmental Psychobiology, 46*, 25–30.

Johnson, M. H. (2006). Developing a social brain. *Acta Pediatrica, 96*, 3–5.

Kandel, E. R. (2001, November 2). The molecular biology of memory storage: A dialogue between genes and synapses. *Science, 294*, 1030–1038.

Kaplan, G. A., Roberts, R. E., Camacho, T. C., & Coyne, J. C. (1987). Psychosocial predictors of depression. *American Journal of Epidemiology, 125*, 206–220.

Karoly, L. A., Kilburn, M. R., & Cannon, J. S. (2005). *Early childhood interventions. Proven results, future promise.* Santa Monica, CA: RAND Corporation.

Keegan Eamon, M. (2000). Structural model of the effects of poverty on externalizing and internalizing behaviors of four- to five-year-old children. *Social Work Research, 24*, 143–155.

Keegan Eamon, M. (2001). The effects of poverty on children's socioemotional development: An ecological systems analysis. *Social Work, 46,* 256–266.

Keegan Eamon, M. (2002). Effects of poverty on mathematics and reading achievement of young adolescents. *Journal of Early Adolescence, 22,* 49–74.

Khazipov, R., & Luhmann, H. J. (2006). Early patterns of electrical activity in the developing cerebral cortex of humans and rodents. *Trends in Neurosciences, 29,* 414–418.

Kishiyama, M. M., Boyce, W. T., Jimenez, A. M., Perry, L. M., & Knight, R. T. (2009). Socioeconomic disparities affect prefrontal function in children. *Journal of Cognitive Neuroscience, 10,* 1–10.

Kleim, J. A., Jones, T. A., & Schallert, T. (2003). Motor enrichment and the induction of plasticity before or after brain injury. *Neurochemical Research, 28,* 1757–1769.

Kleim, J. A., Vij, K., Ballard, D. H., & Greenough, W. T. (1997). Learning-dependent synaptic modifications in the cerebellar cortex of the adult rat persist for at least four weeks. *Journal of Neuroscience, 17,* 717–721.

Klerman, L. V. (1991). The health of poor children: Problem and programs. In A. Huston (Ed.), *Children in poverty: Child development and public policy* (pp. 136–157). Cambridge, England: Cambridge University Press.

Klingberg, T., Fernell, E., Olesen, P. J., Johnson, M., Gustaffson, P., Dahlstrom, K., et al. (2006). Computerized training of working memory in children with ADHD—A randomized, controlled trial. *Journal of the American Academy of Child and Adolescence Psychiatry, 44,* 177–186.

Klingberg, T., Forssberg, H., & Westerberg, H. (2002). Increased brain activity in frontal and parietal cortex underlies the development of visuospatial working memory capacity during childhood. *Journal of Cognitive Neuroscience, 14,* 1–10.

Knudsen, E. I. (2004). Sensitive periods in the development of the brain and behavior. *Journal of Cognitive Neuroscience, 16,* 1412–1425.

Knudsen, E. I., Heckman, J. J., Cameron, J. L., & Shonkoff, J. P. (2006). Economic, neurobiological, and behavioral perspectives on building America's future workforce. *Proceedings of the National Academy of Sciences USA, 103,* 10155–10162.

Korenman, S., Miller, J. E., & Sjaastad, J. E. (1995). Long-term poverty and child development in the United States: Results from the NLSY. *Children and Youth Services Review, 17,* 127–155.

Korkman, M., Kettunen, S., & Autti-Ramo, I. (2003). Neurocognitive impairment in early adolescence following prenatal alcohol exposure of varying duration. *Child Neuopsychology, 9,* 117–128.

Korkman, M., Kira, U., & Kemp, S. L. (1998). *NEPSY—A developmental neuropsychological assessment.* San Antonio, TX: Psychological Corporation.

Kozorovitskiy, Y., Gross, C. G., Kopil, C., Battaglia, L., McBreen, M., Strahahan, A. M., & Gould, E. (2005). Experience induces structural and biochemical changes in the adult primate brain. *Proceedings of the National Academy of Sciences USA, 102,* 17478–17482.

Krebs, J. R., Sherry, D. F., Healy, S. D., Perry, V. H., & Vaccarino, A. L. (1989). Hippocampal specialization of food-storing birds. *Proceedings of the National Academy of Sciences USA, 86*, 1388–1392.

Landry, S. H., Millar-Loncar, C. L., Smith, K. E., & Swank, P. R. (2002). The role of early parenting in children's development of executive processes. *Developmental Neuropsychology, 21*, 15–41.

Laungier, B., Sanders, L., Stevens, C., & Neville, H. (2006, April). *An ERP study of selective auditory attention and socioeconomic status in young children.* Poster presented at the 13th Annual Meeting of the Cognitive Neuroscience Society, San Francisco.

Lenroot, R. K., & Giedd, J. N. (2006). Brain development in children and adolescents: Insights from anatomical magnetic resonance imaging. *Neuroscience and Biobehavioral Reviews, 30*, 718–729.

Leventhal, T., & Brooks-Gunn, J. (2000). The neighborhoods they live in: The effects of neighborhood residence on child and adolescent outcomes. *Psychological Bulletin, 126*, 309–337.

LeVine, R. A., & New, R. S. (2008). *Anthropology and child development.* Oxford, England: Blackwell.

Lilliard, A., & Else-Quest, N. (2006, September 29). Evaluating Montessori education. *Science, 313*, 1893–1894.

Linver, M. R., Brooks-Gunn, J., & Kohen, D. E. (2002). Family processes as pathways from income to young children's development. *Developmental Psychology, 38*, 719–735.

Lipina, S. J. (2006). *Vulnerabilidad social y desarrollo cognitivo: Aportes de la Neurociencia* [Social vulnerability and cognitive development: Contributions of neuroscience]. Buenos Aires, Argentina: Jorge Baudino Ediciones.

Lipina, S. J., & McCandliss, B. D. (2007, September). Cognitive neuroscience and childhood poverty: Progress and promise. In S. Lipina & U. Nayar (Chairs), *Rethinking poverty and children in the new millennium: Linking research and policy.* Paper presented at the CROP/Childwatch International Academic Workshop, Oslo, Norway.

Lipina, S. J., & Colombo, J. A. (2007). Premorbid exercising in specific cognitive tasks prevents impairment of performance in parkinsonian monkeys. *Brain Research, 1134*, 180–186.

Lipina, S. J., Martelli, M. I., Vuelta, B., Injoque Ricle, I., & Colombo, J. A. (2004). Pobreza y desempeño ejecutivo en alumnos preescolares de la ciudad de Buenos Aires (Argentina) [Poverty and executive performance in preschoolers from the City of Buenos Aires (Argentina)]. *Interdisciplinaria, 21*, 153–193.

Lipina, S. J., Martelli, M. I., Vuelta, B. L., & Colombo, J. A. (2005). Desempeño en la prueba A-no-B de infantes Argentinos provenientes de Hogares con y sin Necesidades Básicas Satisfechas [Performance on the A-not-B task of Argentinean infants from unsatisfied and satisfied basic needs homes]. *Revista Interamericana de Psicología, 39*, 49–60.

Lledo, P. M., Alonso, M., & Grubb, M. S. (2006). Adult neurogenesis and functional plasticity in neuronal circuits. *Nature Reviews. Neuroscience, 7*, 179–193.

Lorenz, K. (1965). *Evolution and modification of behavior*. Chicago: Midway Reprint.

Love, J. M., Kisker, E. E., Ross, C., Constantine, J., Boller, K., Chazan-Cohen, R., et al. (2005). The effectiveness of early Head Start for 3-year-old children and their parents: Lessons for policy and programs. *Developmental Psychology, 41*, 885–901.

Luciana, M., & Nelson, C. A. (1998). The functional emergence of prefrontally-guided working memory systems in four- to eight-year-old children. *Neuropsychologia, 36*, 273–293.

Luciana, M., Lindeke, L., Georgieff, M., Mills, M., & Nelson, C. A. (1999). Neurobehavioral evidence for working-memory deficits in school-aged children with histories of prematurity. *Developmental Medicine and Child Neurology, 41*, 521–533.

Ludwig, J., & Miller, D. L. (2005). *Does Head Start improve children's life chances? Evidence from a regression discontinuity design* (Working Paper). University of California, Davis.

Lupie, S. J, King, S., Meaney, M. J., & McEwen, B. S. (2001). Can poverty get under your skin? Basal cortisol levels and cognitive function in children from low and high socioeconomic status. *Developmental Psychopathology, 13*, 653–676.

Mackner, L. M., Black, M. M., & Starr, R. H. (2003). Cognitive development of children in poverty with failure to thrive: a prospective study through age 6. *Journal of Child Psychology and Psychiatry, and Allied Disciplines, 44*, 743–751.

Maggi, S., Irwin, L. G., Siddiqi, A., Poureslami, I., Hertzman, E., & Hertzman, C. (2005). *Knowledge network for early child development. Analytical and strategic review paper: International perspectives on early child development*. Vancouver, British Columbia, Canada: Human Early Learning Partnership—University of British Columbia for World Health Organization.

Maguire, E. A., Gadian, D. G., Johnsrude, I. S., Good, C. D., Asburner, J., Frackowiak, R. S., & Frith, C. D. (2000). Navigation-related structural change in the hippocampi of taxi drivers. *Proceedings of the National Academy of Sciences USA, 97*, 4398–4403.

Majewska, A. K., & Sur, M. (2006). Plasticity and specificity of cortical processing networks. *Trends in Neuroscience, 29*, 323–329.

Mareschal, D., Johnson, M. H., Sirois, S., Spratling, M. W., Thomas, M. C., & Westermann, G. (2007). *Neuroconstructivism. How the brain constructs cognition*. Oxford, England: Oxford University Press.

Markham, J. A., & Greenough, W. T. (2004). Experience-driven brain plasticity: Beyond the synapse. *Neuron and Glia Biology, 1*, 351–363.

Marks, D. J., Cyrulnik, S. E., Berwid, O. G., Santra, A., Curko, E. A., & Halperin, J. M. (2001). Relationship between ADHD ratings and working memory in preschool children. *Journal of the International Neuropsychological Society, 8*, 302–303.

Marmot, M. (2002). The influence of income on health: Views of an epidemiologist. Does money really matter? Or is it a marker for something else? *Health Affaires*, *21*, 31–46.

McAllister, A. K., Lo, D. C., & Katz, L. C. (1995). Neurotrophins regulate dendritic growth in developing visual cortex. *Neuron*, *15*, 791–803.

McCandliss, B. D., Beck, I. L., Sandak, R., & Perfetti, C. (2003). Focusing attention on decoding for children with poor reading skills: Design and preliminary tests of the Word Building Intervention. *Scientific Studies of Reading*, *7*, 75–104.

McCormick, M. C., Brooks-Gunn, J., Buka, S. L., Goldman, J., Yu, J., Salganik, M., et al. (2006). Early intervention in low birth weight premature infants: Results at 18 years of age for the Infant Health and Development Program. *Pediatrics*, *117*, 771–780.

McLoyd, V. C. (1998). Socioeconomic disadvantage and child development. *American Psychologist*, *53*, 185–204.

McLoyd, V. C., Jayaratne, T. E., Ceballo, M. M., & Borquez, T. S. (1994). Unemployment and work interruption among African American single mothers: Effects on parenting and adolescent socioemotional functioning. *Child Development*, *65*, 562–589.

Melhuish, E., Quinn, L., Hanna, K., Sylva, K., Sammons, P., Siraj-Blatchford, I., & Taggart, B. (2006). *Effective pre-school provision in Northern Ireland (EPPNI) project* (Summary Rep. No. 41). Bangor, County Down, Northern Ireland: Department of Education, Northern Ireland Statistics and Research Agency.

Menchini, L., & Redmond, G. (2006). *Child consumption poverty in south-eastern Europe and the commonwealth of independent states* (Innocenti Working Paper No. 2006-04). Rome, Italy: UNICEF-Innocenti Research Centre.

Mendola, P., Selevan, S. G., Gutter, S., & Rice, D. (2002). Environmental factors associated with a spectrum of neurodevelopmental deficits. *Mental Retardation and Developmental Disabilities*, *8*, 188–197.

Mezzacappa, E. (2004). Alerting, orienting, and executive attention: Developmental properties and sociodemographic correlates in and epidemiological sample of young, urban children. *Child Development*, *75*, 1373–1386.

Michel, G. F., & Tayler, A. M. (2005). Critical period: A history of the transition from questions of when, to what, to how. *Developmental Psychobiology*, *46*, 156–162.

Miller, A. L., Seifer, R., Stroud, L., Sheinkopf, S. J., & Dickstein, S. (2006). Biobehavioral indices of emotion regulation relate to school attitudes, motivation, and behavior problems in a low-income preschool sample. In B. M. Lester, A. Masten, & B. McEwen (Eds.), *Annals of the New York Academy of Sciences: Vol. 1094. Resilience in children* (pp. 325–329). New York: New York Academy of Sciences.

Miller, E. K., & Cohen, J. D. (2001). An integrative theory of prefrontal cortex function. *Annual Review of Neuroscience*, *24*, 167–202.

Mills, D., & Mills, C. (2000). *Hungarian kindergarten curriculum translation*. London: Mills Production.

Minujin, A., Delamonica, E., Davidziuk, A., & González, E. D. (2006). The definition of child poverty: A discussion of concepts and measurements. *Environment and Urbanization, 18,* 481–500.

Mistry, R. S., Lowe, E. D., Benner, A. D., & Chien, N. (2008). Expanding the family economic stress model: Insights from a mixed-methods approach. *Journal of Marriage and Family, 70,* 196–209.

Mohammed, A. H., Zhu, S. W., Darmopil, S., Hjerling-Leffler, J., Ernfors, P., Winblad, B., et al. (2002). Environmental enrichment and the brain. *Progress in Brain Research, 138,* 109–133.

Mohammed, A. K., Jonnson, G., & Archer, T. (1986). Selective lesioning of forebrain noradrenaline neurons at birth abolishes the improved maze learning performance induced by rearing in complex environment. *Brain Research, 398,* 6–10.

Mohammed, A. K., Winblad, B., Ebendal, T., & Larkfors, L. (1990). Environmental influence on behaviour and nerve growth factor in the brain. *Brain Research, 528,* 62–72.

Molnar, Z., Métin, C., Stoykova, A., Tarabykin, V., Price, D. J., Francis, F., et al. (2006). Comparative aspects of cerebral cortical development. *European Journal of Neuroscience, 23,* 921–934.

Mooney, C. M. (1957). Age in the development of closure ability in children. *Canadian Journal of Experimental Psychology, 2,* 219–226.

Murname, R. J. (2007). Improving education of children living in poverty. *The Future of Children, 17,* 161–182.

Murname, R. J., & Steele, J. L. (2007). What is the problem? The challenge of providing effective teachers for all children. *The Future of Children, 17,* 15–28.

Najman, J. M., Hayatbakhsh, M. R., Heron, M. A., Bor, W., O'Callaghan, M. J., & Williams, G. M. (2008). The impact of episodic and chronic poverty on child cognitive development. *Journal of Pediatrics, 11,* 1–6.

Narayan, D., Chambers, R., Shah, M. K., & Petesch, P. (2000). *Voices of the poor. Crying out for change.* Washington, DC: International Bank for Reconstruction and Development/The World Bank.

Nation, M., Crusto, C., Wandersman, A., Kumpfer, K. L., Seybott, D., Morrissey, E., & Davino, K. (2003). What works in prevention. Principles of effective prevention programs. *American Psychologist, 58,* 449–456.

National Institute of Child Health and Human Development & the Early Child Care Research Network. (2003). Do children's attention processes mediate the link between family predictors and school readiness? *Developmental Psychology, 39,* 581–593.

National Institute of Child Health and Human Development & the Early Child Care Research Network. (2005). Predicting individual differences in attention, memory, and planning in first graders from experiences at home, child care, and school. *Developmental Psychology, 41,* 99–114.

Nayar, U., & Lipina, S. J. (2007). Summary and conclusions (Group 2): A draft. *Rethinking poverty and children in the new millennium: Linking research and policy.* CROP/Childwatch: Oslo, Norway.

Neddens, J., Brandenburg, K., Teuchert-Noodt, G., & Dawirs, R. R. (2001). Differential environment alters ontogeny of dopamine innervation of the orbital prefrontal cortex in gerbils. *Journal of Neuroscience Research, 63*, 209–213.

Nelson, C. A. (2002). Neurobehavioral development in the context of biocultural co-constructivism. In P. Bates (Ed.), *Lifespan development and the brain: The perspective of biocultural co-constructivism* (pp. 61–81). West Nyack, NY: Cambridge University Press.

Nelson, C. A., Bloom, F. E., Cameron, J. L., Amaral, D., Dahl, R. E., & Pine, D. (2002). An integrative, multidisciplinary approach to the study of brain–behavior relations in the context of typical and atypical development. *Developmental Psychopathology, 14*, 499–520.

Nelson, C. A., Zeanah, C. H., Fox, N. A., Marshall, P. J., Smyke, A., & Guthrie, D. (2007, December 21). Cognitive recovery in socially deprived young children: The Bucharest Early Intervention Project. *Science, 318*, 1937–1940.

Neville, H., Andersson, A., Bagdade, O., Bell, T., Currin, J., Fanning, J., et al. (2008). Effects of music training on brain and cognitive development in under-privileged 3- to 5-year-old children: Preliminary results. In C. Asbury, & B. Rich (Eds.), *Learning, arts, and the brain. The Dana Consortium Report on Arts and Cognition* (pp. 105–116). Washington DC: Dana Press.

Noble, K. G., Farah, M. J., & McCandliss, B. D. (2006). Socioeconomic background modulates cognition achievement relationships in reading. *Cognitive Development, 21*, 349–368.

Noble, K. G., McCandliss, B. D., & Farah, M. J. (2007). Socioeconomic gradients predict individual differences in neurocognitive abilities. *Developmental Science, 10*, 464–480.

Noble, K. G., Norman, M. F., & Farah, M. J. (2005). Neurocognitive correlates of socioeconomic status in kindergarten children. *Developmental Science, 8*, 74–87.

Noble, K. G., Tottenham, N., & Casey, B. J. (2005). Neuroscience perspectives on disparities in school readiness and cognitive achievement. *The Future of Children, 15*, 71–89.

Noble, K. G., Wolmetz, M. E., Ochs, L. G., Farah, M. J., & McCandliss, B. D. (2006). Brain–behavior relationships in reading acquisition are modulated by socioeconomic factors. *Developmental Science, 9*, 642–651.

O'Connor, T. G., Rutter, M., Beckett, C., Keaveney, L., Kreppner, J., & ERA Study Team. (2000). The effects of global severe privation on cognitive competence: Extension and longitudinal follow-up. *Child Development, 71*, 376–390.

Office of Human Development Services. (2008). *Program performance standards for the operation of Head Start programs by grantee and delegate agencies.* Washington, DC: U.S. Department of Health and Human Services, Administration for Children and Families.

Organisation for Economic Co-operation and Development. (2007). *Understanding the brain: The birth of a learning science.* Danvers, MA: Author.

Ornoy, A. (2003). The impact of intrauterine exposure versus postnatal environment in neurodevelopmental toxicity: Long-term neurobehavioral studies in children at risk for developmental disorders. *Toxicology Letters, 140–141,* 171–181.

Pakulak, E., Sanders, L. Paulsen, D. J., & Neville, H. (2005, April). *Semantic and syntactic processing in children from different familial socioeconomic status as indexed by ERPs.* Paper presented at the 12th Annual Meeting of the Cognitive Neuroscience Society, New York.

Pascalis, O., Scott, L. S., Kelly, D. J., Shannon, R. W., Nicholson, E., Coleman, M., & Nelson, C. A. (2005). Plasticity of face processing in infancy. *Proceedings of the National Academy of Sciences USA, 102,* 5297–5300.

Patel, A. D. (2003). Language, music, syntax and the brain. *Nature Neuroscience, 7,* 674–680.

Patrick, P. D., Oriá, R. B., Madhavan, V., Pinkerton, R. C., Lorntz, B., Lima, A. A., & Guerrant, R. L. (2005). Limitations in verbal fluency following heavy burdens of early childhood diarrhea in Brazilian shantytown children. *Child Neuropsychology, 11,* 233–244.

Patterson, P. H. (2002). Maternal infection: Window on neuroinmune interactions in fetal brain development and mental illness. *Current Opinion in Neurobiology, 12,* 115–118.

Pennington, B. F., & Ozonoff, S. (1996). Executive functions and developmental psychopathology. *Journal of Child Psychology and Psychiatry, and Allied Disciplines, 37,* 51–87.

Peretz, I., Zatorre, R. J. (2005). Brain organization for music processing. *Annual Review of Psychology, 56,* 89–114.

Pollit, E. (2000). Developmental sequel from early nutritional deficiencies: Conclusive and probability judgments. *Journal of Nutrition, 130*(Suppl.), 350S–353S.

Posner, M. I. (2008). *Evolution and development of self-regulation.* New York: American Museum of Natural History.

Posner, M. I., & Raichle, M. E. (1994). *Images of mind.* New York: Scientific American Library.

Posner, M. I., & Rothbart, M. K. (2000). Developing mechanisms of self-regulation. *Development and Psychopathology, 12,* 427–441.

Posner, M. I., & Rothbart, M. K. (2005). Influencing brain networks: Implications for education. *Trends in Cognitive Sciences, 9,* 99–103.

Posner, M. I., & Rothbart, M. K. (2007a). *Educating the human brain.* Washington, DC: American Psychological Association.

Posner, M. I., & Rothbart, M. K. (2007b). Research on attention networks as a model for the integration of psychological science. *Annual Review of Psychology, 58,* 1–23.

Pretzlik, U., Olsson, J., Nabuco, M. E., & Cruz, I. (2003). Teachers' implicit views of intelligence predict pupils' self-perceptions as learners. *Cognitive Development, 18,* 579–600.

Qi, C. H., Kaiser, A. P., Milan, S., & Hancock, T. (2006). Language performance of low-income African American and European American preschool children on the PPVT-III. *Language, Speech, and Hearing Services in Schools, 37,* 5–16.

Raizada, R. D. S., Richards, T. L., Meltzoff, A., & Kuhl, P. K. (2008). Socioeconomic status predicts hemispheric specialisation of the left inferior frontal gyrus in young children. *NeuroImage, 40,* 1392–1401.

Rakic, P. (2006). A century of progress in corticoneurogenesis: From silver impregnation to genetic engineering. *Cerebral Cortex 16,* i13–i17.

Ramey, C. T., Campbell, F. A., & Ramey, S. L. (1999). Early intervention: Successful pathways to improving intellectual development. *Developmental Neuropsychology, 16,* 385–392.

Ramey, C. T., & Ramey, S. L. (1998). Prevention of intellectual disabilities: Early interventions to improve cognitive development. *Preventive Medicine, 27,* 224–232.

Ramey, S., & Ramey, C. T. (2003). Understanding efficacy of early educational programs: Critical design, practice, and policy issues. In A. J. Reynolds, M. C. Wang, & H. J. Walberg (Eds.), *Early childhood programs for a new century* (pp. 135–154). Washington DC: Child Welfare League of America.

Rampon, C., Jiang, C. H., Dong, H., Tang, Y. P., Lockhart, D. J., Schultz, P. G., et al. (2000). Effects of environmental enrichment on gene expression in the brain. *Proceedings of the National Academy of Sciences USA, 97,* 12880–12884.

Rauscher, F. H., Shaw, G. L., & Ky, K. N. (1993, October 14). Music and spatial task performance. *Nature, 365,* 611.

Raven, J.C. (1995). *Coloured progressive matrices. Set II.* Oxford, England: Oxford Psychological Press.

Raver, C. C., Gershoff, E. T., & Aber, J. L. (2007). Testing equivalence of mediating models of income, parenting, and school readiness for White, Black, and Hispanic children in a national sample. *Child Development, 78,* 96–115.

Reynolds, A. J. (1994). Effects of a preschool plus follow-on intervention for children at risk. *Developmental Psychology, 30,* 787–804.

Reynolds, A. J., Temple, J. A., Robertson, D. L., & Mann, E. A. (2002). *Age 21 cost–benefit analysis of the Title I Chicago Child–Parent Centers* (Discussion Paper No. 1245-02). Madison, WI: Institute for Research on Poverty.

Reynolds, A. J., Wang, M. C., & Walberg, H. J. (2003a). *Early childhood programs for a new century.* Washington DC: Child Welfare League of America.

Reynolds, A. J., Wang, M. C., & Walberg, H. J. (2003b). Trends in early childhood programs. In A. J. Reynolds, M. C. Wang, & H. J. Walberg (Eds.), *Early childhood programs for a new century* (pp. 11–32). Washington DC: Child Welfare League of America.

Richards, M., & Wadsworth, M. E. J. (2004). Long term effects of early adversity on cognitive function. *Archives of Disease in Childhood, 89,* 922–927.

Richardson, L., & Le Grand, J. (2002). Outsider and insider expertise: The response of residents of deprived neighbourhoods to an academic definition of social exclusion. *Social Policy and Administration, 36,* 496–515.

Richter, L. M., Cameron, N., Norris, S. A., Del Fabro, G., & MacKeown, J. (2004). *Birth to Twenty Research Programme dissemination report.* Johannesburg, South Africa: University of the Witwatersrand.

Ripple, C. H., & Zigler, E. (2003). Research, policy, and the federal role in prevention initiatives for children. *American Psychologist, 58,* 482–490.

Rogoff, B. (2003). *Cultural nature of human development.* Cary, NC: Oxford University Press.

Rogoff, B., Goodman Turkanis, C., & Bartlett, L. (2001). *Learning together. Children and adults in a school community.* New York: Oxford University Press.

Roosa, M. W., Deng, S., Nair, R. L., & Lockhart Burrell, G. (2005). Measures for studying poverty in family and child research. *Journal of Marriage and Family, 67,* 971–988.

Rosenzweig, M. R., & Bennett, E. L. (1996). Psychobiology of plasticity: Effects of training and experience on brain and behavior. *Behavioural Brain Research, 78,* 57–65.

Rothbart, M. K., Ahadi, S. A., & Hershey, K. (1994). Temperament and social behavior in childhood. *Merrill-Palmer Quarterly, 40,* 21–39.

Rueda, M. R., Chueca, P., & Santoja, M. (2008, April). *Training executive attention: Lasting effects and transfer to self-regulation.* Paper presented at the 15th Annual Meeting of the Cognitive Neuroscience Society, San Francisco.

Rueda, M. R., Fan, J., McCandliss, B. D., Halparin, J. D., Gruber, D. B., Lercari, L. P., & Posner, M. I. (2004). Development of attentional networks in childhood. *Neuropsychologia, 42,* 1029–1040.

Rueda, M. R., Rothbart, M. K., McCandliss, B. D., Saccomanno, L., & Posner, M. I. (2005). Training, maturation, and genetic influences on the development of executive attention. *Proceedings of the National Academic of Sciences USA, 102,* 14931–14936.

Rutter, M. (2003). Poverty and child mental health. Natural experiments and social causation. *Journal of the American Medical Association, 290,* 2063–2064.

Sabourin, L., Pakulak, E., Paulsen, D. J., Fanning, J. L. & Neville H. J. (2007, April). *The effects of age, language proficiency and SES on ERP indices of syntactic processing in children.* Paper presented at the 14th Annual Meeting of the Cognitive Neuroscience Society, New York.

Sack, K. (1998, January 15). Georgia's governor seeks musical start for babies. *New York Times,* p. A12.

Sameroff, A. J., & MacKenzie, M. J. (2003). Research strategies for capturing transactional models of development: The limits of the possible. *Development and Psychopathology, 15,* 613–40.

Sandeman, R., & Sandeman, D. (2003). Development, growth, and plasticity in the crayfish olfactory system. *Microscopy Research and Technique, 15,* 266–277.

Scerif, G., & Karmiloff-Smith, A. (2005). The dawn of cognitive genetics? Crucial developmental caveats. *Trends in Cognitive Sciences, 9,* 126–135.

Schroeder, D., Martorell, R., Rivera, J., Ruel, M., & Habicht, J. (1995). Age differences in the impact of nutritional supplementation on growth. *Journal of Nutrition, 125,* 1051S–1059S.

Schweinhart, L. J., Montie, J., Xiang, Z., Barnett, W. S., Belfield, C. R., & Nores, M. (2005). *Lifetime effects: The High Scope Perry Preschool study through age 40.* Ypsilanti, MI: High Scope Educational Research Foundation.

Scott, J. (1999). *Análisis del programa de educación, salud y alimentación progresa: Informe final* [Analysis of the Program of Education, Health and Nutrition Progress: Final report]. Mexico City, México: RIMISP-FAO.

Segretin, M. S., Lipina, S. J., Benarós, M. S., Hermida, M. J., & Colombo, J. A. (2008, April). *Predictors of cognitive control processing increments in preschoolers from poor homes after cognitive training interventions.* Paper presented at the 12th Annual Meeting of the Cognitive Neuroscience Society, New York.

Shallice, T. (1982). Specific impairments of planning. *Philosophical Transcripts of the Royal Society of London, 298,* 199–209.

Share, D. L., Jorm, A. F., MacLean, R., & Mathews, R. (1984). Sources of individual differences in reading acquisition. *Journal of Educational Psychology, 76,* 1309–1324.

Shaw, P., Eckstrand, K., Sharp, W., Blumenthal, J., Lerch, J. P., Greenstein, D., et al. (2007). Attention-deficit/hyperactivity disorder is characterized by a delay in cortical maturation. *Proceedings of the National Academy of Sciences USA, 104,* 19469–19654.

Shaw, D. S., Vondra, J. I., Hommerding, K. D., Keenan, K., & Dunn, M. (1994). Chronic family adversity and early child behavior problems: A longitudinal study of low income families. *Journal of Child Psychology and Psychiatry, and Allied Disciplines, 35,* 1109–1122.

Shaywitz, B. A., Shaywitz, S. E., Blachman, B. A., Pugh, K .R., Fullbright, R. K., Skudlarski, P., et al. (2004). Developments of left occipitotemporal systems for skilled reading in children alter a phonologically-based intervention. *Biological Psychiatry, 55,* 926–933.

Sheese, B. E., Voelker, P. M., Rothbart, M. K., & Posner, M. I. (2007). Parenting quality interacts with genetic variation in dopamine receptor D4 to influence temperament in early childhood. *Developmental Psychopathology, 19,* 1039–1046.

Sheridan, M., Khalea, S., D'Esposito, M., & Thomas, B. W. (2008, April). *Establishing a relationship between prefrontal cortex function, socioeconomic status and cortisol reactivity in children.* Paper presented at the 15th Annual Meeting of the Cognitive Neuroscience Society, San Francisco.

Sherry, D. F., Jacobs, L. F., & Gaulin, S. J. C. (1992). Spatial memory and adaptive specialization of the hippocampus. *Trends in Neuroscience, 15,* 298–303.

Shi, L., Fatemi, H. S., Sidwell, R. W., & Patterson, P. H. (2001). A mouse model of mental illness: Maternal influenza infection causes behavioral and pharmacological abnormalities in the offspring [Abstract]. *Society for Neuroscience Abstracts.* Available at http://www.sfn.org/index.cfm?pagename=abstracts_ampublications

Shipler, D. K. (2004). The working poor. *Stanford Social Innovation Review, 2,* 36–43.

Shonkoff, J. P., & Phillips, D. A. (2000). *From neurons to neighborhoods: The science of early childhood development.* Washington, DC: National Academic Press.

Shors, T. J., Miesegaes, G., Beylin, A., Zhao, M., Rydel, T., & Gould, E. (2001, March 15). Neurogenesis in the adult is involved in the formation of trace memories. *Nature, 410,* 372–376.

Siegler, R., DeLoache, J., & Eisenberg, N. (2003). *How children develop.* New York: Worth.

Sirois, S., Spratling, M., Thomas, M. S. C., Westermann, G., Mareschal, D., & Johnson, M. H. (2008). Précis of neuroconstructivism: How the brain constructs cognition. *Behavioral and Brain Sciences, 31,* 321–356.

Smith, E., & Farah, M. J. (2008, April). *Childhood poverty and learning: Medial temporal versus striatal learning systems.* Paper presented at the 15th Annual Meeting of the Cognitive Neuroscience Society, San Francisco.

Society for Neuroscience. (2008). *Brain facts: A primer on the brain and nervous system.* Washington, DC: Author.

Sowell, E. R., Thompson, P. M., Leonard, C. M., Welcome, S. E., Kan, E., & Toga, A. W. (2004). Longitudinal mapping of cortical thickness and brain growth in normal children. *Journal of Neuroscience, 24,* 8223–8231.

Sparling, J., & Lewis, I. (1991). Partners: A curriculum to help premature, low birthweight infants get off to a good start. *Topics in Early Childhood Special Education, 11,* 36–55.

Stanton-Chapman, T. L., Chapman, D. A., Kaiser, A. P., & Hancock, T. B. (2004). Cumulative risk and low-income children's language development. *Topics in Early Childhood Special Education, 24,* 227–237.

Sternberg, R. J. (2004). Culture and intelligence. *American Psychologist, 59,* 325–338.

Sternberg, R. J. (2005). There are no public-policy implications. A reply to Rushton and Jensen. *Psychology, Public Policy, and Law, 11,* 295–301.

Sternberg, R. J., & Grigorenko, E. L. (2004). Successful intelligence in the classroom. *Theory Into Practice, 43,* 274–280.

Sternberg, R. J., Lautrey, J., & Lubart, T. I. (2003). Where are we in the field of intelligence, how did we get here, and where are we going? In R. J. Sternberg & E. L. Grigorenko (Eds.), *Models of intelligence* (pp. 3–26). Washington, DC: American Psychological Association.

Stevens, C., Currin, J., Paulsen, D., Harn, B., Chard, D., Larsen, D., et al. (2008, April). *Kindergarten children at-risk for reading failure: Electrophysiological measures of selective auditory attention before and after the Early Reading Intervention (ERI).* Paper presented at the 15th Annual Meeting of the Cognitive Neuroscience Society, San Francisco.

Stevens, C., Fanning, J., Coch, D., Sanders, L., & Neville, H. J. (2008). Neural mechanisms of selective auditory attention are enhanced by computerized training: Electrophysiological evidence from language-impaired and typically developing children. *Brain Research, 1205,* 55–69.

Stevens, C., Sanders, L., & Neville, H. (2006). Neurophysiological evidence for selective auditory attention deficits in children with specific language impairment. *Brain Research, 111,* 142–152.

Stipek, D. J., & Ryan, R. H. (1997). Economically disadvantaged preschoolers: Ready to learn but farther to go. *Developmental Psychology, 33*, 711–723.

Sturney, P., Thorburn, M. J., Brown, J. M., Reed, J., Daur, J., & King, G. (1992). Portage Project. *Child Care Dual Health Development, 18*, 377–394.

Sylva, K., Melhuish, E., Sammons, P., Siraj-Blatchford, I., & Taggart, B. (2004). *The final report: Effective preschool education* (Technical Paper 12). London: Institute of Education, University of London.

Szucs, D., & Goswami, U. (2007). Educational neuroscience: Defining a new discipline for the study of mental representations. *Mind, Brain, and Education, 1*, 114–119.

Taylor, E. H. (2000). Curriculum in Head Start. *Head Start Bulletin, 67*, 1–35.

Technau, G. M. (1984). Fiber number in the mushroom bodies of adult *Drosophila melanogaster* depends on age, sex and experience. *Journal of Neurogenetics, 1*, 113–126.

Temple, E., Deutsch, G. K., Poldrack, R. A., Miller, S. L., Tallal, P., Merzenich, M. M., & Gabrieli, J. D. (2003). Neural deficits in children with dyslexia ameliorated by behavioral remediation: Evidence from functional MRI. *Proceedings of the National Academy of Sciences USA, 100*, 2860–2865.

Thomas, M. S. C., & Johnson, M. H. (2008). New advances in understanding sensitive periods in brain development. *Current Directions in Psychological Sciences, 17*, 1–5.

Thompson, R. A., & Nelson, C. A. (2001). Developmental science and media. *American Psychologist, 56*, 5–15.

Thorell, L. B., Lindqvist, S., Bergman Nutley, S., Bohlin, G., & Klingberg, T. (2009). Training and transfer effects of executive functions in preschool children. *Developmental Science, 12*, 106–113.

Toga, A. W., & Thompson, P. M. (2005). Genetics of brain structure and intelligence. *Annual Review of Neuroscience, 28*, 1–23.

Toga, A. W., Thompson, P. M., & Sowell, E. R. (2006). Mapping brain maturation. *Nature Neuroscience, 29*, 148–159.

Townsend, P. (1979). *Poverty in the United Kingdom*. London: Penguin-Harmondsworth Press.

Trasande, L., Landrigan, P. J., & Schechter, C. (2005). Public health and economic consequences of methyl mercury toxicity to the developing brain. *Environmental Health Perspectives, 113*, 590–596.

Turkheimer, E., Haley, A., Waldron, M., D'Onofrio, B., & Gottesman, I. I. (2003). Socioeconomic status modifies heritability of IQ in young children. *Psychological Science, 14*, 623–628.

United Nations Children's Fund. (1999). *Voices of children and adolescents in Latin America and the Caribbean*. New York: Author.

United Nations Children's Fund. (2000). *A league table of child poverty in rich nations* (Innocenti Report Card Issue No. 1). Florence, Italy: United Nations Children's Fund Inoccenti Research Center.

United Nations Children's Fund. (2005). *The state of the world's children*. Washington, DC: Author.

United Nations Procurement Division. (2005). *PNUD: Informe sobre el desarrollo humano 2005* [UNPD: Human development report 2005]. Madrid, Spain: Editorial Mundi-Prensa.

U.S. Department of Health and Human Services. (2000a). *Child Health USA 2000*. Washington, DC: U.S. Government Printing Office.

U.S. Department of Health & Human Services. (2000b). *Healthy people 2010*. Washington, DC: U.S. Government Printing Office.

Valenzuela, M. (1997). Maternal sensitivity in a developing society: The context of urban poverty and infant chronic under nutrition. *Developmental Psychology, 33*, 845–855.

Vandell, D. L. (2004). Early child care: The known and the unknown. *Merrill-Palmer Quarterly, 50*, 387–414.

Van del Pol, A. N. (2006). Viral infections in the developing and mature brain. *Trends in Neuroscience, 29*, 398–406.

Van Praag, H., Kemperemann, G., & Gage, F. H. (2000). Neural consequences of environmental enrichment. *Nature Reviews. Neuroscience, 1*, 191–198.

Varma, S., McCandliss, B. D., & Schwartz, D. L. (2008). Scientific and pragmatic challenges for bridging education and neuroscience. *Educational Researcher, 37*, 140–152.

Verkhratsky, A., & Toescu. E. C. (2006). Neuronal–glial networks as substrate for CNS integration. *Journal of Cellular and Molecular Medicine, 10*, 826–836.

Volpe, J. J. (2000). Overview: Normal and abnormal human brain development. *Mental Retardation and Developmental Disabilities Research Reviews, 6*, 1–5.

Wagner, R. K., & Torgesen, J. K. (1987). The nature of phonological processing and its causal role in the acquisition of reading skills. *Psychological Bulletin, 101*, 192–212.

Walker, S. P., Wachs, T., Gardner, J. M., Lozoff, B., Wasserman, G. A., Pollit, E., et al. (2007). Child Development: Risk factors for adverse outcomes in developing countries. *Lancet, 369*, 145–157.

Warner, T. D., Behnke, M., Eyler, F. D., Padgett, K., Leonard, C., Hou, W., et al. (2006). Diffusion tensor imaging of frontal white matter and executive functioning in cocaine-exposed children. *Pediatrics, 118*, 2014–2024.

Wasik, B. H., Ramey, C. T., Bryant, D. M., & Sparling, J. J. (1990). A longitudinal study of two early intervention strategies: Project CARE. *Child Development, 61*, 1682–1696.

Wasserman, G. A., Liu, X., Pine, D. S., & Graziano, J. H. (2001). Contribution of maternal smoking during pregnancy and lead exposure to early child behavior problems. *Neurotoxicology and Teratology, 23*, 13–21.

Wassermann, C. R., Shaw, G. M., Selvin, S., & Gould, J. B. (1998). Socioeconomic status, neighborhood social conditions, and neural tube defects. *American Journal of Public Health, 88*, 1674–1680.

Westermann, G., Mareschal, D., Johnson, M. H., Sirois, S., Spratling, M. W., & Thomas, M. S. C. (2007). Neuroconstructivism. *Developmental Science, 10,* 75–83.

White, H., Leavy, J., & Masters, A. (2002). *Comparative perspectives on child poverty: A review of poverty measures* (Working Paper No. 1). London: Young Lives—Save the Children Fund.

Wilkinson, R. G. (1999). Health, hierarchy, and social anxiety. In N. E. Adler, M. Marmot, B. S. McEwen, & J. Stewart (Eds.), *Annals of the New York Academy of Sciences: Vol. 896. Socioeconomic status and health in industrial nations: Social, psychological, and biological pathways* (pp. 46–83). New York: New York Academy of Sciences.

Williamson, D. L., Salkie, F. J., & Letourneau, R. N. (2005). Welfare reforms and the cognitive development of young children. *Canadian Journal of Public Health, 96,* 13–17.

Wilson, A. J., Dehaene, S., Pinel, P., Revkin, S. K., Cohen, L., & Cohen, D. (2006). Principles underlying the design of "The Number Race," an adaptive computer game for remediation of dyscalculia. *Behavioral and Brain Functions, 2,* 19.

Wilson, A. J., Revkin, S. K., Cohen, D., Cohen, L., & Dehaene, S. (2006). An open trial assessment of "The Number Race," an adaptive computer game for remediation of dyscalculia. *Behavioral and Brain Functions, 2,* 20.

Winders Davis, D., Chang, F., Burns, B., Robinson, J., & Dossett, D. (2004). Lead exposure and attention regulation in children living in poverty. *Developmental Medicine and Child Neurology, 46,* 825–831.

Winocur, G., Moscovitch, M., Fogel, S., Rosenbaum, R. S., & Sekeres, M. (2005). Preserved spatial memory after hippocampal lesions: Effects of extensive experience in a complex environment. *Nature Neuroscience, 8,* 273–275.

Wismer Fires, A. B., Ziegler, T. E., Kurian, J. R., Jacoris, S., & Pollak, S. D. (2005). Early experience in humans is associated with changes in neuropeptides critical for regulating social behavior. *Proceedings of the National Academy of Sciences USA, 102,* 17237–17240.

Woodcock, R. N. (1998). *Woodcock Reading Mastery Tests—Revised.* Circle Pines, MN: American Guidance Service.

Zelazo, P. D., Frye, D., & Rapus, T. (1996). An age-related dissociation between knowing rules and using them. *Cognitive Development, 11,* 37–63.

Zigler, E., & Finn-Stevenson, M. (2007). From research to policy and practice: The school of the 21st century. *American Journal of Orthopsychiatry, 77,* 175–181.

Zigler, E., & Styfco, S. J. (2003). The federal commitment to preschool education: Lessons from and for Head Start. In A. J. Reynolds, M. C. Wang, & H. J. Walberg (Eds.), *Early childhood programs for a new century* (pp. 58–73). Washington DC: Child Welfare League of America.

INDEX

ABOUT THE AUTHORS

Sebastián J. Lipina, PhD, is an assistant investigator of the Consejo Nacional de Investigaciones Científicas y Técnicas, Buenos Aires, Argentina; codirector of the Unidad de Neurobiología Aplicada at the Centro de Educación Médica e Investigaciones Clínicas "Norberto Quirno," Buenos Aires, Argentina; and professor of social vulnerability and cognitive development at the School of Humanities, Universidad Nacional de San Martin, Buenos Aires, Argentina. He works in the area of cognitive neuroscience, analyzing processes of brain organization and reorganization and carrying out experimental and applied models with humans and nonhuman primates with an interdisciplinary team of colleagues directed by Jorge A. Colombo. One of these projects involves the study of poverty's impact on cognitive development and the design of interventions aimed at improving children's cognitive performance through cognitive exercises and training in laboratory and school settings.

Jorge A. Colombo, MD, PhD, performed research in the field of comparative neuroendocrinology at Bernardo A. Houssay's Instituto de Biología y Medicina Experimental, Buenos Aires, Argentina; at the Department of Anatomy, University of California, Los Angeles (UCLA), directed by Charles Sawyer; and at the Brain Research Institute, UCLA, as a fellow of the Ford Foundation's Fund for Research in Psychiatry. During the 1980s, he was a professor at the College of Medicine, University of South Florida, Tampa, where he used several research models to explore hypothalamic control of pituitary function and started work on neural cell transplantation. A recipient of several fellowships, professorships, and grants, he researched cell transplantation procedures in A. Bjorklund's and Y. Ben-Ari's laboratories in Sweden and France, respectively. He returned to his home country of Argentina a few years after the fall of the military coup, where he became principal investigator of the Consejo Nacional de Investigaciones Científicas y

Técnicas, Buenos Aires, and founder and director of the Unidad de Neurobiología Aplicada at the Centro de Educación Médica e Investigaciones Clínicas "Norberto Quirno," Buenos Aires. During this period, his most visible work included cell transplantation in nonhuman primates and the characterization of the interlaminar astroglia. He performed collaborative work with Karl Zilles (Dusseldorf, Germany) and Andreas Reichenbach (Leipzig, Germany) as a fellow of the Alexander von Humboldt Foundation. More recently, he has included research on the impact of poverty on child brain development among his social and scientific concerns.